Getting Started in
Internet
Auctions

The Getting Started In Series

Getting Started in
Internet
Auctions

Alan C. Elliott

John Wiley & Sons, Inc.

New York • Chichester • Weinheim • Brisbane • Singapore • Toronto

This book is printed on acid-free paper. ∞

Copyright © 2000 by Alan C. Elliott. All rights reserved.

Published by John Wiley & Sons, Inc.

Published simultaneously in Canada.

The screen captures of AOL software are copyright 1999 America Online, Inc. and are printed with permission. America Online, AOL, and the AOL logo are registered trademarks of America Online, Inc. in the United States and other countries.

This publication is designed to provide accurate and authoritative information in regard to the subject matter covered. It is sold with the understanding that the publisher is not engaged in rendering legal, accounting, or other professional services. If legal advice or other expert assistance is required, the services of a competent professional person should be sought.

Library of Congress Cataloging in Publication Data:
Elliott, Alan C., 1952–
    Getting started in internet auctions / Alan C. Elliott.
      p. cm.—(The getting started in series)
    Includes index.
    ISBN 0-471-38087-3 (paper : alk. paper)
    1. Internet auctions.   2. Internet (Computer network)   I. Title.   II. Getting started in.
5478.E45 2000
381'.17—dc21   99-055243

Printed in the United States of America

10 9 8 7 6 5 4 3 2 1

Contents

Chapter 13

Chapter 14

Chapter 15

Acknowledgments

I wish to thank a number of people who helped in the development of this book: Janice Bennett, Betty Brooks, Ryan and Valerie Cooper, Annette Elliott, Patsy Summey, Melanie Walker, and Wayne Woodward. In addition, Susie Cooper, John Kelly, John A. Williams, John H. Williams, and Elvis contributed valuable information. Thanks also to Nicholas Smith, Debra Englander, Gowri Ramachandran, Michael Detweiler, and Missy Garnett who made this book possible.

Special thanks to my understanding network of family and friends for their encouragement and patience. Hey, guys, you're the greatest!

Introduction

Congratulations! You're about to enter a whole new era of shopping and selling in the world of Internet auctions. You've heard about how commerce on the Web has skyrocketed in the past years—and there's a reason. It's easy and fun to shop online—plus there are more items available online than you'd ever find in a single physical store.

BUYING AND SELLING ON INTERNET AUCTION SITES

Like millions of other people, you want to participate in Internet auctions, but you're concerned about getting your feet wet in this new ocean of commerce. It's unfamiliar and perhaps a little daunting. That's what this book is for! Now you don't have to figure out all the secrets of buying and selling on an Internet auction by yourself. You'll learn tricks and tips from people who've already traveled down the Internet auction highway. Just come along and discover how Internet shopping will change everything you've ever known about buying and selling.

Where did all this excitement about Internet auctions come from anyway? Most of the flurry of activity is from one site: www.eBay.com. The eBay auction site is the king of auctions on the Internet. How successful is eBay? There are usually more than 2 to 4 million items being auctioned on eBay at any time of the day or night—24 hours a day, 365 days a year. That's right. There's no typo. Two to four million! And about 250,000 new items are added every day.

What's being sold? eBay began as a site for Pez collectors—you know, those little candy dispensers with character heads. It grew quickly to include items for other collectors: Beanie Babies, coins, dolls, comics, and more. Today you'll find a huge variety of items including mobile homes, cars, rare books, jewelry, autographs, tickets, computers, collectibles, music, one-of-a-kind items, and yes, there are still hundreds of Pez dispensers for sale every day.

And, if you can't find what you want on eBay, you have hundreds of other auctions to choose from. Several major companies have tried to replicate eBay's success by offering similar auction sites. These include Amazon (auctions.amazon.com), Yahoo! (auctions.yahoo.com), and Excite (auctions.excite.com.) There are also other more specialized Internet auction sites where you'll find computers, wine, automotive parts, antiques, and much more. Still other auction sites are designed to sell only merchandise from a particular company (such as egghead.com and onsale.com). You'd need lots of free time to sort out the hundreds of sites on the Web—or you can just read this book.

GETTING SUCCESSFULLY STARTED AS A BUYER OR SELLER

There's no doubt about it. Whether you are a buyer or seller, participating in an online auction *is* fun. For some people it's downright addictive. But first there are a few rules, courtesies, and business practices that you need to know about to make your auction experience really enjoyable and perhaps even profitable.

LEARNING HOW TO BUY AT AUCTION

The first five chapters in this book are mostly concerned about buying items at auction. Your auction experience will be much more fun and successful if you know some of the secrets of the trade. You could spend hours and hours sifting through the information on the Web, or you can quickly learn what you need to know in the first few chapters of this book.

- ✔ **Chapter 1: Getting Started** Learn how Internet auctions work, what kinds of auctions are available, and how you can sign up to become a registered auction participant. Then, once you're registered, you can begin bidding. But wait! Know what all of the information on the auction sales page means before you submit that first bid.

- ✔ **Chapter 2: The Opening Bid** The auction page may seem full of mysterious information. This chapter will let you in on the secrets. You'll see how to use safe and smart bidding practices, set limits, time your bids, and spot real bargains.

- ✔ **Chapter 3: The Winning Bid** One of the great benefits of Internet auctions is that you may get a once-in-a-lifetime chance to bid on that item you've always wanted. But you have to compete with others in a bidding war. How can you increase your chances to win?

✔ **Chapter 4: Money Matters** Any time money changes hands, there's potential for profits, bargains, and fraud. In this chapter you'll learn how to safely conduct financial transactions.

✔ **Chapter 5: Participating in the Collector's Paradise** eBay traces its roots to a Pez collector who wanted to get in touch with other "Pezzies." Since that time, eBay has been one of the best collectors' sites on the Web—not just for buying and selling, but also for keeping in touch with other collectors. This chapter presents ways you can enhance your collection not only by buying and selling your items, but by participating in collector communities, online conventions, and promoting your interests to others.

SELLING YOUR OWN ITEMS AT AUCTION

Not long after buying a few items on Internet auctions you'll begin to think, "I can make some money selling my extra stuff." And, you *can* make money. However, the planning strategies for selling on the Internet are more complicated than for buying. Chapters 6 through 12 of this book describe how to successfully sell items on Internet auctions—whether you have only a few items or you plan to make a career of it. These chapters teach you the business and computer skills you'll need to sell your merchandise. The eBay auction site will be used for most of the examples, but much of what will be covered is relevant to any open market auction site. The chapters covering selling are:

✔ **Chapter 6: Selling Your Own Merchandise** What should you know about selling in an Internet auction before jumping into the fray? Are you going to be an occasional seller or considering making a business of it? Are there sales tax and income tax ramifications? Have you considered how you'll ship your items—are you in a big city near a post office or UPS office, or are you in an out-of-the-way place with few shipping resources?

✔ **Chapter 7: What to Sell and How to Sell It** One-third of the merchandise offered for auction on the Internet is never sold. Why? Because no one wants the item at the price offered or because the item is improperly described or marketed. This chapter looks at what items sell best. It also presents information about wording ads to increase interest and sales.

✔ **Chapter 8: Creating a Winning Ad** Like any other business, successful selling in Internet auctions takes marketing skills. Bidders must feel comfortable dealing with you as an individual. Do you present yourself as someone who can be trusted? Is your item correctly and clearly described? With a little marketing sense you can word your ads and choose selling options that will increase the chances of getting a good price for your merchandise.

✔ **Chapter 9: Creating and Using Pictures in Your Ad** Possibly the most important part of your ad is a picture of your merchandise. This chapter teaches you the fundamentals of creating digital pictures using cameras, scanners, and video equipment. It shows you how to upload a picture to the Internet and how to include it in your ad description.

✔ **Chapter 10: Improving Your Presentation** How do you make your ad stand out from the rest? Add some "gee-whiz!" to your ad. This chapter looks at options for including color graphics, animation, and sound. A tutorial on using hypertext markup language (HTML) and ad preparation software is also included.

✔ **Chapter 11: Managing Your Auction** Now that you've created an ad, it's time to start the auction. But wait! There are also strategies for *when* and *how* to place your ads. This chapter describes methods for setting up auctions on eBay and other open market auction sites and gives you information to help you decide when the optimal time for your auction to end will be.

✔ **Chapter 12: Completing the Auction** Once your item has been placed on the auction block, you're in business. But what does that mean? You now have to communicate with your customer, handle payments, ship the merchandise, and possibly deal with deadbeat customers. This chapter covers the basics of running an auction business.

GETTING PAST THE BASICS

The basics of buying and selling through Internet auctions are easy enough for most people to accomplish readily. If you want to learn more and go further with your auction hobby or business, there are a few more topics you'll want to explore. The final chapters in this book cover additional material for those serious about their auction experience.

✔ **Chapter 13: Controlling Risks** Although certain kinds of risks are discussed in previous chapters, it's an important enough concern for both sellers and buyers that it needs to be covered in detail by itself. Most auction houses are aware that many people are wary of purchasing items on the Internet. Some of the risks are similar to those for the mail-order business, but other risks are unique to Internet auctions. Users must be aware that both sellers and buyers sometimes commit fraud. This chapter looks at specific methods major auction sites use to protect their customers. It also gives users tips for avoiding problems and provides resources for rectifying problems if they occur.

✔ **Chapter 14: Making a Living on Internet Auctions** Some people are making a steady and significant income from Internet auctions. What do they sell and how do they do it? Can you duplicate their success?

✔ **Chapter 15: Other Auction Resources** This chapter looks at the top auction sites on the Web. It describes what each site sells, how to access the site, and what advantages and disadvantages each includes. However, with new auctions coming online all the time, how can you know what's available? Ongoing information about auctions and auction resources can be found at this book's own Internet web site, www.alanelliott.com/auction.

SUMMARY

Internet auctions have grown rapidly because they are fun and easy to use and because they give you a way to buy interesting items and make money selling your own merchandise. Although some people have had to learn about auctions by trial and error, you now have a resource that will help you get started quickly and easily. This book will teach you how to successfully and safely participate in Internet auctions both as a buyer and as a seller. So buckle up your seat belt, put on your driving gloves, and enjoy the ride.

Getting Started in

Internet
Auctions

Chapter

1

Getting Started

Live auctions have been held for thousands of years. Now with the advent of the Internet, a new generation of auctions for the masses is taking form. The Internet auction engine got started in the mid-1990s and is now revving up to full power and at breakneck speed. By the late 1990s a single auction site stepped out and began to lead the pack. That site is eBay. Although eBay is not the only auction site on the Net, it is by far the most active. This chapter will introduce you to the types of auctions on the Web and will show you how to start participating in these auctions right now.

HOW DO INTERNET AUCTIONS WORK?

Before the Internet, an auction generally took place at a single location. One or more companies or families consigned merchandise to be sold and the merchandise was auctioned one item at a time. The auctioneer received a portion of the sale as his payment.

Internet auctions are different in a number of ways. Instead of being held in a building, an Internet auction is held electronically on an Internet web site. An auction host such as eBay provides the Web space where auctions are held. Individuals "rent" a piece of that space to auction their own merchandise. On eBay, registered participants can place an ad for a modest fee. The merchandise remains with the seller and eBay never sees or has possession of any auctioned items. When a bidder wins an auction, it is up to the seller and buyer to conclude the transaction one-on-one.

eBay collects its fee for being the auction host, and that's how it makes its money. (More about auction fees is covered in Chapter 11, "Managing Your Auction.")

For example, suppose you want to buy a rare *Star Wars* poster. You find it listed on eBay at a starting price of only $1. Wow! What a bargain! You've seen the same poster sell for more than $50. However, the starting price is just the beginning of the auction. Once the poster is online, it can be seen by millions of eBay shoppers. Since you've been looking for the poster, you open the bidding by placing a bid for $1. Another *Star Wars* collector sees the poster, wants it, and bids $2. A third collector sees the poster and really wants it. He bids $10. Now you discover that you've been outbid, so you raise your bid to $12. Soon you have a bidding war going on! The bidding continues for the duration of the auction—usually seven days. In the last hour the bids quickly go from $18 to $24 to $33 to $39. Just before time runs out, you make a final bid of $48! The auction ends and you've won! You are the high bidder. You're elated. But that's only the beginning. Now you and the seller must contact each other by e-mail, arrange payment and shipping terms, and conclude the transaction. It sounded easy until you reach the "business" part.

Once the seller receives payment, she ships the merchandise to the buyer and the transaction is completed. eBay sends the seller a bill by e-mail for hosting the auction. These fees are modest, often less than $1. (Specific information on seller's fees is given in Chapter 11, "Managing Your Auction.") There are no additional fees collected by eBay from the buyer.

Although buying and selling through an Internet auction is fairly simple, there are some "gotchas" you'll want to avoid. Just keep reading—this chapter will get you started on the right track.

UNDERSTANDING THE TYPES OF AUCTIONS ON THE WEB

Before becoming involved in Internet auctions, you should know something of the types of auctions available on the Web. They are not all the same. In fact, there are two primary kinds of auctions. The first type of auction was created to sell surplus merchandise from a single company or store. The only way you can participate in these auctions is as a buyer. These sites are called *Store Auctions*. Example Store Auctions include egghead.com, ubid.com, and onsale.com. Occasionally, these auctions will also accept consigned merchandise from an individual or a company.

These auctions are a good resource for new merchandise. They often carry last year's models, surplus items, and overstocks. Many of these auctions specialize in electronics and computing equipment. Chapter 15, "Other Auction Resources," lists a number of these auctions with descriptions of the items they specialize in selling.

The second kind of Internet auction is designed to allow you to easily be a seller as well as a buyer. In this kind of auction you can put your own merchandise up for sale for little or no cost to you, and you can also easily bid on and purchase merchandise from other participants. These sites are called *Open Auctions*. eBay (www.ebay.com) is the primary example of an Open Auction. Other major auction sites include Amazon (auctions.amazon.com), Excite (auctions.excite.com), and Yahoo! (auctions.yahoo.com).

Open Auctions are causing the greatest amount of excitement on the Internet. Most of this book will concentrate on how you can successfully become both a buyer and a seller in the Open Auction model, and eBay will be the primary example of how the Open Auction concept works.

GETTING STARTED WITH eBAY

You can get to the eBay Internet auction site by pointing your browser to www.ebay.com. When you enter eBay's main page, you see an inviting and colorful opening page similar to the one in Figure 1.1. What you actually see may look a little different because eBay changes its home page on a regular basis. However, the main sections will always be there—item categories, a list of featured items, and links for new users, how to bid, how to sell, how to register, and more. At the top right of the eBay page is a menu. this menu appears on all eBay pages and is useful for navigating to all sections of the eBay site. Throughout the book references will be made to this menu to help you move to various pages within the eBay system. You'll be introduced to many of these features in this chapter. So hold on and keep reading. You are about to enter the world's largest online marketplace.

Becoming a Registered eBay User

Every major auction site requires that you become a registered user before you can participate in any of the auctions, either as a buyer or seller. This restriction is for your protection and it's usually free. Registering every participant is one way eBay tries to keep sales on the up-and-up. For example, one of the results of being registered is that buyers and sellers can leave either positive or negative feedback about other users. Every user on eBay can look at your feedback score to determine if you

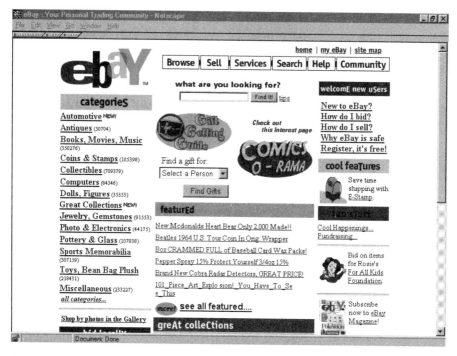

Figure 1.1   The eBay Opening Page.

are a good customer or a good seller. To play it safe as a buyer or seller it's recommended that you pay attention to the feedback score of the person you're doing business with. You may want to avoid doing business with users who have negative feedback. However, if a user's feedback is full of positives, then you can feel relatively safe that your transaction will proceed smoothly.

Registration is simple. From the main eBay page, click on the link <u>Register, it's free!</u>. You will see a series of pages that will ask you what country you are from, your e-mail address, full name, address, and phone number. Users must be at least 18 years old to register.

Don't panic at all the personal information it requests. eBay does not give all of the information out that you enter. However, users *can* get your e-mail address on request—but you'll be notified that they've requested it. All of this formality takes away some of the anonymity of the Web and should make any honest person more comfortable in dealing with other eBayers. If registered users turn out not to be so honest, then their registrations will be cancelled, and they will no longer be able to buy or sell on eBay. However, only a very small percent of users have ever had to face this fate.

During registration, you may select an eBay handle to use instead of your actual name—for example *ELVIS*, or *ebayjunkie*, *icollectdolls*, or *takethecake*. Some users choose to specify their e-mail address as their User ID. So how do other users know who you really are if you use an eBay handle? Throughout eBay, when you see someone's User ID, it will be followed by a numbered link in parentheses and one or more icons. For example, you might see

takethecake (31) ⭐

This tells you that the registered user called *takethecake* has accumulated 31 positive feedback points. The color of the star is based on the feedback number:

A *Yellow Star* represents a Feedback Profile of 10 to 99.

A *Turquoise Star* represents a Feedback Profile of 100 to 499.

A *Purple Star* represents a Feedback Profile of 500 to 999.

A *Red Star* represents a Feedback Profile of 1,000 to 9,999.

A *Shooting Star* (⭐)represents a Feedback Profile of 10,000 or higher.

You may also see one or two other icons next to a person's eBay User ID. The sunglasses icon (🕶) tells you that the user has changed his or her ID within the last 30 days. This icon will disappear after the user has maintained the same User ID for a 30-day period. The "About Me" icon (**me**) is a link to an eBay user's "About Me" personal page. This page allows users to display personal information about themselves. Just click on the **me** icon to view it. (For information on creating your own personal page, see the section later in this chapter called "About Me.")

Registered users are awarded a point for every positive feedback left for them by other users. A negative feedback takes away a point. A neutral feedback does not affect the feedback score one way or the other. Therefore, it is possible for a user to have a positive feedback score but have multiple negative feedback points. How can you tell? In the Feedback Forum you can view the feedback history of any user and see if they have been given any negative points. Figure 1.2 shows the feedback results for the user called *takethecake*. Notice that this user has 31 positive feedback points and no neutral or negative feedbacks.

If a user has negative feedback points, you'll have to use your own

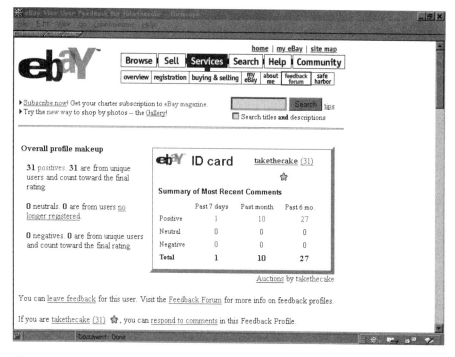

Figure 1.2   An eBay Feedback Profile Page.
(This material has been reproduced by John Wiley & Sons, Inc. with permission of eBay, Inc. Copyright © eBay, Inc. All rights reserved.)

judgment to determine if you want to do business with him. However, if a person has accumulated hundreds or thousands of positive points and only a few negative ones, then you might want to give him the benefit of the doubt. Knowing the importance of the feedback score should tell you that it is important for you to be honest and prompt in your own dealings on eBay.

Okay, you're an official eBay registered user. Now what? Now is the time to explore some of the resources available to you on the eBay site. Go back to the main eBay page (www.ebay.com) and click on <u>New Users Click Here</u>. This takes you to the eBay "Help Basic" page. You'll see that eBay describes itself as "the world's first, biggest, and best person-to-person online trading community. eBay is your place to find the stuff you want, to sell the stuff you have, and to make a few friends on the way! Think of eBay as a marketplace that provides efficient, one-to-one trading in an auction format on the Web."

Click the "Back" button to go back to the "Help Basic" page and look at the series of links available on this page. They include the following topics:

- ✔ **New to eBay** The links under this list provide an overview of all major components of eBay including how to register, descriptions of the different auction types, and how to find out what's happening.
- ✔ **Glossary Terms** When you see an auction or eBay term you don't understand, go to the <u>Glossary Terms</u> link. Dozens of words, icons, and procedures are explained here.
- ✔ **Direct Help** If you need help regarding a topic that cannot be found in the glossary or tutorials, you can ask questions on one of the Direct Help forums and usually get an answer from an expert who has already solved the same problem you're experiencing.
- ✔ **FAQ** New users to eBay have standard questions they ask. <u>Frequently Asked Questions</u> (FAQ) links answer many of the questions you may have about eBay or auctions.
- ✔ **New to** The eBay "New to" tutorials present step-by-step instructions for many of the most commonly performed tasks on eBay. Refer to these if you are having a problem understanding how to register, search, place a bid, sell items, or add images to your listings.

Unfortunately, even with all of the tutorials and links provided by eBay, it is easy to become overwhelmed. One of the purposes of this book is to help you wade through the morass of cyber-knowledge so that you can more efficiently and quickly become a successful Internet auction participant.

Becoming a Part of the Community

Since eBay originally began as a web site for collectors, it's understandable that it retains many aspects of its once tight-knit community. Therefore, if you're a collector, it's likely you'll be able to find and make friends here. One of the best ways to become an active part of the eBay community is to visit the chat rooms. The main eBay chat room is called the "eBay Café." You're invited to come on in and pour yourself a cup of mocha. Talk to people who've been eBayers since its inception as well as newbies trying to learn the ropes. You can get to the eBay Café by clicking on the

<u>Community</u> link from the main eBay page, then click on U.S. "eBay Café" under the chat header.

The topics in the eBay Café are wide and general—from "I'm having a baby!" to "What's the best way to ship a six foot lamp from Alaska to Ohio?" You must be a registered user to participate. Simply type in some question in the "Your Message" text box, press "Save My Message," and voilà, you're chatting! Click on your browser's "Reload" button periodically to see the progression of new messages in the chat room.

When something about eBay puzzles you or you don't know where to turn for help, you can usually find a listening ear in the eBay Café. You should visit it often and become a known member of the community. It will make your auction experience easier and more rewarding. For more information about using eBay chat rooms, refer to the section titled "Using the Chat Rooms" in Chapter 5, "Participating in the Collector's Paradise."

Fun Stuff and Cool Features

Tucked away on the eBay main page, usually in the lower right quadrant, are links to <u>Fun Stuff</u> and <u>Cool Features</u>. The information in this area changes on a regular basis. These links usually contain information about items such as advertisements for eBay merchandise and eBay community information, as well as links to celebrity charity auctions and holiday gift links.

About Me

Another feature of eBay that can help you be a part of the community is the "About Me" personal page. If you click on the <u>Site Map</u> link at the top of any eBay page, then click on the <u>About Me</u> link in the Services listing, you'll see a page that will allow you to create your own personal eBay page. Once you create a personal page, the "About Me" icon (**me**) will appear next to your User ID anytime it is displayed in eBay. Then, users can click on the icon to display your personal page.

To create a page you must first enter your User ID and password. You are then given the opportunity to select from three available page styles (column, newspaper, and centered). Once you've selected a style, a page containing a fill-in form will appear where you'll enter a title for your page, a welcome message, and a picture. You can also choose to have your recent feedback results posted on the page as well as links to the items you're currently selling. The personal page is a good way to help you participate in a chat room—people can find out what your interests are and they can see what you really look like! A portion of the fill-in form is shown in Figure 1.3.

BUYING AT AUCTION

Now that you've browsed around the eBay site, and perhaps snooped around in some of the chat rooms, you should be eager to take the leap from being an observer to becoming a participant. However, if you have limited experience buying at auction, you may be intimidated with the process. It's not like going to your local department store where prices are fixed. It even differs from a flea market where you might be able to negotiate a price for an item from a vendor. In an auction you are competing with other customers who also want the same item. You're in a war fought with money, and the one willing to spend the most wins the battle.

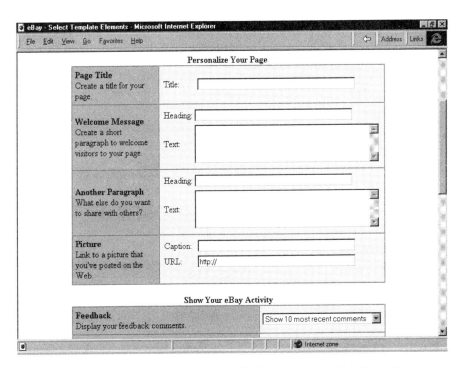

Figure 1.3 A portion of the "About Me" eBay Personal Web Page Form.

THREE VARIETIES OF eBAY AUCTIONS

One variety of auction is not enough to meet the needs of those who want to sell items on eBay, so three forms of auctions have developed. These are the Standard Auction, the Dutch Auction, and the Private Auction.

The Standard Auction

The first and most common form of auction on eBay (and most other Internet auctions) is based on a form called the English Auction. In the eBay Standard Auction, the seller first posts a minimum bid. If a customer wants to bid on an item and she is the first person to bid on the item, she has to offer the minimum (opening) bid price. If another bidder wishes to raise the bid, he must raise the bid by a specified incremental amount. The bid increment is specified by eBay according to the value of the current bid. See Table 1.1.

Of course, a bidder may bid higher than the minimum acceptable bid. This brings up a new auction term—the *proxy bid*. If you bid more than the minimum increment required on an auction, eBay will only raise the reported high bid by an amount to make you the high bidder. That is, if the current bid is $1.00, and the minimum bid increment is $0.25, and you bid a maximum bid of $3.00, eBay will report your high bid as $1.25. What happened to the other part of the bid? It is held in "proxy" to pro-

TABLE 1.1 Bid Increments in an eBay Standard Auction	
High Bid	*Bid Increment**
$0.01 to $0.99	$.05
$1.00 to $4.99	$0.25
$5.00 to $24.99	$0.50
$25.00 to $99.99	$1.00
$100.00 to $249.00	$2.50
$250 to $499.99	$5.00
$500 to $999.99	$10.00
$1,000 to $2,499.99	$25.00
$2,500 to $4,999.99	$50.00
$5,000 and up	$100.00
*At time of publication.	

tect you from being outbid by another customer. Therefore, if someone else comes along and bids $2.00, eBay's proxy service will automatically place a bid in your name for $2.25 to make you the high bidder again. However, if another bidder places a bid of $4.00, you are outbid. Using the proxy bid is a tactic you might take advantage of when you *really* want an item, and know the maximum price you'd be willing to pay. Then, if someone bids on the item in the dead of night, eBay will be there to represent you and regain the high bid status for you (up to your specified limit). A complete description of bidding tactics is covered in Chapter 3, "The Winning Bid."

A further wrinkle in eBay's Standard Auction is the *reserve price* option. Usually you expect the highest bidder in an auction to win the auction, but on eBay this is not always the case. The seller may specify a reserve price auction. In this case, if the bidding does not reach a specified level, the seller has no obligation to sell the item at the highest bid. For example, if a seller specifies a $10.00 reserve price, and the bidding only reaches $8.00, the highest bidder will probably not get the item. (The seller has the option to go ahead with the sale, but he is under no obligation to do so.) Furthermore, the amount of the reserve price is *unknown* to the buyer unless the seller specifies it in the item description. This technique is designed to protect the seller from having to sell an item too cheaply. However, many bidders look with disdain on reserve price auctions and some even refuse to bid on them.

Tip: You'll know if an auction is reserve price by looking at the current maximum bid. If the phrase "reserve not yet met" appears next to the bid, it means that a reserve price has been set and that the current high bid does not exceed that reserve price. When the maximum bid exceeds the reserve price, the message "reserve price met" will appear next to the maximum bid.

The Dutch Auction

An eBay Dutch Auction is used to sell multiple copies of the same item in a single auction listing. In a Dutch Auction, the seller indicates an opening bid and the number of items to be sold. When a bidder places a bid on the item, she specifies not only a bid but also how many of the items she wants if she wins. For example, suppose a seller has eight copies of a

Yellowstone Night Sounds CD. He places the item in a Dutch Auction and specifies a minimum bid of $9.99. The first bidder may bid the minimum $9.99 and specify that he wants five copies. Bidder number 2 comes along and bids $9.99 and specifies three copies. If the auction ends now, both bidders will get the copies they wanted at $9.99 each. However, suppose bidder 3 bids $10.99 and specifies two copies. Now when the auction ends, bidder 3 gets the two copies he wanted—at the price of $9.99—not at the price he bid. What? How's that? The final price the buyer must pay is the *lowest winning bid*. Therefore, in this auction, since two copies were bid at $10.99 and the rest at $9.99, the lower of the two prices is the selling price. So which of the two bidders that bid $9.99 will get the CDs? The priority goes to the bidder who bid first. Thus, bidder 1 will get his five copies. The one remaining copy of the CD goes to bidder 2—even though he had wanted three copies.

The Private Auction

Private auctions are the least-used type of eBay auction. The auction itself works like the standard auction except that identities of bidders are not publicly known. This variety of auction is used primarily when the seller believes that his potential customers would be more likely to bid if they can do so anonymously.

EVALUATING THE AUCTION ITEM

When you find an item for sale in an Internet auction, its description usually contains details about the item and shipping, plus a picture. For example, Figure 1.4 shows a copy of a typical eBay item description.

The important features of this description are:

✔ **The item description** Before getting too involved with an item, make sure it is exactly what you want. Important considerations are condition, completeness, grade (for collectibles), and authenticity (Is proof included?). If the item sounds exactly like what you're looking for, check out the picture.

✔ **The picture** Although pictures are optional, the vast majority of items contain one or more pictures. The picture allows you to visually verify the textual description. If the picture checks out, take a look at the current bid.

MECHANICAL CAST IRON MONKEY BANK W/ACTION NR

Item #180112202

Collectibles:Banks:Mechanical

Description

Bid!

Starts at	**$4.99**	
Quantity	1	
Time left	**6 days, 12 hours +**	
Started	10/11/99, 18:51:09 PDT	
Ends	10/18/99, 18:51:09 PDT	

First bid	**$4.99**
# of bids	0 (bid history) (with emails)
Location	**Cedar Hill**

✉ (mail this auction to a friend)

🎁 (request a gift alert)

Seller **takethecake** (38) ☆ **me**

(view comments in seller's Feedback Profile) (view seller's other auctions) (ask seller a question)

High bid --

Payment See item description for payment methods accepted

Shipping See item description for shipping charges

Update item **Seller:** If this item has received no bids, you may revise it.
Seller revised this item before first bid.

Seller assumes all responsibility for listing this item. You should contact the seller to resolve any questions before bidding. Currency is U.S. dollar ($) unless otherwise noted.

Description

MECHANICAL MONKEY BANK This cast iron monkey bank allows you to put a coin in the monkey's mouth, then it will jump up and put the coin in the organ grinder's box. This is a reproduction of a turn of the century type mechanical bank. Paint and action are in great condition. It even comes with a few coins already in the organ grinder's box.

Winning bidder pays $3.50 for postage in the U.S. Mastercard, Visa and American Express accepted. Texas residents add 8.25% sales tax.

Bid with confidence. This item is guaranteed to be to your liking or your bid is refunded.

Have a great day, and thanks for bidding.

Figure 1.4 A typical eBay auction item description.

✔ **The current bid** This tells you what the highest bid (so far) has been offered for this item. If no one has yet bid on the item, the current bid will be $0. Now you must make the decision to either outbid the current high bid or look elsewhere. If you decide to bid, first check out the bid restrictions.

✔ **The bid restrictions** There are two kinds of bid restrictions, both of which are set by the seller. One is the opening bid, which is the minimum amount you can bid for an item. The other restriction is the minimum winning bid, in which the seller specifies a reserve price auction. In a reserve auction, the bidder does not know what the minimum bid is. In eBay, if you see the message "reserve bid not met" next to the current bid, it means that the current bid is not high enough to win the auction. If you are comfortable with the bid restrictions and want to continue, check the ending time for the auction.

✔ **The ending time** This is the time the auction officially ends. Most auctions on eBay run for seven days, although auctions may run either 3, 5, 7, or 10 days at the discretion of the seller. The "time left" tells you how much time remains until the auction ends. If there are still several days remaining, it means that there is plenty of time for you and other customers to bid on the item. If you bid now, you'll need to check back periodically to make sure you are not outbid. (eBay will notify you by e-mail if you are outbid.) If there's little time left in the auction, say a few minutes, then you better get your bid in quickly. Specific strategies for bidding are covered in Chapter 3, "The Winning Bid." Before bidding, however, you should look at the item location.

✔ **The item location** This information is important because of shipping considerations. If the item is located overseas, you might have a problem receiving it, or shipping may be too expensive. Before bidding, make sure you are comfortable with the method and cost of shipping.

✔ **The shipping method** Most sellers will include a specific cost for shipping the item to the winner within the United States. Or you may be given several options to select how you want to ship the item. You may also be offered the option to purchase insurance. Beware—some sellers try to make additional money on shipping by charging excessive amounts. Make sure you feel that the shipping is in line with the value of the article.

✔ **Guarantee** Serious and honest sellers will usually offer you some sort of guarantee for the item. This gives you assurance that if you misunderstood the description and do not get the item you bargained for, you have a chance to send it back. Don't assume that you'll get the cost of shipping back—usually it's just the bid amount.

✔ **The seller's feedback score** The eBay feedback score was defined earlier in this chapter. Generally, a high score means that the seller has made many successful transactions and that the customers are happy. If the seller has a low score, you may want to examine his feedback details to determine if you feel comfortable doing business with him.

If you're satisfied with all of the above considerations, then you can feel safe about bidding on the item you want. Be aware of these details. However, don't let them stop you from the enjoyment of browsing and bidding. The vast majority of all auction transactions are concluded quickly and to the satisfaction of both the buyer and seller.

WHAT DO THE ABBREVIATIONS MEAN?

When you begin looking at auction titles and descriptions, you'll soon see that there are certain abbreviations and phrases that are used as quick ways to describe some aspect of an item. Once you've browsed around eBay or other auctions for a while, you'll be reading these abbreviations like a pro. To give you a head start, here's a list of some of the common terms and abbreviations you're likely to see:

✔ **BU (Brilliant Uncirculated)** Usually refers to a coin that has never been circulated and still retains its luster.

✔ **CC (Credit Cards)** When you see this in a title or description it means that the seller accepts credit cards for payment.

✔ **DJ (Dust Jacket)** When referring to a book, the dust jacket is the paper cover that is often present on hardbound books. The presence and condition of a dust jacket can influence the value of the book.

✔ **Fox (Foxing)** In book descriptions you might see a phrase like "foxing around the page edges." This refers to a discoloration or stain, often the reddish-brown color of a fox.

✔ **HC/1st (Hard Cover, 1st Edition)** This refers to a book that is bound with a hard cover, and is a first edition. Note that first "book club" editions are generally worth considerably less than original retail first editions.

✔ **NIB (New in Box)** The item is brand-new and still in its original box. This is very important for collectibles, since the original box can add significantly to an item's value.

✔ **NR (No Reserve)** This refers to the eBay option to place a hidden reserve as a minimum acceptable bid. NR means that the seller did *not* set a reserve price on the item. Many bidders despise auctions that contain a reserve price. Thus, the NR indication is a positive statement about the sale.

✔ **MINT** This item is in brand-new condition, never used or refurbished to like-new condition.

✔ **MWMT (Mint with Mint Tags)** This usually refers to plush toys such as Beanie Babies. The tag is the manufacturer's ID tag. Items with mint tags are worth more than those whose tag has been removed or damaged.

✔ **MSRP (Manufacturer's Suggested Retail Price)** This is the price set by a manufacturer that often appears on an item's box or cover. It is the price you'd expect an item to sell for in a retail store that does not offer a discount.

✔ **MS65** This refers to a grading system used for coins. You'll often see MS64, MS65, up to MS70 for highly desirable coins. Make sure you understand this grading before bidding on a coin since one number difference can make a large difference in the coin's value. See the description of PCGS below.

✔ **PCGS (Professional Coin Grading Service)** This independent coin grading service authenticates coins and rates them on a 70-point scale. Having a PCGS rating on a coin gives assurance to the buyer that the coin is real and in the condition described.

✔ **V/MC (Visa/MasterCard)** The seller accepts Visa and Master-Card for purchases.

There are many abbreviations and terms unique to particular categories that are too numerous to list here. If you are interested in a particular collectible, you should study the market to understand what the abbreviations mean and any grading standards that are available for the collectible before making any significant purchases.

SUMMARY

Participating in online auctions is fun and exciting. When you use a little common sense, it is also safe and rewarding. Go ahead and take a drive on the Internet highway to experience the auction frenzy for yourself. You are now ready for your first opening bid!

Chapter 2

The Opening Bid

S hopping on an Internet auction site is exciting and full of sur-
prises. You never know what interesting piece of merchandise
may be offered for sale. Sometimes you may want to browse
through the seemingly endless lists of items for sale while other times
you might be hunting for a very specific item. Fortunately, most auction sites allow you to shop both ways, browsing and searching.
Whichever method you use, when you find an item you want, that's
when the bidding fun begins.

BROWSING AND SEARCHING

If you're "window shopping" for something, but don't exactly know what
you want, then browsing is a fun way to see what's available at auction.
Browsing allows you to discover unusual items that you may not think to
look for on your own. Who would have thought that you'd find a copy of
your old high school yearbook, or a brand-new teddy bear just like the
one you used to sleep with when you were a kid, or a restored 1958 Buick
just like the one you went to Yellowstone in back in 1962? You have to
watch yourself when you begin browsing—the memories can start to
flood back quickly and relentlessly. You'll be looking for the "bid" button
quicker than you can say "Howdy Doody." What! Is that an old Howdy
Doody puppet being auctioned? Cool!

Featured Auctions

One of the first places to begin browsing is on eBay's main page. Right in the middle of the page you'll see a short list of featured items for sale. This is only a teaser. After looking through the short list, click the <u>more featured . . .</u> link to see additional items. Why do some items appear in this highly visible "Featured Auctions" area? You guessed it. Each seller paid an extra fee ($99.95) to have his item included in this highly visible list. The fee should tell you something about these particular sellers—either they have to sell a lot of items (as in a Dutch Auction) or one expensive item to justify the fee. The kind of items you'll find here usually include new merchandise such as office consumables (for example, ink cartridges), popular toys, software, small electronics, and the like. For example, a recent set of Featured Auctions included a *Day You Were Born* software CD, bulk bubble wrap, T-shirt iron-ons, Epson printer cartridges, a haunted house soundtrack CD, cell phone batteries, Beanie Babies, special blend coffee, and a complete English Pub bar (with a starting bid of $4,000).

Because most of the items in the featured list are Dutch Auctions, buying a featured item at the bid price is almost a sure thing. In fact, most of these items have a hundred or more copies available, and there are rarely enough bidders to buy them all. If you're looking for very popular toys or office consumables, the Featured Auction area may be the best place to begin. However, if you're looking for more interesting one-of-a-kind items, you're more likely to find what you want by browsing in a category. To view items by category, go to the eBay main page (click on "Home" at the top of any eBay page), and click on the "Categories" icon.

Browsing Through Auction Categories

Because there are usually more than two million items for sale each day on eBay, you could easily spend your entire day browsing through the listings and still only see a fraction of the items. Fortunately, eBay has evolved in a way that makes it easy to search for a particular item by using category listings.

As you view the eBay main page, at the left side is a listing of some of the major categories. Click on the "Categories" icon to view the entire list of categories. The eBay Categories page appears; note that this page is actually a part of the Featured Auctions page described in the previous section. The category listings begin about halfway down the page and are in alphabetical order by major category types. For example, the listing begins with the first major category, Antiques, then the Antiques subcategories, followed by the Automotive listing, and so on:

Antiques (49877)

General (6679)

Ancient World (2078)

Architectural (1912)

Asian Antiques (1857)

Books, Manuscripts (3904)

Ceramics (768)

Ethnographic (594)

European (700)

Folk Art (1449)

Furniture (1885)

Glass (975)

Medical (757)

Metalware (8399)

Musical Instruments (698)

Primitives (2014)

Prints (6637)

Reproductions (477)

Science Instruments (714)

Textiles, Linens (2913)

Toleware (276)

Woodenware (720)

Antiques (post-1900) (3471)

Automotive (32885)

Collector Vehicles (10464)

General Vehicles (15196)

Motorcycles (7225)

Notice the numbers in parentheses next to each category name. These tell you how many items are currently for sale in that category. Also notice that the categories are divided into major categories and subcategories. In the example above, Antiques is the major category, and the subcategories under Antiques include General, Ancient World, and so on. Most major categories have ten to 20 subcategories.

At this time, the major eBay categories include: Antiques; Automotive; Books, Movies, and Music; Coins and Stamps; Collectibles; Computers; Dolls and Figures; Jewelry and Gemstones; Photo and Electronics; Pottery and Glass; Sports Memorabilia; Toys and Bean Bag Plush; and Miscellaneous. Furthermore, if you click on one of the popular subcategories, a secondary list will be displayed with an even more detailed breakdown of the item. For example, if you click on the Music category under Books, Movies, and Music, another page of categories will appear: General, CDs, Records, and Tapes. Under the CD subcategory are listings for General, Big Band/Swing, Blues, Children's, and many more. In all, there are well over a thousand different categories of items on eBay.

The list of major eBay categories may change at any time, but you can always get the current list by clicking on the "Categories" option on the main eBay page and then simply clicking on the category name. The resulting page will first list any featured items in that category followed by the general list of items for the category. If there are items in the category that currently have 30 or more bids, they will be listed in a "Hot List." The Hot List is where you'll find the most popular items for sale. But one word of warning: When an auctioned item is hot, it means that a bidding war is going on, and the chances for you to get the item at a reasonable price diminishes significantly.

If you're an avid collector, you can keep up with what is for sale and what is popular within a particular category by browsing through that category's entire list. This gives you a chance to discover that unique item you've never heard of or never expected to be for sale. However, as you might notice, even within some of the subcategories there might be ten thousand or more items—still too many to look through in a reasonable amount of time. What's your next option? Perform a Gallery search.

The Auction Gallery

The eBay "Auction Gallery" is another way to search through listings by category. You can get to the Gallery either from a link on the main eBay page or by selecting the <u>Site Map</u> link, then click on <u>Gallery</u> from the Browse listing. Figure 2.1 shows the eBay Gallery page. Notice that this page contains links to major category listings.

When you select one of the <u>Gallery</u> category links, another page of links will be displayed that allows you to narrow your search. Once you click on one of the sublinks, a page of images will appear for items from that category. Figure 2.2 shows a page from the Gallery listing for ancient

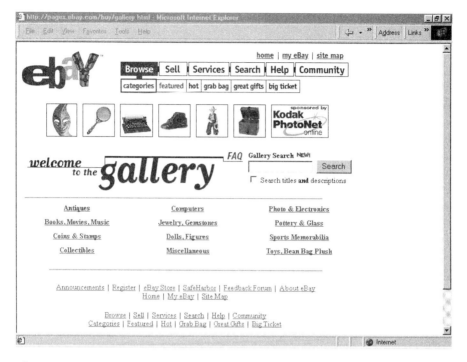

Figure 2.1　The eBay Gallery Page.

world antiques. Items get placed in the Gallery listing in one of two ways. For a small charge of $0.25, a seller can place her auction in the general Gallery listings. For $19.95, a seller can place an item in the Featured Gallery listing. The images for Featured Gallery items are larger than those of the general Gallery listing and they appear first in any list. Obviously, Featured Auctions will typically be for expensive items or Dutch Auctions. Items that are featured in the Gallery are different that those in the general Featured Auctions. To become featured in both places, the seller must pay both fees associated with the Gallery and general Featured Auctions.

When would you want to use the Gallery? If you are a visual person, then looking through the Gallery listing will be much more pleasant to you than looking at lines and lines of words from the normal listings. The Gallery allows you to get a quick feel for an item. For certain items such as artwork, antiques, and collectibles, a picture of the item can give you a quick way to determine if you want to know more.

If you see an item in the Gallery that you want to know more about,

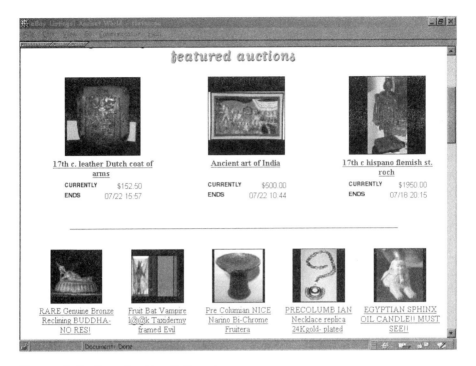

Figure 2.2 Sample eBay Gallery Images.

click on the link directly below the picture. This will take you to the standard auction listing where you can read the details about the item and bid on the item if you wish.

Another way to use the Gallery is to perform a specific search by entering one or more keywords in the Gallery Search field. This search field is located on the main Gallery page, as shown in Figure 2.1. Only those auctions that are in the Gallery will be displayed as a result of a Gallery search. This is a great way to shop from pictures rather than from titles. To learn more about specific search techniques, refer to the next section.

NARROWING YOUR SEARCH

If you want to find a particular type of item, the quickest method might be to perform a simple search. The first place you'll see a "Search" entry box is on the eBay main page. If the type of item you're looking for can be described in a word or two, simply type the descriptive word(s) into the

"Search" entry box and click on the "Search" button. For example, a collector of Dr Pepper memorabilia might enter *Dr Pepper* and a collector of *Star Wars* action figures might enter *Star Wars Figures*. (Note that case does not matter when you enter your search words. A search for *Star Wars Figures* is the same as for *star wars figures*.) Each of these searches will typically result in listings of 200 to 500 items. As another example, if you're interested in New York memorabilia not related to sports, and you enter *New York*, you'll come up with thousands of items whose titles contain the words *New York*. However, many (if not most) of the items found in the search will be collectibles related to the various sports teams in the Big Apple. Fortunately, there's a way to narrow this search. For example, if you enter *New York–yankees–mets–knicks* (putting minus signs in front of the search words you want to exclude), the resulting list of items will include all matches containing *New York*, but only if they *do not* also include the words *yankees*, *mets*, or *knicks*. Thus, the eBay search engine is not limited to searching for simple lists of words. By knowing a little of the eBay search syntax, you can easily create sophisticated searches to find exactly what you're looking for.

General eBay Search Rules

When you enter a list of words into the eBay search engine, every word in your search list is used as a search word. This means that if you enter *Bell and Disney*, eBay will search for items containing the three words *Bell*, *and*, and *Disney*. (Some other search engines use the words *and*, *or*, and *not* as Boolean logicals, meaning that the *Bell and Disney* search would look for an item containing both the words *Bell* and *Disney*.) The bottom line is *do not* use the words *and*, *or*, or *not* in your searches unless you really want to search for a title or description that contains those specific words.

Another general eBay search rule is that you may specify an exact phrase by placing the words in quotation marks. For example, a search for *"Dr Pepper"* would only find items that contained that exact phrase. However, if you leave off the quotation marks and searched on *Dr Pepper*, the search might find any listing that contains the words *Dr* and *Pepper* anywhere in the description—such as a listing for "Salt & Pepper Shakers from Dominican Republic (DR)."

When you enter a search from the eBay main page, eBay searches the title of the item up for auction—not the words in the item's longer description. However, once you make an initial search from the main page's "Search" box, you'll see a new set of search options displayed on the top of the screen with your search results, as shown in Figure 2.3. This figure

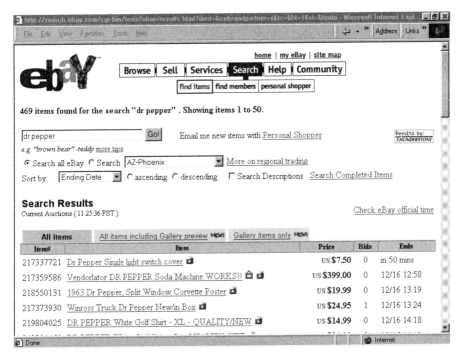

Figure 2.3 Results of a simple eBay search.

(This material has been reproduced by John Wiley & Sons, Inc. with permission of eBay, Inc. Copyright © eBay, Inc. All rights reserved.)

shows that a search of *Dr Pepper* yielded 469 items. Notice that the new search box that appears has a "Go!" button next to it, and several other search options below the box. This setup allows you to further narrow your search by specifying several other search options.

Just under the search box you can select to search all of eBay, or to limit your search only to auctions from sellers in a specific geographical area. Below the location option is a "Sort by" options list box. Within this box, you can select to have the listing of items sorted by Ending Date (the default), Starting Date, Bid Price, or Search Ranking. (Click on the down arrow next to the "Sort by" box to display the option list.) The Search Ranking option sorts the items according to how well the item matches the search criteria.

Click on "ascending" or "descending" order to select how you want the listing displayed. If you want eBay to search words in the item descriptions as well as words in the title, click on the "Search Descriptions" checkbox. The Search Descriptions option is probably the most useful of the list options because oftentimes you are looking for a specific item, and the seller does not have enough room in the title field to enter all the details needed to describe the item fully. By including the item's longer description in the search, you can narrow your search to very specific criteria. For example, suppose you're looking for an old TI Transistor Radio. You might use the search *TI Transistor Radio* and come up with no matches. However, by including the descriptions in the search you might find a listing whose title is "Antique Transistor Radio Still Works LOOK!" Notice that *TI* is not in the title. However, if the description includes a phrase such as *Manufactured by TI* then the search that includes the description will find the item. The down side of including the description is that because eBay must search through more text, the search might take considerably longer than a search that only included the title.

> **Tip:** From any "Search" box you can initiate any new search. You're not limited to searches on the items or categories that originally brought you to that page.

eBay Search Syntax

There are several additional eBay syntax rules that can come in handy to help you perform a successful search. For example, suppose you want to find an item that could be listed as *coin*, *coins*, or *coinage*. eBay allows you to use the asterisk (*) as a wild card letter to specify any combination of letters following several initial letters. Thus, if you enter *coin** as a search word, eBay will find listings that include the words *coin*, *coins*, and *coinage*.

Use a negative sign (–) before a word in your list to tell eBay to find items that *do not* include that specific word. For example, suppose you want to search bears, but not teddy bears. You could enter the search *bear –teddy*. (Note that there's no space between the minus sign and the word *teddy*.)

Use parentheses to specify a search that performs an "or" search. For example, suppose you're looking for a computer mouse, but you're only interested in either the Microsoft or Compaq brand. You could enter the search *mouse (Microsoft,Compaq)*. This would perform a search for listings that include the word *mouse* and either the word *Microsoft* or *Compaq*.

TABLE 2.1 Using eBay's Search Syntax

If you enter the search phrase	eBay will search for
Doctor Who	Items containing both the words *Doctor* and *Who*.
"Doctor Who"	Items that contain the specific phrase *Doctor Who*.
(ty,beanie)	Items that contain either the word *ty* or *beanie*.
bear –teddy	Items that contain the word *bear*, but not the word *teddy*.
penny –(lincoln,indian)	Items that contain the word *penny* but not the words *lincoln* or *indian*.
americ*	Items that contain words including *american*, *americana*, *americas*, etc.
#1999	Items that include the exact number or date *1999*.

Table 2.1 shows how you can use eBay's search syntax to specify just the kind of search you want to perform. Note that search words may be in lowercase, or uppercase, or mixed—the case does not matter.

Searching within Categories

In addition to the search box on the main eBay page, you'll also find a search box when you select a category listing. Figure 2.4 shows a category listing of Dolls and Figures. Notice the "Search" text box in the upper right section of the screen. Under this "Search" box are two options:

Search only in *Dolls, Figures*

Search titles *and* descriptions

If you select *Search only in Dolls, Figures*, then the search will only look for items in that specified category. If you select *Search titles and descriptions*, then the search will look for matches both in the item title as well as in the item description. As described in the *Dolls and Figures* example above, this option can come in handy to limit searches by words that might normally not be used in the title.

28

Figure 2.4 Category listing of Dolls and Figures.
(This material has been reproduced by John Wiley & Sons, Inc. with permission of eBay, Inc. Copyright © eBay, Inc. All rights reserved.)

Complex eBay Searches

If the previous search options are not enough to help you hone in on exactly what you're looking for, eBay has an even more comprehensive way to search. To display the eBay "Find Items" screen, click on the "Search" option at the top of any eBay page. The "Find Items" screen is shown in Figure 2.5.

This screen allows you to select from five different searches to help you locate a item. They are:

✔ **By Title** This type of search looks for matching words in the item's descriptive title. Within this search form you may also specify other information to be used in the search, such as a category, a price range, and the region where the item is located. It also allows you to request several sort criteria and even allows you the option to search completed auctions. For example, if you live in Texas and want to find antique tables only from dealers in

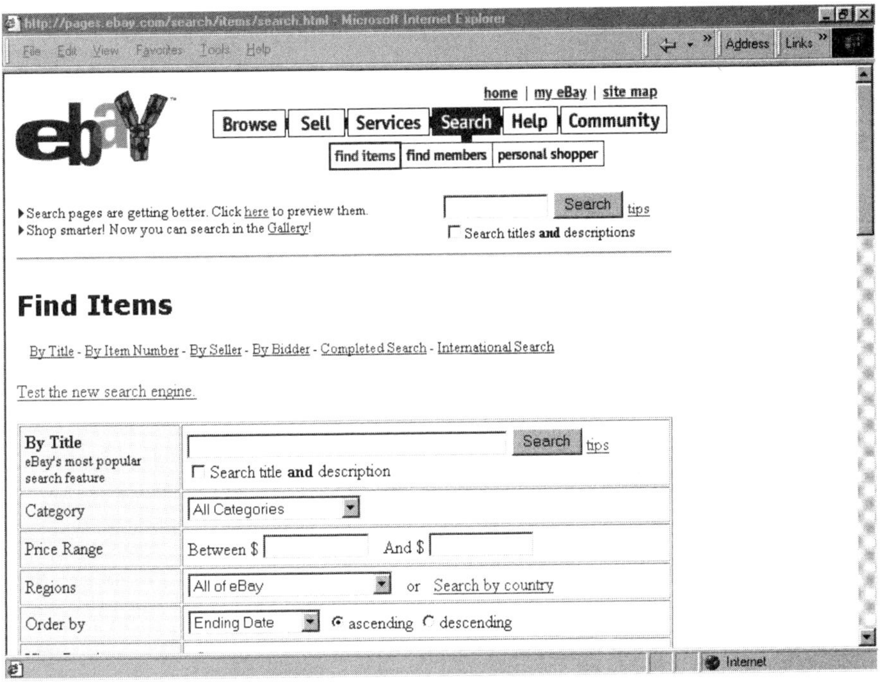

Figure 2.5 eBay Find Items Search Page.
(This material has been reproduced by John Wiley & Sons, Inc. with permission of eBay, Inc. Copyright © eBay, Inc. All rights reserved.)

Texas (because of shipping concerns), you could use this search form.

✔ **By Item Number** This option allows you to search for an item by its unique eBay item number. Each eBay auction item is assigned a number, and this search allows you to quickly find it (whether the auction has ended or not).

✔ **By Seller** This search allows you to find auctions from a particular seller. You must know the seller's User ID. In fact, if you are a seller, this search method is a quick way to display all of your own auctions to monitor their progress. If you're a fan of a particular seller (perhaps you like the service or quality of their products), you can use this search to find all of the seller's current (and past) auctions.

✔ **By Bidder** This search allows you to find all of the auctions a particular bidder is currently involved in. If you bid on a lot of items, you may lose track of what you've bid on. This search is a quick way to find out where you stand on those items.

✔ **Completed Auctions** This search allows you to find auctions that have been completed. This comes in handy when you are researching prices to see what items have sold for in the past. For example, suppose you're interested in purchasing a movie poster for a classic movie. You might do a search to find out what prices similar posters recently sold for. This can help you judge what you might have to bid in order to win an auction in the future.

A recent addition to the eBay search options is the *Regional Search*. eBay is in the process of creating regional eBays for some of the more active areas of the country, beginning with the Los Angeles area. If you're in this area and want to search for local goods or save shipping on large items, a regional search might be helpful.

Finding Bargains

One method of searching that is *not* automated in eBay is the search for bargains. However, there are some tricks you can use to spot auctions that might end up with a lower bid than usual—thus being a bargain. Usually, bargain auction prices are caused by sellers who don't pay attention to the search capabilities within eBay or who are naive about the way eBay works. These sellers make fundamental mistakes about how to list their item on eBay, and the result is that they do not usually get the maximum bid price for their merchandise.

One mistake some sellers make in their listing is misspelling words in the item title. Suppose you're searching for a book by the English fantasy author J. R. R. Tolkien. Just for kicks, you might also search for *Tolkein* (a common misspelling of his name). Most people looking for Tolkien's books will not do the second search, and so they will miss any auctions that are using the misspelled version of the name. Unfortunately for sellers and buyers, misspellings are fairly common on eBay. Savvy customers can take advantage of this error. Another way to locate items that may not show up in searches is to browse through categories that interest you. Since you can't always guess at the misspellings people may use, sometimes the only way to find an errant item is to browse through the entire list.

Another mistake sellers make is to create a poor descriptive title. For example, a seller might have a Disney animation cel to offer, but uses a title such as "Cool painted scene from an old classic cartoon." (An animation cel is a picture painted on a piece of celluloid. A cel had to be painted for every frame in a cartoon feature. These cels were then photographed in sequence to create the cartoons. Cels from popular cartoon features, es-

pecially rare Disney ones, often sell for a hefty price.) This kind of uninformative description does not attract knowledgeable buyers who might
enter search words like *Animation, cel,* and *Disney*. Therefore, if you find
this item, you may be one of the few people who see it; thus you have the
potential for winning the auction with a low bid. (Sellers who create poor
titles have obviously not read this book!)

Understanding auction timing can also help you find bargains. Timing is important in Internet auctions because it is not uncommon for several buyers to place last minute bids on a certain item. For example, if you
make a bid on a popular item a few days before it closes, there's a good
chance you'll be outbid. Therefore, if you really want that item, you'll be
online when the bidding is scheduled to end. Then you can see if you're
outbid and possibly get in a last-second bid to beat your competitor. However, what if an auction ends at a really bad time—say 2:00 A.M. or midday
on a workday? In that case there will probably be fewer bidders online at
that time and the likelihood of there being a flurry of last-second bids is
diminished.

When is eBay the busiest? Typically, on Wednesday evenings and
weekend evenings because these are the most common times for auctions
to end. Late nights and working hours (except for lunch hour) are times
of lower activity. Therefore, if you find an auction that ends at an odd
time, you might have a better chance at getting the item for a bargain
price than if the auction ends during a busier time. For more information
on auction timing, see Chapter 3, "The Winning Bid."

Finally, your own expertise in a particular area can help you spot
and buy bargains. If you are an expert on a particular type of pottery,
for example, you should keep a sharp eye on the auctions within that
category. If a seller and other bidders don't recognize the value of an
item up for auction, then you might be able to get a bargain. In fact,
some eBay sellers buy the merchandise from other eBay sellers, repackage it with a more complete description, and sell it on eBay at a handsome profit.

Searching Other Auctions

If you're looking for a particular item that you can't find on eBay, don't
give up. There are plenty of other popular auctions available on the Web,
such as Amazon, Yahoo!, and Excite.

For example, suppose you want to see what kinds of Dr Pepper collectibles are available on the Amazon auction site. The search on that site
will be very similar to the one on eBay. To perform a search on Amazon,
enter the www.amazon.com address into your Internet browser's location

box. The main Amazon page will appear. Select the "Auction" tab from the menu and the Amazon Auction main page will appear. Enter *Dr Pepper* into the "Auction Search" text box and click on the "Go!" button. Figure 2.6 shows the results of a search for *Dr Pepper* on the Amazon auction site. Although there are significantly fewer hits, there might be something you'd like to get, and there might be fewer people bidding on it, which could result in a lower price for you. For more information about other auctions, see Chapter 15, "Other Auction Resources."

Using Automated Searching

Many auction participants log onto the Internet to search for the same few items time after time. Because computers are good at these kinds of repetitive tasks, automated ways have been developed to perform these searches for you. One of these automated search engines is eBay's "Personal Shopper." This automated search feature allows you to specify up to

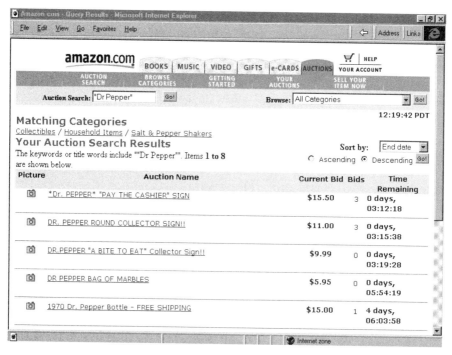

Figure 2.6 Amazon Auction Search Results screen.

three different searches. Even when you are not logged into the Web, it will search through its two million items and come up with a list of matches. When you log onto your e-mail the next time, you'll see a message that tells you what auctions have been found. You can then go directly to the auctions to see if the matches are what you're looking for. An example of the kind of message you'll receive from eBay's Personal Shopper is given below:

```
Hello imabuyer@myisp.com
Good news! Based on what you told us you were looking for:
Search:          Brass Bell* Japan
Search Scope:    Item Title and Description
Price Range:     Over $0.00
E-mail Frequency: Daily
E-mail Duration:  90 days (ending on December 18, 1999 PDT)

There are 28 auctions that we found. Here are the most re-
cent new auctions since we last e-mailed you. Please click
on any of the URLs to see what Personal Shopper has found
for you.

1
Item #:  234694046
Item:    A small BRASS BELL with inlaid ivory from Japan
Price:    $5.99
Bids:    0
Started: 11/20 19:09
URL:     http://grass.ebay.com/go/101/10398195/234694046

2
Item #:  234502104
Item:    Lot of 15 bells, some brass some silver, Japan,
         China
Price:   $9.99
Bids:    0
Started: 11/20 13:52
URL:     http://grass.ebay.com/go/101/10398195/234502104

To access the rest of the search results, please click here:
http://grass.ebay.com/go/1/10398195/252712
```

Simply click on the link to view the auctions you're interested in. Notice that eBay will list only the first few auctions it has found. To see the remainder of the list you must click on the link provided at the end of the message.

To set up your own Personal Shopper searches, click on the <u>Site Map link</u> at the top of any eBay page, then select the <u>Personal Shopper</u> link from the "Search" list. Or from a search results screen, you can click on the <u>Personal Shopper</u> link. You'll be required to enter your User ID and password to access the Personal Shopper system. Once in the system, you may define up to three searches. You can also select how often the search will be performed (for example, daily or every three days), a price range, how long you want the searches to take place, and how often you want eBay to notify you of its findings (for example, daily or every three days). When eBay performs a search and finds matching auctions, it will send you an e-mail like the one described above.

Another way to search for items you want is to do a search across several auction sites. One software program that will perform an automatic search over eBay, Yahoo!, and Amazon is Auction Explorer by ExpressDev Company. This is a program that you can download from www.expressdev.com. For the program to work, you must have accounts at the sites you want it to search. Auction Explorer allows you to enter search criteria for a number of searches at a time. It will then search all sites and display a list of the auctions matching your criteria. You can also choose to display only auctions ending within one day or only new auctions. Other options within this program allow you to set how often you want it to check the Web for auctions, choose to have it alert you a few minutes before an auction ends, and automatically dial into the Web (for those with dial-up connections.)

BIDDING

You've found an item you're interested in buying, but you want to know more. To display the item's description and shipping terms, click on the

Description

"Description" icon   or scroll down the page. As we mentioned earlier, before you decide to bid, you should read the item description, analyze the seller's feedback, agree with the shipping terms, and verify that the picture of the item shows exactly what you want. Now you're ready to bid. But how much is a good price? This is where you might utilize the "Completed Search" feature described earlier in this chapter to compare what other similar items have recently sold for. Having this information should help you make a clear decision about what you're willing to pay.

How Much Should You Bid?

There are usually two objectives to bidding in an auction. You want to win the bidding war but you also want to pay as little as possible. There-fore, if the current bid on the item you want is $1.00, you might want to raise the bid to $1.50 and see if you get outbid. Then you could raise your bid again. The problem is that you can't stay online and watch your bid indefinitely. Fortunately, eBay has an automated way of allowing you to outbid competitors without being online. It's called bidding by proxy, which we talked a little about in Chapter 1.

To recap, when you bid by proxy, it means that you can place a bid for the maximum amount you are willing to pay for an item, but only the amount necessary to win the current bid will be used. For example, sup-pose you bid $5.00 on an item whose current bid is $1.00. After you place the bid, you notice that eBay reports that the high bidder is now $1.25. What happened to your $5.00 bid? The rest of your bid is held in reserve in case someone else comes along and outbids you. Suppose another bid-der places a bid for $2.00. Then eBay automatically raises your bid by the minimum incremental amount to $2.25, keeping you as the top bidder. The other bidder is immediately notified that he's been outbid, and he may continue to raise his bid until he tops your $5.00 bid, or he may stop bidding and let you maintain your high bid status.

If more than one person is interested in the same item, a bidding war may erupt and your proxy bid amount may be quickly used up. If you *re-ally* want this item, you'll have to use another bidding technique. Chapter 3, "The Winning Bid," describes strategies you can use to maximize your chances of being the winning bidder on a particular item.

Placing a Bid

Before you place a bid on eBay (or on most other Internet auctions), you need to be a registered user. (Refer back to Chapter 1 for information on registering.) When you're ready to enter and place a bid, click on the

"Bid" icon **Bid!** . Figure 2.7 shows the bid screen for an "Old Small Dr Pepper Bottle." Notice that the current bid is $3.25 and the lowest the

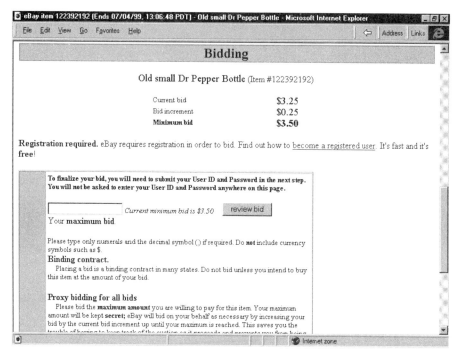

Figure 2.7 Entering an eBay bid.

(This material has been reproduced by John Wiley & Sons, Inc. with permission of eBay, Inc. Copyright © eBay, Inc. All rights reserved.)

new bid can be is $3.50. Enter your bid in the "Your Maximum Bid" text box. Remember that if you enter a bid of more than $3.50, *only the amount needed to make you the highest bidder* will be used. After you enter the amount you want to bid, click on the "Review Bid" button. Also notice the Binding Contract statement:

> Placing a bid is a binding contract in many states. Do not bid unless you intend to buy this item at the amount of your bid.

The next page is called "Reviewing bid for: Old Small Dr Pepper Bottle." It summarizes your bid amount and warns you that "Once you place a bid you cannot cancel it." (Actually, there are occasions when you can cancel a bid; these are covered in Chapter 4, "Money Matters.")

At the bottom of the bid page you must enter your eBay User ID and password to finalize the bid. Click on the "Place Bid" button to lock in your bid. Figure 2.8 shows the screen where you finalize your bid.

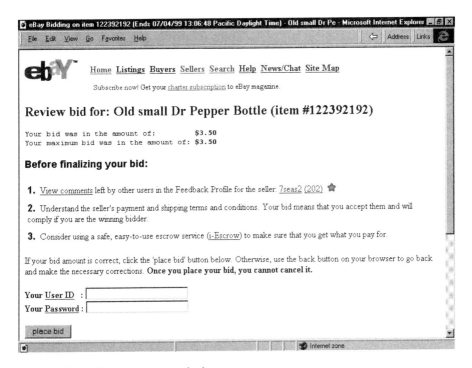

Figure 2.8 Placing an eBay bid.
(This material has been reproduced by John Wiley & Sons, Inc. with permission of eBay, Inc. Copyright © eBay, Inc. All rights reserved.)

If you're the high bidder, eBay will display a message that you are now the high bidder. However, if the previous bidder has a proxy bid higher than yours, you'll see the message

NOTICE! You have been OUTBID by another bidder.

Now you have to make a choice. If you want to bid again, you can click on a link provided on the outbid notice called Follow This Link. This link will send you back to the original bid page for the item, where you can bid again. Knowing that there is a bidder already using the proxy method of upping the bid, you might want to consider entering the highest amount you'd be willing to pay for the item in the hopes that your maximum bid will be higher than your competitor's.

Once you place a bid, eBay notifies you by e-mail of the status of the bid. Any time you are outbid on an item you've bid on, you'll be notified by e-mail. As long as there's plenty of time left in the auction, this message can help you go back and reestablish yourself as the high bidder before the auction ends. However, keep in mind that if someone outbids you too close to the end of the auction, there will not be enough time for you to get the outbid notice by e-mail.

SUMMARY

Bidding is a competition. That's one of the factors that makes auctions exciting. It allows you and your fellow bidders to establish a price for an item. That's the free enterprise system at its best! However, if you're going to be a consistent winner in the bidding competition, you have to have a competitive advantage. Part of that advantage can be the information you learn in the next chapter, "The Winning Bid."

The Winning Bid

Online auctions can be an adrenaline-pumping, heart-pounding contest. Okay, auctions aren't always *that* dramatic. But when you've found something you *really* want, a simple purchase can turn into a mission. That's part of the fun! Enjoy the thrill of victory and console yourself in the agony of defeat. This chapter is about winning—but not just winning at any cost. Using the strategies in this chapter you can get the items you want—even highly desirable items—at prices that won't break the bank.

BIDDING STRATEGIES

Some people play checkers for fun; others see it as a contest akin to the Olympics. Guess who wins more games? If you're going to win at auctions, you must have a good strategy. Of course, there are always auctions that turn out to be easy to win. Perhaps you're the only person interested in the product. In that case, you'll win with a simple opening bid. However, when you want to win an auction for a more popular item, you'll find yourself in a contest with other bidders. Now you have to decide how much you want the item. Is it worth a bidding war? Bidding strategies fall into two basic categories: bargain bidding and aggressive bidding.

Bidding for Bargains

It's easy to find bargains in Internet auctions. In fact, many of the items that are routinely won at auction end up being purchased for less than what would normally be charged in a retail store. How can you tell? First, you must know the retail prices so you can compare them to the auction prices. For example, Annette recently became interested in a china pattern that was retired in the 1970s. She bought her first pieces at antique stores. Then eBay came along. Suddenly, she found that pieces of her pattern routinely sold for less—often as much as half of the cost of the same items in antique stores. Now she suspects that many of the antique dealers buy their pieces on eBay auctions, then double the price when they sell them in stores! Thus, Annette found that most eBay prices she paid for her china pattern were "bargains."

However, not all auctions on eBay result in bargains. For example, I was interested in purchasing a particular book on tape. When I found a used copy on eBay, I put in a bid of $5. Someone else also wanted the tape and raised the bid to $8. I countered with a $10 bid, and the other bidder countered with a $13 bid. By this time I began to wonder how much this tape was really worth. I hopped over to the Amazon online bookstore (amazon.com) and looked up the cost of a brand new copy of the tape. It was selling for $11.89. Needless to say, I let the other bidder have the used copy and I purchased my own new copy from Amazon. This is why it's important to do comparison shopping when you're not sure what a reasonable price might be for a particular item.

What if an item is not normally sold at a retail store? How can you estimate its actual value? You can start by performing a search on eBay for completed auctions. If you find an auction that matches the item you're interested in, you'll be able to see the auction's ending bid price. This should give you an estimate of the item's value—and what it might expect to bring in the next auction. For collectibles and antiques you might also check standard price guides and stores specializing in these items. There are a number of price guides available for coins, stamps, bottles, dishes, Beanie Babies, and many other collectibles. If you're near a large metropolitan area, you might look for collectors' conventions. Compare the price of your item to the retail, convention, and book value to see if the eBay auction price is a bargain.

One way to spot potential bargains on eBay or at other Internet auction sites is to find items with incomplete or inappropriate titles or descriptions. A few examples of this kind of bargain were described in Chapter 2, "The Opening Bid." These auctions often result in bargain prices because they do not attract many bidders. Just as in any business, you must be able to effectively market your product to get the best price. If you do a poor job of marketing, then you'll attract fewer customers. In the auction business, this means that your item will probably sell for less than it would if the item were properly described.

Here are some of the ways to find bargains that result from poor marketing:

✔ **Watch for misspelled keywords in the auction title.** If you can think of a possible misspelling of a word for an item you're looking for, do a search on that misspelled word. For example, search for *diseny* instead of *disney*, *tupper ware* instead of *tupperware*, or *star treck* instead of *star trek*. (Remember that case does not matter in a search.) A recent search yielded these results:

> star trek: 7468 matches
>
> startrek: 104 matches
>
> star terk: 1 match
>
> star treck: 8 matches

Be creative in your misspellings. You might find a bargain!

✔ **Watch for titles that do a poor job of describing the item for sale.** If you can't tell what the item is by reading the title, then look at the item anyway. Be a contrarian. When it seems like most people would skip the item because of its bad description, be different and take a look.

✔ **Watch for items without pictures.** When looking at a listing of auctions, notice the ones that *do not* contain the "camera" icon ![camera icon] next to the description. Many people don't like to bid on something they can't see. If you know the item well enough to bid on it without seeing it, you might get a bargain. You also might e-mail the seller and ask questions for clarification or see if they could at least fax you a picture.

✔ **Watch for items whose auctions end in the dead of night.** You need to know that eBay time is West Coast (Pacific) time. Therefore, when it's 1 A.M. on the East Coast, there are still plenty of bidders online out west where the time is only 10 P.M. The lowest times of activity are between 1 A.M. and 7 A.M. West Coast time. (You'll have to translate that to your own time zone.) Auctions that end at these times will probably not get much last-minute action. On the other hand, the most active times for auctions are at noon and between 3 P.M. and 10 P.M. West Coast time. The lowest days of the week for activity tend to be Monday, Tuesday, and Thursday. The most active days of the week are Sunday, Wednesday, and Saturday.

✔ **Watch for items that are placed in an inappropriate category.** With over a thousand eBay categories, it is often hard for an inexperienced seller to know where to place an item. For example, does a book about Beanie Babies go in the Book category or the Beanie Baby category? If you're looking for items in a particular category, you might also browse through other possible categories to see if an item you're looking for has been misclassified. This is also a reason for you not to limit your searches to a single category. To do so might make you miss out on a potential bargain.

✔ **Be willing to travel.** Although eBay began as a collectors' site, it has quickly grown to include expensive and sometimes large items such as cars, boats, and motor homes. When the item for sale cannot be easily shipped, some potential buyers may be reluctant to bid on it. However, if the large item is near you or you are willing to travel to get it, it may be a bargain.

✔ **Be willing to buy an expensive item.** This bargain hunting technique may seem a little far-fetched, but consider that most people who purchase items on the Internet are concerned about transaction safety. They might be willing to take a chance on a $20 item, but once the bidding gets to $100 or so, worry sets in and bidders may become reluctant to risk losing that much money if the deal goes sour. Actually, most transactions on eBay are smooth and worry-free. However, fraud does exist. (See Chapter 4, "Money Matters.") If you're looking for an expensive item—even a car, a diamond, or fine art—take a look at what's for sale in auctions. If you're careful, you might be able to get a bargain.

✔ **Buy in Quantity.** If you're a reseller, buying office expendables, or buying gifts, you might consider looking at Dutch auctions or multiple item auctions as a bargain buying strategy. Oftentimes, buying items in quantity can save you money. The most obvious reason is shipping. Usually, it is much cheaper per item to ship multiple items than it is to ship one at a time. Also, many sellers are willing to sell multiple items for less than selling one at a time. For the seller, there's less paperwork, less correspondence, and fewer hassles. Dutch auctions are the obvious place to buy in quantity. They allow you to choose how many of the item you want to buy. However, you'll also see instances of auctions where the seller is offering multiple items in a lot. Sometimes these are closeouts of merchandise where the seller is just interested in getting rid of his inventory. In that case you might consider buying the lot, then breaking it up and offering it again on eBay as individual items.

Here are a few examples of how these bargain tips paid off for some savvy eBay users. A recent search for *Dr Pepper* (including searching descriptions) resulted in a listing whose title was "Old Coke Bottle." That was the complete title! This kind of a description should make your bargain antenna quiver. First of all, the listing is a possible misclassification. It was found with a Dr Pepper search, yet it says "Coke Bottle." That's a mystery in itself.

Furthermore, this listing is very uninformative. What kind of Coke bottle? Six and one-half ounce? Twelve ounce? Returnable? To find out more about this item, you had to go to the longer description. The actual long description of the item was "This is an old Dr Pepper Coke bottle." What? That's confusing. At least the description included a picture—which was the only way to actually verify that the item was an old twelve ounce 1960s era returnable Dr Pepper bottle.

To understand what's going on here you have to know a little bit about the southern United States. In some parts of the South, any kind of soda pop is called a "coke." A Dr Pepper is a "coke," a Pepsi is a "coke," and even a 7-Up (the Uncola) is a "coke." The Coca-Cola Company hates this fact because the word *Coke* is a registered trademark. But old habits die hard. Obviously the seller of this Dr Pepper bottle is one of those people who still use that unfortunate terminology. He's also not very good at marketing because his description is woefully inadequate. Therefore, when you see descriptions like this, pay attention. The item in this auction is begging to be sold at a bargain price.

Another example of misclassification comes from the "Dolls/Figures/General" category. An eBayer who collects ceramic items made in occupied Japan recently happened to run across a small ceramic Santa Claus up for auction. In the description and title, the seller never mentioned that the Santa figure was made in occupied Japan (it was clearly stamped on the bottom of the item and visible in the item's picture). Because the words *occupied Japan* did not appear in either the title or description, the item would never be listed in a search for *occupied Japan*. This mistake by the seller made Santa sell for much less than he would have usually fetched had the description been more accurate.

How much is an auction picture worth? Its value became obvious in a recent auction for a popular Disney license plate holder. A search of completed sales for this item revealed that several previous auctions had ended with prices ranging from $28 to $51. However, in one auction the seller did not include a picture of the license plate holder, though she offered to send a picture by e-mail. While an auction for the *identical* item that ended one day prior to this auction's closing had a winning bid of $36, the winning bid for the auction *without the picture* was only $17.

An example for large items comes from an eBayer in Dallas. He was in the market for a particular kind of recreational boat. In the Dallas market, these boats typically sold for $25,000 to $30,000. One night as he was browsing eBay he noticed the exact boat he wanted being offered by a seller in Indiana. Just on a lark, he put in a bid for $12,500. When he woke up the next morning and checked his e-mail, he found out that he'd won! After corresponding with the seller, the buyer arranged to pick up the boat the following weekend. He drove his pickup to Indiana and came back with the boat in tow and a smile on his face. His willingness to travel earned him a bargain!

Of course, you shouldn't bid on an item just because it might be sold at a bargain price. When you *do* spot a potential bargain, you might ask yourself:

- ✔ Do I want to buy the item for myself (if the price is right)?
- ✔ Do I want to buy the item for someone else?
- ✔ Do I want to resell the item?

These are the three most probable reasons for buying a bargain on eBay. When you find an item that you think may result in a bargain price and you've determined that it's worth buying, go ahead and place a low bid on it. Of course, if the minimum bid is already higher than you want to pay, pass the item up. If the item has a reserve price, you can still enter a low bid to see if it meets the minimum price. If you are also an eBay seller, you might want to consider whether the item could be sold for a higher price if its description were more appropriate. If that's the case, you could take the risk to buy it and then resell. You should be aware that sometimes a seller will become aware of his mistake. eBay allows sellers to add to the description even after the auction has begun; so an errant description is sometimes corrected midway through an auction.

However, don't get caught buying an item just because it looks like it might be a bargain. When you see that no one else has bid on an item and it's approaching the end of the auction, ask yourself if the reason may be because no one *wants* the item. A bargain is not a bargain just because the price is low. If you can't use it or sell it, then it's not worth buying at any price.

Bidding for Unique or Popular Items

Buying for bargains is one way to shop eBay. Another is to shop for items you *really* want. For example, if you collect Beatles autographs and you already have Ringo, Paul, and George, you might be willing to pay a hefty price for John Lennon's autograph. Now you're shopping for a one-of-a-kind item (or at least a fairly rare item). This category is where eBay really stands out and is one reason it is so popular. Before the Internet, how many antique or collector's stores would you have to visit to find that unique item that you need to make your collection complete? If you live in a small city or town, it could be impossible to find what you're looking for. eBay specializes in having odd and unique items for sale.

If you're motivated to find a unique item, you might think that you'd have to throw any thought of a bargain out of the window. But that's not true. Yes, some eBay auction prices do hit astronomical heights, but just as many end up with winning bids that are less than you'd pay at a retail store. With some simple auction strategies, you can increase your chance of winning a bid while keeping the price from going through the roof.

Suppose you're still searching for that John Lennon autograph to fill out your Beatles collection. A recent search for completed sales for "John Lennon Autograph" yielded the following results:

JOHN LENNON Autograph 8X10 Photo*Fantastic**	$760.00
John Lennon ink autograph cut	$305.00
BEATLES ~ JOHN LENNON AUTOGRAPH ~ LOW RSV!	$202.51
SEAN LENNON AUTOGRAPH TAPE son of John & Yoko	$17.01
JOHN LENNON AUTOGRAPH	$500.00
Yoko Ono-John Lennon (Beatles) autograph photo	$26.75

Once you study the descriptions on this list you see that the autograph selling for $17.01 was actually for a Sean Lennon autograph, and the one selling for $26.75 was of Yoko Ono. This leaves actual autographs of John Lennon selling for a price range of $202 to $760. The $202 autograph is simply a scrap of paper with John's signature and the $760 autograph is a nice autographed picture of John. This information should give you an idea of how much a future autograph may auction for.

Now, when another John Lennon autograph appears on an auction, you have some concept about what the final winning bid might need to be. With this in mind, use the following information to develop a strategy for how you'll bid.

Going, Going, Gone

Sometimes an item makes it through an auction with nary a bid, or with only one or two low bids. If you could find these items and they were in a category you wanted, would you be interested in bidding for them? There's a way to locate these items on eBay. First, select the category you're interested in. When the listing of current items is displayed, you'll see the following links at the top of the listing:

Current || New Today || Ending Today || Completed || Going, Going, Gone

By clicking on the Going, Going, Gone link you'll list items whose auctions are about to end within the next few hours. These auctions are based on when eBay last updated the listings. At the top of the page, you'll see a statement like this:

Updated: 12/15/99, 08:25 PDT Check eBay official time

It's not uncommon for there to be a gap of several hours between the time eBay last updated the listing and the current time. Therefore, to find the auctions that are actually ending in the next hour, you sometimes have to scroll through the listing of those that have already ended until you find those that are still active. For long listings, you'll see a message at the bottom of the screen that shows how many pages of listings are available:

For more items in this category, click these pages:
= 1 = 2 3 4 5 6 7 8 9 10 11 12 13 (next page)

This example shows that there are thirteen pages of listings available. Usually, eBay lists five hours of listings. Therefore, if the current eBay time is 2:00 (Pacific Time) and the last update to the page was at 11:00 (Pacific Time), then you'll have to begin looking about three-fifths of the way down the list to get to the auctions that are current. In this case, that would be at about page 7 or 8.

Once you've located the active listings, you can browse through the titles and number of bids to find those auctions with no or few bids. If you see an item you're interested in, then you may be able to win the item without competition and for a low bid.

Planting an Initial Bid

When you find an item you really want, you may be tempted to make a generous bid immediately. However, if there are several days left in the auction, that bid will continue to tempt other potential bidders until one of them possibly gets enough courage to outbid you. Therefore, it may be better if you enter a minimum bid just to lock in your interest for this item. That way you can use the bidder search on the "Find Items" page to quickly keep in touch with how the bidding process is going—it will tell you the current high bid for every auction you're bidding on and will indicate if you currently own the high bid. It also tells you how long the auction has before it ends. If you're a busy bidder and you don't lock in an initial bid for an item, you may forget about the item or miss the deadline for putting in a final bid.

Using Automatic Bidding

If the bidding for an item ends when you can't be around, you can use proxy bidding to try to keep on top of the bidding war. If you really want an item and this is your only avenue, then you should bid the absolute highest bid you'd be willing to pay for this item. Keep in mind that in proxy bidding, eBay will only raise your bid to the point required to win the auction. Therefore, if you put in a maximum bid of $200 and other bidders are only willing to bid $150, then eBay will put in your bid at $152.50 (raised by the minimum bid increment) and you'll win the auction.

TIMING COUNTS WHEN YOU REALLY WANT TO WIN

Sometimes an item is so important that it doesn't matter to you how much you pay (up to a point)—you're just interested in WINNING. Perhaps the item is so unique that you've never seen it come up before and don't expect that it will come up again. One of the strongest areas of interest on Internet auctions (as well as in antique stores) is Baby Boomer nostalgia—board games, Erector sets, Barbie dolls, GI Joe action figures, first editions of books like *Mike Mulligan and the Steam Shovel* and *The Cat in the Hat* and much more. Those toys and books that we played with as kids in the 50s and 60s have an emotional grip on millions of people who can afford to pay a hefty price to get that warm fuzzy feeling again.

There are two strategies to winning—using an outlandish proxy maximum bid and last-second bidding. If you have the money and want an item enough, then you can simply enter a maximum bid that is way beyond the normal value of the item. For example, if you've determined by a *Completed Sales* search that the Barbie you want sells in the range of $20 to $40, then you might enter a $100 bid to give you almost complete assurance that you'll win any potential bidding war. This is the safe way to bid, but for the adventurous soul, it is not as much fun as bidding for the lowest winning price.

Therefore, if you don't want to pay an exorbitant price and you're willing to be online when the bidding ends, you can wage war against other bidders. Veteran eBayers call this *sniping*. For this strategy you'll need a quick mouse and a steady hand. Some eBayers dislike this type of bidding because those who don't know what's going on can get their high bid jerked out from under them a second before an auction closes. In reality, if other bidders are going to use sniping, then you need to know how it's done so you can also use it if you wish. In sniping, the clock is all-important. You must pay attention to the time (remember that eBay is on Pacific time). You'll need to be online about five to ten minutes before the bidding ends. Here are some tips about how to win a bidding war.

To set up your command center for bidding, start up two copies of your browser. You can do this by simply starting Netscape or Internet Explorer, then clicking on the resize button at the top right of the screen and opening another copy of the same program. To see both programs at once (in Windows), right click on the program bar, then select *Tile Windows Vertically* or *Tile Windows Horizontally*. Other operating systems have similar features. Figure 3.1 shows two browsers opened at once to the same item—one showing the bidding page and the other showing the description page.

When you're ready to place a bid, display the bid window in one of the browsers. This will be the browser that you'll use to place the bid. Open the other browser so you can see the top part of the auction screen where the time to go and current bid is visible. You can periodically click on the "Reload" (or "Refresh") button to see if the maximum bid has changed.

Now you're set up to wage war. If you notice that one or more people are placing last minute bids, then the battle has started. You're not sure how badly your opponent wants the item, but if she wants it as much as you, then the winner will be the last one to place a bid. In this case, seconds will count.

Remember that the eBay clock is the critical factor in this battle. You must place your bid before time runs out, but late enough to prevent any other bidder from squeezing in a last second bid after yours. Therefore, you continue to watch the progress of the bidding closely. It would be easy to wait until the last second, but you have to consider how quickly your bid will travel down the Internet wires to the eBay computer in California. To run a quick test of your Internet access speed, do these steps:

1. With two copies of your browser open, enter a bid on one browser screen, enter your User ID and password, but don't click on the "place a bid" button.

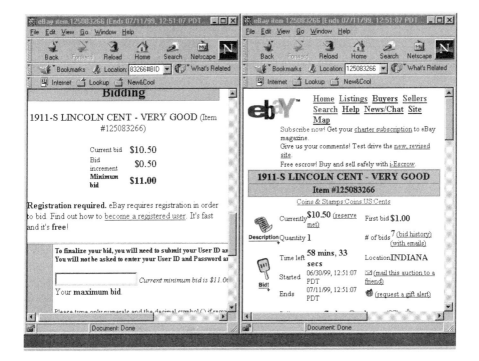

Figure 3.1 Two browsers open at once.
(This material has been reproduced by John Wiley & Sons, Inc. with permission of eBay, Inc. Copyright © eBay, Inc. All rights reserved.)

2. On the other screen, where the time left in the auction is shown in minutes and seconds, press the "Reload" button to get an accurate time to end (say it's 8 minutes and 50 seconds).

3. Click "Reload," then while counting the seconds (one thousand, two thousand, three thousand) move to the other window and click on the "place a bid" button to submit your bid. Now stop counting. Let's say it took you five seconds from the time you clicked "Reload" until you clicked on "place a bid." That means that you actually placed your bid at about 8 minutes and 45 seconds before the end of the auction (50 seconds – 5 seconds = 45 seconds).

4. Click "Reload" again on the window containing the item description. Is your User ID displayed as the high bidder? If yes, go to the next step. If no, try again.

5. On the "Item Description" window, find the link next to the number of bids called "bid history." Click on the "bid history"

link and look at the time your bid was recorded. Compare this time to the end of the auction time to find out how many seconds were left in the auction by the time your bid was recorded. (You'll have to do a little math.) For this example, let's say that the bid was recorded 8 minutes and 39 seconds before the end of the auction.

6. This tells you that it took about 6 seconds from the time you clicked the "place a bid" button until the time the bid was recorded (45 seconds − 39 seconds = 6 seconds).

What did you learn from this exercise? You learned that it takes your bid about 6 seconds to go from your computer to eBay's computer. Every Internet connection is different. Some connections are faster than others, and a signal from a computer on the East Coast may take longer to reach eBay's site than a computer's signal from Arizona. Therefore, you have to do this test from *your own computer* to find out what time it takes for your computer's connection. In fact, you should repeat the test a few times to make sure the estimate is accurate. Also note that signal speed may be slower during busier times of the day—typically during the lunch hour and in the evenings.

After learning the time it takes for a bid to get recorded, you have the information you need to win the battle of the bids. With your two browsers open—one prepared to bid and the other keeping track of the current bids—keep a close watch on the bidding. You might submit a bid a few minutes before the auction is scheduled to end, then watch to see if it is outbid. If you are high bidder for a few seconds and then you are outbid, it means that you have a live adversary! If you are immediately outbid, it means that you are bidding against a proxy.

When you're bidding against a proxy, there is no other way to outbid it other than to enter a significantly higher single bid or continue to bid smaller increments until you become the high bidder.

Bidding against a live bidder means that you'll have to judge how to time your bid in the hopes of outbidding him. If there are only seconds left in the auction, you have to make a decision. You can bid just enough to outbid the current high bid, but your opponent may have a proxy bid set up that will outbid you automatically. Then you may not have time to counter with another bid. Thus, it is probably best to wait until the last possible second and bid the highest bid you're willing to pay.

What will your highest bid be? Only you can decide that. However, there are a few strategies in selecting a high bid. If you think $25.00 will win the item, your opponent might think the same thing. Therefore, add a little padding to your high bid, say $25.52. Then, if your opponent bids

$25.00, or $25.50, or even $25.51, you'll still win. Winning is worth 52 cents to you, isn't it? Also remember that when you place a high bid only a bid sufficient to beat out the next highest bidder will be placed by the proxy system on your behalf. Therefore, if you bid $101.00 and the next high bidder only bids $55, then you'll win the auction with a bid of $56.00 ($55.00 plus the next bid increment of $1.00)

Closely watch the high bid amount by clicking on the "Reload" button every five seconds. The time is quickly ticking away. There are twenty seconds left. Should you go ahead and bid? No! If you bid now, your opponent will have enough time to counter. Continue waiting. Fifteen seconds. Make sure your high bid, User ID, and password is entered in the second browser. Twelve seconds. Remember that it took six seconds for your bid to be recorded. However, the Internet speed is not a constant. The actual time to record your next bid may be a few seconds either way. How long can you hold out? Ten seconds left. Nine seconds. Eight seconds. Quick! Click on "place a bid." Hold your breath. Go back to the other browser and click on "Reload" until the time left changes to "Auction has ended." Are you the high bidder? Chances are very good that if you waited until the last second and placed a generous bid that you won the contest.

Remember, no strategy is perfect. There's the possibility that your opponent also read this book and submitted a higher bid just a second after your bid was posted. Is all lost? Not necessarily. You can either hope another similar item will come up for bid soon, or you can contact the seller and tell her that you really wanted the item. Let her know that if the winning bidder reneges, you'll be willing to buy the item at your high bid. You might also inquire if the seller has another similar item to sell.

YOU'RE THE WINNER!

You know you are the winner of an auction when you display the item description page, the time says "Auction has ended," and your User ID is listed as the winning bidder. If you're not online when the bidding ends, you may first find out that you're the winner when you receive an e-mail notification from eBay. This notification is sent out shortly after (but not immediately after) the auction ends. The notification subject is "eBay End of Auction Notification Item #XXXXXXXXXX (Title of Auction Item)" and the message will read something like the one shown below. Note that eBay periodically changes the message a little, but it will basically contain this information:

Dear imaseller and imabuyer,
DO NOT REPLY TO THIS MESSAGE. PLEASE ADDRESS YOUR MAIL
DIRECTLY TO BUYER OR SELLER.
••
Check out the new Help section, and test drive the
future eBay site. See it at http://pages-new.ebay.com/
welcome-new.html

Change in Credit Request Policy!

Please see the Announcement Board for other important news!
http://www2.ebay.com/aw/announce.shtml
••
BUYERS PLEASE REMIT PAYMENT TO SELLER

This message is to notify you that the following auction
has ended:

    R2D2 Star Wars Beanie Buddies (Item #110789558)

    Final price: $6.01
    Auction ended at:12/05/99 14:10:45 PDT
    Total number of bids: 3
    Seller User ID: imaseller
    Seller E-mail: imaseller@dallas.net
    High-bidder User ID: imabuyer
    High-bidder E-mail: imabuyer@aol.com

Seller and high bidder should now contact each other to
complete the sale.

IMPORTANT: buyer and seller should contact each other
within three business days, or risk losing their right to
complete this transaction.

The official results of this auction (including e-mail
addresses of all bidders) can be found for 30 days after
the auction closes at:

http://cgi3.ebay.com/aw-cgi/eBayISAPI.dll?ViewItem&
item=110789558

If you won an auction in which the seller has at least a
positive feedback rating of 10, you can send a gift
alert. This is a great feature if you're buying gifts or
if you're a little late on your gift-giving. To use this
feature, see: http://cgi3.ebay.com/aw-cgi/eBayISAPI.
dll?ViewGiftAlert&item=110789558&userid=imaseller

If you have trouble contacting each other via email:
http://pages.ebay.com/aw/user-query.html

Please leave feedback about your transaction:
http://cgi2.ebay.com/aw-cgi/eBayISAPI.dll?LeaveFeedback
Show&item=110789558

For other valuable "after the auction" needs:
http://pages.ebay.com/aw/postauction.html
• •
eBay has a new mailing address for sellers who mail
checks and money orders:

eBay, Inc.
P.O. Box 200945
Dallas, TX 75320-0945

This address is for check and money order payments only!

All other correspondence should still be mailed to:

eBay, Inc.
2005 Hamilton Avenue, Ste 350
San Jose, CA 95125
• •
Thank you for using eBay! If you have not already done so
today, it wouldn't hurt to mention eBay to a few of your
friends!

http://www.ebay.com

Item Description:

R2D2 Where are you? He's here — a cute little 5 1/2 inch
beanie "Star Wars Buddy." Mint condition made with silver,
white and blue fabric. Tag attached. For all ages, Created
by Kenner, 1997, copyright Hasbro. Inside tag has
information on how to join the Star Wars Fan Club.

Thanks for bidding on this auction.

Good luck. Successful bidder pays $3.20 postage. I'll get
your merchandise to you as quickly as possible - as soon
as I get payment or your check clears. Texas residents
pay sales tax.

This official looking document is both your notification about the
outcome of the auction and a reminder of your obligations as a buyer (or
seller) that eBay has now turned over the rest of the transaction to the

participants. Up to now, the auction was a lot like a game. Now you have to come back to the real world and conclude the transaction.

RETRACTING A BID

Sometimes you make a mistake when you place a bid. You meant to bid only $9 but your fingers slipped and you actually bid $99. That's a bad mistake. What can you do? When you placed your bid, you carefully read that the bid was binding. Fortunately, eBay recognizes that there are occasional circumstances that will require you to cancel a bid. Therefore, they have established a mechanism you can use to retract a bid—*if* you have a good reason for the retraction. A few reasons eBay recognizes as legitimate are:

- ✔ The seller has substantially changed the description of the item, making it no longer what you want.
- ✔ You accidentally entered an incorrectly large bid.

Reasons that eBay believes are *not* legitimate include:

- ✔ You've changed your mind.
- ✔ You decide you can't afford the item.
- ✔ You found another item you want more.

If you feel that you need to retract a bid, click on the "Site Map" from any eBay page, then click on the <u>Retract Bid</u> link under "Services/Buyer Tools" listing. A page will be displayed explaining how to retract a bid, and when it is appropriate to do so. Since eBay (and sellers) don't like it when users retract bids, it is designed to carry a stigma with it. The following warning is included on the page

> Your retraction will be publicized in the bidding history for this auction, and you may be asked to explain your retraction to the seller or other bidders. If the retraction was not legitimate, you open yourself to potential negative feedback from other users.

To retract your bid, fill out the retraction form, along with an explanation of up to 80 characters. Although it is not strictly required, it's also a good idea to contact the seller directly and tell her why you had to do it. If the seller is sympathetic to your explanation, she may accept your reasoning and not leave you negative feedback. If you retract a bid and do not contact the seller, she may be less likely to be forgiving. Also, if you're going to retract a bid, *don't do it at the last minute*. Your high bid may have caused others to shy away from bidding. Therefore, if you cancel your bid right before the auction closes, you don't leave time for others to bid on the item, and you will have potentially cost the seller money she would have rightfully deserved. Some scam artists run a scheme where a partner places a low bid, which is followed by a high bid from another partner. When the high bid is retracted at the last minute, the buyer is left with an artificially low bid to end the auction. Knowledgeable sellers are aware of this scam and will complain loudly to eBay and to other authorities if they suspect that your retraction is an attempt at fraud.

The bottom line is that retracting a bid is not something you need to get into the habit of doing. Use it sparingly and only when you have a very, very good reason.

SUMMARY

You took on all competitors and won the auction. Your warm fuzzy should arrive in the mail any day now. But wait, your job isn't over yet. You have to finalize the transaction. If you and the seller follow the instructions in the end of auction notification, everything should work smoothly. However, there are a few "gotchas" you need to avoid. The next chapter, "Money Matters," will guide you through the final stages of the auction: contacting the seller, arranging payment, and receiving the merchandise you've purchased.

Chapter 4

Money Matters

You successfully placed a bid on an item and now it's time to complete the transaction. You might expect that this is where the fun ends and reality begins. However, eBay has renewed something in the American psyche that many of our generation have missed up to now. At the turn of the century when the Sears and Montgomery Ward catalogs were the phenomena of the era, people all over the country began getting stuff in the mail. People in the rural areas could buy the same goods that the millionaire on Fifth Avenue could buy. It was a revolution. Now another mail-order revolution is taking place. This time the goods come not from large warehouses but from individuals selling to individuals. Therefore, don't let the money matters spoil the fun. With a little common sense and caution, the financial part of your eBay experience will go very smoothly. You may even make friends with the postal carrier and think of him as Santa Claus bearing your eagerly awaited purchases.

YOU WON! NOW WHAT?

When an Internet auction is over, your host (such as eBay) turns over the remainder of the transaction to the buyer and seller. Shortly after the auction is over, the buyer and seller both receive an official notification that the auction has ended. An example end-of-auction e-mail was shown in the previous chapter. For the vast majority of the transactions, the steps toward concluding the sale go like this:

1. The seller contacts the buyer by e-mail and provides information about how the buyer should pay for the purchase.

2. The buyer then sends the seller a payment and the seller mails the merchandise to the buyer.

3. When the buyer receives the item in good condition, then the transaction is finished.

4. Optionally, the buyer and seller leave each other a feedback score and a comment on the "Feedback Forum."

A few transactions do need a little more attention and the sloppy buyer (or seller) can overly complicate a sale. This chapter provides information about how to avoid common pitfalls, head off potential misunderstandings, and make your transactions proceed without problems.

Contacting the Seller

Give the seller a few days to contact you after an auction has finished and don't get too anxious. You're usually dealing with an individual and not a well-oiled company. She might be out of town visiting Aunt Minnie or involved in a major project at work. Give her three days at least. If the seller has not contacted you within three days, go ahead and e-mail her a polite message. For example,

Dear imaseller,

I'm the winner on your auction for the size 32/30 Levi's 501 jeans, auction number 12345678. Please send me information about where to send payment. If I understand correctly, the amount due is $10.00 (my winning bid) plus $3.20 postage = $13.20. I will be paying by cashier's check. I look forward to hearing from you.

Thanks,
John J. Jones
"imabuyer"
jones@myisp.com

Once you've sent this e-mail, give her two days to reply. If she hasn't replied within that time frame, you might start to get a little concerned. Don't panic. Go to the eBay "Feedback Forum" and check out the seller's feedback rating. If the seller has only a few feedback points, it could mean that she is a beginning eBay seller and is not used to concluding sales. In that case, try to contact her again by e-mail with a repeat of the letter above.

If you discover from the "Feedback Forum" that the seller has a poor rating caused by multiple negative feedback points, then ask yourself why you didn't look at this before you bid. If you do not hear from the seller within ten days, go to the section in this chapter titled "What If the Transaction Goes Bad?"

Choosing the Best Payment Method

Payment for your winning item is always the point of most concern for buyers. You're going to send your money in the mail and hope that your merchandise is sent promptly. But you've heard horror stories about how people sent money and never received anything. Has this ever happened? Yes, but not very often. To avoid becoming one of those few individuals whose money vanished, take a few precautions.

- ✔ **Check out the seller.** Before sending your money, make sure you are comfortable with the reputation of the seller by checking out his status on the "Feedback Forum." If the seller has transacted dozens of sales with no negative feedback, then you can feel confident that he's not a charlatan.

- ✔ **Make payment according to the auction guidelines.** Most sellers specifically state how they prefer payment to be made. If you're given an option, select the payment method you prefer. However, if a seller states "payment by money order or cashier's check only," don't be disappointed if they refuse to take your personal check. If you don't like paying by money order or cashier's check, don't bid on future auctions that have that payment restriction.

- ✔ **Do not send cash.** It is tempting to send cash for small purchases, but there is no way to track cash or to verify that it ever arrived at its destination. Do people send cash for payments? Yes, though it is never recommended.

- ✔ **Can you pay by credit card?** If you can pay for your purchase by credit card, do so. This is the safest option since you have the power of the credit card company behind your transaction. Some credit cards give you protection for your purchases. Plus, you may be able to cancel a charge under certain circumstances. You'll have to check with your own card's policy to see what protections are actually provided for you.

✔ **Paying by money orders or checks.** Many auctions request payment in the form of money orders or cashier's check. This is a clean way for the seller to get her money since it can be cashed immediately. Most sellers will not send you the merchandise until they have verified payment. This is why sending a personal check can delay shipping the merchandise by about a week to ten days. If you live outside the United States and want to send a money order, make sure it is a governmental postal money order made out in United States currency. The United States Post Office will usually cash a postal money order from another country. However, some United States banks will charge up to $15 to cash a money order from a foreign bank. Of course, the problem in paying with money orders is that it adds additional cost to your purchase.

✔ **Using an escrow service.** For transactions involving a large sum of money you may want to use an escrow service to assure a smooth and safe transaction. The escrow service acts as a neutral third party in a transaction, collecting payment for the merchandise from the buyer until the seller sends the item to the buyer. Once the buyer accepts the merchandise, the escrow service forwards the payment to the seller. eBay recommends a service named i-Escrow. It charges 5 percent of the final value of the item up to $5,000, with a $5 minimum fee with discounts for transactions above $5,000. The buyer typically pays for the escrow fees; however, payment of fees could be decided between the buyer and seller prior to the beginning of the transaction. More information about escrow services is found on eBay by selecting the "Site Map" option at the top of any eBay page, then selecting "Escrow" under the "Services/Buyer Tools" section.

✔ **Conclude the sale person to person if possible.** If the seller lives near enough and if the transaction is big enough, you may want to conclude the sale face to face. If you can't meet face to face but you have concerns about shipping or payment, call the seller on the phone and work out arrangements. E-mail can be impersonal and it's easy to be misunderstood. If you talk to the seller, you may be able to prevent problems before they occur. Plus, you might make a friend with a fellow afficionado.

✔ **Include detailed information about the purchase.** It's amazing how many buyers send a check or money order to sellers without sending information about what they bought or where to send the item. Some sellers have dozens of auctions ending every day. If they receive a check or money order in the mail without proper identification, it can slow the process considerably. The best idea is to include a copy of the end of auction e-mail message from eBay with your payment. And be sure to include your complete and *legible* address. Also, put a return address on your envelope if you mail payment. Some buyers send the seller an address label containing their address. This eliminates any possibility that the seller will accidentally put the wrong address or zip code on the package.

✔ **Make sure you send the correct amount.** Occasionally buyers will forget to include shipping costs with their payment. On most auctions, shipping must be paid by the buyer. Make sure in your correspondence with the seller that you know the *full* payment amount you need to send, and don't just send the amount of the winning bid.

Problems that delay the completion of transactions include checks that don't clear, illegible addresses, incomplete information about what item you're paying for, and failing to send the correct payment amount. Before sending your payment, double check everything. You might even make a photocopy of your check or money order as documentation of what you've sent.

If you send a check that bounces, the seller will not be very happy. It can cost him $10 to $25 depending on what his own bank charges him. The only legitimate way to correct this problem is to send the seller a cashier's check or money order for the correct amount *plus* the amount his bank charged him for the bounced check. Don't whine about having to pay more for the item than you intended. Don't ask the seller to accept another check. Act promptly on this problem to protect your own reputation and to prevent negative feedback on your record.

Shipping Options

On some items the seller fixes the shipping method and cost and describes them in the auction description. In this case, the buyer usually has no option but to pay the shipping costs stated. Be aware that some sellers try to make extra income from shipping. They may state a $5 shipping charge in the auction description when it only cost them $2 to actually ship the merchandise. Some sellers will claim that "postage and handling" should include labor and materials for shipping. However, if you see excess postage being charged, you might consider not dealing with that seller again. Also, if you don't like the shipping method or price, you can negotiate with the seller. Nonetheless, you're obligated to go with what was described in the auction description if the seller refuses to offer you other options.

Fortunately, many sellers allow users to select from a list of shipping options and most sellers will only charge the buyer the actual price of the postage. Which method should you use to have your item shipped? Usually, the faster you want to receive the item, the more it will cost you in postage. The three most commonly used delivery methods are the United States Postal Service (USPS), United Parcel Service (UPS), and Federal Express (FedEx). Prices for delivery in certain parts of the United States differ according to distance, and delivery outside of the United States costs more. Therefore, for definitive prices on delivery you'll need to contact the delivery service you plan to use. Here are some price guidelines for the most popular shipping methods (current at the time of publication):

- ✔ **First Class United States Postage** Small items such as postcards and lightweight small paper goods are often sent in an envelope with first class postage. Cost is 33 cents for the first ounce and 22 cents for each additional ounce for envelopes thirteen ounces or less. Maximum size is $4^1/_4$-by-6-inches by 0.016-inch thick.

- ✔ **USPS Priority Mail** This is a popular shipping method for sellers since the post office generally will supply the shipping container free of cost. The price is $3.20 for the first two pounds, $4.30 for up to three pounds, and $5.40 for up to four pounds.

- ✔ **USPS Express Mail** If the item is sent in the flat envelope provided by the U.S. Post Office, the cost is $15.75 regardless of weight or destination. For other rates, check with USPS. (www.usps.gov)

- ✔ **USPS Book Rate** Generally used for books (at least eight pages), film (16 mm or narrower), printed music, printed test materials, sound recordings, play scripts, printed educational charts, loose-leaf pages and binders consisting of medical information, and computer-readable media. Packages must measure 108 inches or less in combined length and girth. Cost is $1.13 for the first pound, $1.58 for 2 pounds, and $2.03 for 3 pounds. Check with the USPS for additional costs for packages up to seventy pounds.

- ✔ **COD** The United States Postal Service provides a "Cash On Delivery" option that allows you to pay for an item when you receive it. If the seller is willing to use this payment option, it allows you to have the package in hand before you pay for it.

However, you should expect to pay an additional charge for this service. The post office charges $4.00 for a COD up to $50.00, $5.00 for a COD up to $100.00, and so on up to a maximum fee of $10 for a COD of $600.00. FedEx and UPS also provide a COD service for an extra fee.

✔ **UPS** Rates are based on weight and destination. For example, a one-day delivery from Dallas to New York for a two-pound package will cost between $19.75 and $47.95 depending on how early in the day you want delivery. (www.ups.com)

✔ **FedEx** Rates are based on weight and destination. A one-day delivery of a two-pound package using the Federal Express Pak from Dallas to New York will cost from between $9.05 for the FedEx Saver rate to $50.25 for FedEx First Overnight service. (www.fedex.com)

Use the information above to select the kind of shipping you feel most comfortable using and that provides you with the speed and safety of shipment you want. However, receiving the item is just one goal—you also want to receive it without damage. How can you protect against that? Consider purchasing insurance.

Shipping Insurance

If your merchandise is breakable or expensive, consider asking the seller to include shipping insurance. Of course, the buyer is usually responsible for paying the extra cost for insurance. USPS fees for insurance begin at $0.85 for coverage up to $50, $1.80 for coverage up to $100, and so on up to a maximum coverage of $5,000. UPS offers automatic insurance for up to $100. Additional insurance is available for an extra fee. FedEx does not provide insurance, but it is available through brokerage services.

Automatic Insurance Coverage through eBay's SafeHarbor

With over a million auctions ending weekly, an occasional problem occurs. Sometimes the problem comes from accidents, sometimes from misunderstandings, and sometimes from fraud. To give its users added confidence in purchasing through auctions, eBay has created a service called SafeHarbor that provides insurance coverage for transactions that go bad. The limitations of this coverage are automatic and free to all eBay participants as long as you meet the following guidelines:

✔ Both the buyer and seller are in good standing at eBay (feedback ratings of both users must be nonnegative).

✔ The auction item must be in accordance with the User Agreement.

✔ The final value of the item must be greater than $25 (a deductible of $25 is required; Lloyds will deduct $25 before reimbursing your claim).

✔ Actual fraud has been committed.

✔ The buyer has sent the money in good faith to the seller and never received the item.

✔ The item received is significantly different from the auction's description. (Items damaged during shipping are not covered. Please contact your shipping carrier for information on their reimbursement policy.)

✔ The buyer must register his/her complaint in eBay's "Fraud Reporting System" within 30 days after auction's close.

✔ The buyer must not file more than one claim per month for the first six months of this program.

If you feel that a transaction meets these criteria, you can submit a report to eBay by selecting the Site Map link from any eBay page, then select Insurance under "Services/Buyers Tools," and then click on the Fraud Reporting System link.

WHAT IF THE TRANSACTION GOES BAD?

There are a number of reasons why a transaction can go bad. Unfortunately, one of the most common reasons is miscommunication. Although the vast majority of sellers are willing to work with you to get a transaction completed, some sellers are as hard-headed as an old donkey. If you try to challenge his way of doing business, he'll dig in and refuse to move. He may have never taken a psychology class in his entire life and he probably has no idea what "customer service" means. If you're going to deal with this kind of seller, you sometimes have to bend your own ways a little to gracefully finish a transaction. Then you can avoid ever buying anything from him again. What are the situations that cause the most problems?

✔ **You want to use a method of payment the seller refuses to accept.** Some sellers are very adamant about how they want to receive payment. They like to get their money quickly. Impatient sellers hate personal checks. Therefore, if an auction did not include personal checks as a payment method and you insist on paying with a personal check, you may be in for a fight.

✔ **You're unable to pay for the item you've won.** What if you suddenly find that you cannot pay the winning bid? Suppose you lose your job, or you have a disabling accident or your car's engine blows up and is going to cost you $1,000 to get it fixed. What can you do? Technically, *you're obligated* to pay the seller. Practically, he can't make you pay. If you find yourself in this kind of position, the best policy is honesty. Tell the seller about your problem. Depending on what you think you can do, ask if you can make payments until the item is paid for. If you simply can't pay for the item, tell the seller and at least offer to pay a nominal fee—say 10 percent of the winning bid. Why pay the seller anything? If *you* do not compensate them for the auction, they have the right to ask eBay for a refund for their listing fee. When this happens, eBay will automatically send you a warning e-mail. If you receive three warnings, you will be suspended from bidding for 30 days. A fourth offense will result in indefinite suspension from eBay.

✔ **You suspect fraud.** Before making a payment, it's good to revisit the "Feedback Forum" to make sure the seller is maintaining a positive record. If negative feedback begins to appear, read the explanations. There have been instances where a new seller offers popular items such as Beanie Babies that he has no intention of actually selling. He may get away with collecting bidders' money for a while, but eventually he'll begin getting negative feedback. If you send payment and never receive the item, you should contact the seller first. If you cannot resolve the problem, contact Safe-Harbor@ebay.com with a description of your case. They will follow up on the information as quickly as possible and will suspend users who are found to be violating auction rules. Plus, you may be eligible for coverage under eBay's insurance.

✔ **You paid for an item but never received it.** eBay provides free insurance for transactions from $25 to $200 for cases when you do not receive your merchandise after making payment. They state "An item is covered when the high bidder of an auction sends money to the seller, in good faith, and does not receive the item or the item received is significantly different than the item described in the auction." eBay may change its policy and begin charging for this type of insurance in the future. If your winning bid was over $200, they recommend that you use an escrow service for payment. If you did not, they will not reimburse you more than the $200, less a $25 deductible. This insurance will not apply if the shipping company has lost the package or if the item has been damaged in transit. If your package was lost or damaged in transit, you must contact your shipping carrier for their reimbursement policy.

✔ **You received your item but it was damaged.** Your first option for damage coverage is from the shipping carrier. Check with them on their insurance or reimbursement policy. If you cannot receive coverage from the carrier, then you must negotiate with the seller for help. Depending on the level of damage, the seller might be willing to offer you a partial refund. If your seller offered a guarantee, you should be able to send the item back for reimbursement. Let the seller know the condition of the item before you send it back. Communication is very important when you're trying to negotiate. However, don't expect reimbursement beyond the winning bid. Sellers will not usually refund shipping costs.

✔ **You don't receive what you thought you bought.** Your first course of action should be to contact the seller. You may want to return the item or negotiate a partial refund. If the sale carried a guarantee, you should be able to send it back for a refund of the bid price. If you cannot get satisfaction from the seller, contact eBay's "SafeHarbor/Investigations" (listed under "Services" on the eBay "Site Map"). You may be covered under the eBay insurance plan for a partial refund.

If you spend much time in the eBay chat rooms, you'll see both buyers and sellers complaining about transactions where they were "ripped off." Usually, communication and cool heads could have easily resolved most of these problems. If their respective mothers had been able to get them in the same room, they would have made these complainers work out their problems in a reasonable way and shake hands. Unfortunately, that's usually not possible. Sometimes the problem maker is a real criminal. Sellers have been known to offer nonexistent items in auctions and sell fakes as genuine articles. In this case, you have no alternative but to contact eBay at SafeHarbor@ebay.com and possibly the United States Postal Service if you think mail fraud has occurred.

OTHER AUCTION SAFEGUARDS

Generally, eBay has set the standard for safety in all major auction sites. Like eBay, the Amazon and Yahoo! auction sites utilize a feedback system to identify and verify the status of buyers and sellers. An additional safeguard offered by Amazon is that every registered user's identity has been validated with a credit card. This gives you an added measure of assurance that the participant is not there to commit a crime. Amazon and Yahoo! also provide escrow services for their buyers. Plus, Amazon offers a guarantee of up to $250 that protects sellers using similar guidelines as eBay's guarantee. Before participating in any of the other auctions on the Internet, check out their guarantees, seller services, and fraud prevention network before bidding.

Fortunately, most people participate in hundreds of eBay auctions and never have a substantial problem. Don't let the potential of a problem take away your ability to enjoy and participate in Internet auctions. Be careful, take advantage of the services to help you keep your transactions safe, and enjoy the ride.

LEAVING FEEDBACK

If you've ever been a member of a Crime Watch patrol in your neighborhood, you know that one of the goals is to make each member of the group a "nosey neighbor." That is, everyone should keep an eye out for anything unusual happening in the neighborhood. In the same way, the eBay community wants members to watch out for one another. If you have a great experience buying an item from a seller, tell the rest of the members about it. If you've had a bad experience, let others know about that as well. The mechanism for making other members of the community aware of good or bad auction experiences is the "Feedback Forum." To make feedback work, you have to participate. Therefore, when you've received your item in the mail, make sure you take a little time to leave feedback. Here's how you do it.

Click on the Site Map link at the top of any eBay page then select the Leave feedback on a member link from the site map "Services" listings. Figure 4.1 shows the form you use to leave feedback about an eBay user. You'll need to enter:

✔ Your eBay User ID
✔ Your password

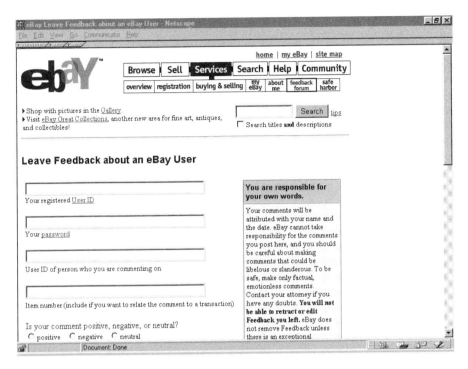

Figure 4.1 The eBay Feedback Form.
(This material has been reproduced by John Wiley & Sons, Inc. with permission of eBay, Inc. Copyright © eBay, Inc. All rights reserved.)

✔ The User ID of the person you're commenting on

✔ Optionally, the item number of the auction

Once you've entered the information above, you must then select to leave either positive, neutral, or negative feedback by clicking on the appropriate item. Below the rating selection (and not seen in the figure) is a text box where you can leave a comment of up to 80 characters. Notice the following statement at the bottom of the feedback form page:

WARNING: Once placed, comments cannot be retracted. If you later change your mind about someone, you'll have to leave another comment. See the Feedback Forum for an explanation about how your comments affect a user's Feedback Rating.

If you're leaving negative feedback, try not to do it while you're too upset. You don't want your words to come back and haunt you later. Also take note of the other warnings on the feedback page:

> If you regret a comment you made or if you have previously left a negative comment and have since been able to resolve your misunderstanding, we encourage you to leave a positive or neutral Feedback comment for that person and explain that the misunderstanding has been resolved.

You're also reminded that "You are responsible for your own words." Be careful not to make libelous or slanderous charges. Every eBay member will be able to see what you write here. The best policy is to report only facts.

When you leave negative comments about others, they have the right to leave negative comments about you. Keep this in mind when you see that a seller has a few negative comments. It could be that he simply reported a few deadbeat customers, and they retaliated. Or, it could be that a customer reported on some unfair practices of a seller, and he retaliated. Before you leave any negative comment, try to work out your problem with the seller. Sellers don't want negative comments. If you have a legitimate complaint, try to come up with a workable solution.

A compromise to negative feedback is neutral feedback. If you feel that you must leave a nonpositive message, but you don't think it warrants a negative comment, then you can leave a neutral message. This does not affect the user's feedback score one way or the other—it just gives you a chance to vent a mild complaint.

Fortunately, the vast majority of the feedback you'll leave will be positive. Sellers and users love positive feedback. It makes their rating number climb and this helps their reputation among other users. When you leave most sellers positive feedback, they will reciprocate and leave you positive feedback as well. It's a mutual admiration society! You get a chance to thank a good seller for her prompt and efficient service, and she'll thank you for being such a great customer. The whole process just makes the auction that much more fun.

The idea of feedback is so important to the success of auctions that it has been adopted and is used on other auction sites as well. For example, Yahoo! and Excite auctions have the same positive, neutral, negative rating system used by eBay. Amazon has a rating system that gives members a score of between 1 and 5, with 1 being bad and 5 being good.

Feedback is an essential part of keeping Internet auctions as legitimate and safe as possible. It's good citizenship to leave feedback each time you conduct business with another user. Just like in your own neighborhood—if we look out for each other we can prevent bad things from happening and can make our neighborhood safe and fun to live in.

SUMMARY

Auctions mean good news for your postal workers. The more you participate in Internet auctions, the more goodies you'll find in to your mailbox. Sure, you have to pay for the items, but there's something magical about opening a package and seeing what's inside. You may enjoy the feeling so much that you'll want to become a citizen of one of the eBay online communities. That's what you'll learn about in the next chapter, "Participating in the Collectors' Paradise."

Chapter 5

Participating in the Collector's Paradise

One of the culture-changing aspects of the Internet has been its ability to bring people together from all parts of the United States and the world into an electronic community. Now people in Idaho and Los Angeles can chat with people in Atlanta and Singapore. For collectors, the Internet has allowed people with similar interests to meet, compare notes, trade, sell and buy merchandise in a continuous and virtual collector's convention. This is the atmosphere that birthed the concept of eBay. It all started when Peter Omidyar's girlfriend, Linda, asked him if there were a good way to buy and sell Pez candy dispensers on the Web. She wanted to be able to communicate and trade easily with other users around the country. Peter took a look at the idea, but the result was more than Linda could have expected. He created the electronic marketplace that became eBay. Today, millions of people use eBay for buying and selling items from all over the world.

Although eBay has grown far beyond its beginnings as a resource for collectors, it has continued to maintain its roots as an active electronic collector's forum. However, it's possible that you could participate in eBay's Internet auctions without ever stumbling upon the collector's community. If you are a collector, you'll benefit by exploring what eBay offers you. This chapter will introduce you to the resources on the Internet that can help you make friends, enhance your knowledge, and improve your collection.

ACCESSING THE INTERNET COLLECTOR'S COMMUNITY

The eBay community is just a click away on any eBay page. At the top of any eBay page, click on the Community link to display the "Community Overview" page as shown in Figure 5.1. (Or click on Site Map, then Community Overview.) This page contains additional links to "eBay News," chat rooms, "eBay Life," "Library," "Charity," "eBay Store," "Suggestion Box," and "About eBay." These links are ways to participate in the eBay community. The following sections describe how to use each of these resources.

eBay News

You can keep up with the status of the eBay site through the announcement in "eBay News." These announcements often contain information

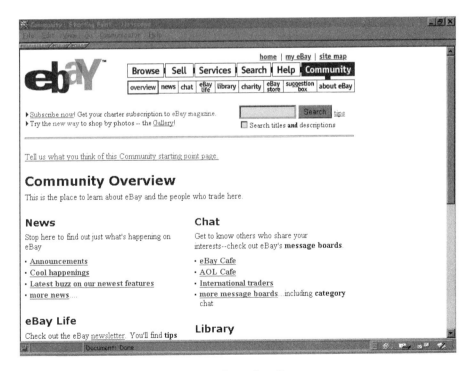

Figure 5.1 The eBay Community Overview Page.

about outages in the system and updates. If you can't get a search to work or have a problem getting some other part of eBay to respond properly, come to the news area and look through the latest announcements. Usually there will be information about when the problem is expected to be resolved.

Using the Chat Rooms

One of the best ways to get to know your fellow eBayers is to participate in chat rooms. The most general chat room is the "eBay Café," which is used as an informal meeting room for new and seasoned users. When you enter the chat room, you should scroll to the bottom of the page and begin reading the messages from the bottom up—that's the order in which they appear. Don't worry, you're not listening to someone's private conversation. You've got to read a few messages to see who's currently chatting and what they're chatting about. Many of the comments are humorous—or at least an attempt at humor. The topics range from personal to business. Don't be surprised if you see some ranting and raving about a seller or buyer who did somebody wrong. You'll get a quick education about what kind of conduct is expected from users—mostly it boils down to being honest, having a little common sense, and treating other people like you want to be treated. (Didn't we learn this behavior in kindergarten or Sunday School?) Here are some samples of messages (although changed a bit to protect the innocent) that were recently displayed. Notice that there are typically several conversations going on at once in every chat room. Remember—read this conversation from the bottom up.

Posted by imabuyer: Got to get back to work. Nice talking to you all. Bye! bye!

Posted by muleshoe: I'm still signed up to play in a tournament next weekend—I sure hope the leg heals up quickly.

Posted by wiseman: Sometimes people go out of town—I'd give them a few more days, then send a gentle reminder.

Posted by imanewby: I wanted to give a reasonable amount of time before saying "Hey! Send me my money!" I don't want to appear to be too gullible—the buyer has good feedback.

Posted by wiseman: When did they claim to have sent the payment? I usually give them a week—more if there is a weekend involved.

Posted by imanewby: It's U.S.

Posted by wiseman: imanewby—depends on what country—was it from the U.S. or overseas?

Posted by imabuyer: I guess that'll keep you off the tennis court for a while!

Posted by imanewby: Can I have an opinion? What is a good or reasonable space of time to wait for a promised payment to arrive for an item? 10 days or 14 days?

Posted by muleshoe: Doctor says to keep it elevated for a day.

Posted by imabuyer: Howdy back to you muleshoe. How's the leg?

Posted by muleshoe: Hi imabuyer, what's doing?

Each time a message is posted, information about the sender is displayed along with the message. Figure 5.2 shows a sample message as it is displayed in the chat room. Notice that the message contains the information "Posted by" followed by the User ID of the person who sent the message. The feedback number in parentheses plus the icons following the name give you some idea of the person's eBay experience. You can click on the person's User ID to send them direct e-mail, or click on the feedback number to see the user's feedback information, or click on the "me" icon to see the user's eBay home page. At the upper right of the message is an Auctions link. When you click this link, you'll see all currently active auctions by that user.

Once you've caught up with the talk in the current eBay chat room, you might want to enter a hello to let everyone know you're online and participating. If you have a question about bidding or selling, this is a good place to ask it. People rarely hold back their opinion; so don't be surprised if you get some interesting and conflicting answers.

eBay sponsors a number of chat rooms to meet a variety of user needs. Although the list may change over time, chat rooms recently available on eBay include:

- ✔ **The eBay Café** Sit down. Relax. Have a mocha. This chat room is a general forum for all eBay users.

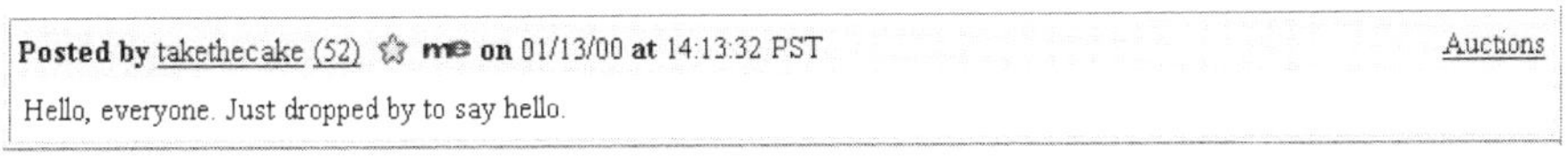
Posted by takethecake (52) **me on** 01/13/00 **at** 14:13:32 PST Auctions

Hello, everyone. Just dropped by to say hello.

Figure 5.2 A message in an eBay chat room.

(This material has been reproduced by John Wiley & Sons, Inc. with permission of eBay, Inc. Copyright © eBay, Inc. All rights reserved.)

✔ **The eBay Café for AOL users** This is the same as the regular eBay Café, but with emphasis on AOL (America Online) topics.

✔ **Collectibles Forums** There are a number of chat rooms designated for specific types of collectibles. Currently, eBay supports chat rooms for these items: Toys, Jewelry, Gemstones, Pottery, Porcelain, Computers, Trading Cards, Coins, Stamps, Dolls, Advertising collectibles, Antiques, Beanie Babies, Glass, Photo Equipment, Elvis, Comics, Sports, Garage, Diecast, Music, Books, and Furbies.

✔ **The eBay Q & A Board** This forum is for users who have questions about buying, selling, shipping, or services. You can get answers and advice from other members of the eBay community about their experiences.

✔ **The eBay Wanted Board** If you're looking for a particular item that you can't find in an auction, this is the place to come.

✔ **Discuss eBay's Newest Features** The sole purpose of this board is for users to provide input to eBay staff concerning recent and proposed new features of the eBay service.

✔ **Live Support for New Users** On this board eBay provides answers to questions 24 hours a day, 7 days a week.

✔ **Emergency Contact** This forum is designed to help you get messages to the eBay staff quickly or to contact other eBay users.

✔ **Holiday** Use this discussion board to celebrate the holidays with members of the eBay community.

✔ **Images/HTML** If you have questions (or answers) about the use of images or the use of the Hypertext Markup Language (HTML) on eBay, this is the forum to use.

✔ **Location specific forums** Several forums are designed for members of the eBay community in various locales including Canada, Japan, the United Kingdom, Los Angeles, and International.

Other Internet Auction Chat Rooms

Other Internet auctions also contain chat rooms or clubs for their members. For example, Yahoo! (auctions.yahoo.com) supports Collector's Clubs with dozens of topics ranging from John Deere Tractors to Christmas ornaments. Excite (auctions.excite.com) supports a few collector-oriented chat rooms plus a room specifically about auctions. Most other Internet sites don't come close to matching the extensive community resources available on eBay.

Read All About eBay Life

The "eBay Life" electronic newsletter is a place for eBayers to read about what's happening in the eBay community. It contains articles about eBay's corporate plans as well as information about specific users. Past articles have included stories about an eBayer who found a lost cousin in an eBay café, how a collector of neckties used eBay to enhance his collection, and how a toy truck collector found a truck he'd been trying to find for years. There's always some way you can participate in "eBay Life" by answering a monthly question—such as, "What one item would you take on a camping trip?" or "What's the most unusual thing you've purchased on eBay?" View the latest "eBay Life" by clicking on the Site Map link at the top of any eBay page. Then look under the "Community" listings for the eBay Life link.

Accessing the eBay Library

Want to know more about a particular kind of collectible? The "eBay Library" is full of articles that can help you learn how to recognize, grade, and evaluate different kinds of items. For example, suppose you want to bid on a set of 1952 coins to give your sister for her birthday. She collects coins, but you don't know the first thing about grading or authentication. To fill in your knowledge gap about coins, you can read through the material in the eBay Library about coins. It contains information about how to find and buy coins, how to understand coin grading, and the meanings of terms such as *Brilliant Uncirculated*, *Proof*, and *MS-70*.

   If you're bidding on a pricey collectible, it's always a good idea to check with the eBay Library for tips on grading, spotting fakes, and valuing the item. The eBay Library contains this information for many popular collectibles, including antiques, coins, computers, jewelry, pottery, stamps, Beanie Babies, dolls, photography equipment, sports memorabilia, toys, and collectibles in general. To get to the "eBay Library," click on the Site Map link at the top of any eBay page; then look under the "Community" listings for the Library link.

Participating in eBay Charities

One of the greatest American character traits is our concern for others who are in need. The eBay community exhibits that spirit through its charitable opportunities. Throughout the year eBay sponsors charity auctions for a variety of causes. One of the most visible charity auctions has been hosted by Rosie O'Donnell. Proceeds from her auctions have helped support the All Kids Foundation. If you have a charity, you can also sponsor a charity auction through eBay. Check out the requirements on the Charity link from the "Community" listings on the site map.

Another way eBay supports others is through its "Giving Board." On this board, users post needs of individuals and families. You'll find requests as simple as "Please send Johnny a get-well card" to "I'm a Boy Scout collecting medical supplies to be shipped to the relief effort in Guatemala." You can respond to these requests by clicking on the User ID of the person who posted the information.

The corporate side of eBay has chosen to participate in helping others through the formation of the eBay Foundation. It was established in June 1998 as a separate entity from eBay Inc. and was funded by eBay's donation of 107,250 shares of its common stock to Community Foundation Silicon Valley (CFSV). This public charity's mission is to promote philanthropy and build a strong community by assisting donors in making effective charitable donations and making grants to a variety of nonprofit organizations across the nation. In November 1998, a team of eBay employees volunteered to form a governance committee to direct the Foundation's efforts. A cross section of eBay employees from such departments as engineering, marketing, and customer support are responsible for selecting grant recipients. You can submit a request for support for your charitable mission by sending e-mail to foundation@ebay.com.

Visiting the eBay Store

People wear T-shirts to support their favorite sports teams; so why shouldn't eBay fans wear eBay shirts? That way, when you're at the supermarket, at Disney World, or in the Grand Canyon, you'll probably meet up with like-minded eBayers. The "eBay Store" is a place from which you can buy all sorts of wearables and toteables sporting the cool eBay logo. True fans will want to snatch up some of these items for themselves or give them to their friends who are also eBay fanatics. You can get to the "eBay Store" by clicking on the Site Map link from any eBay page; then click on "eBay Store" under the "Welcome" listings.

Sending eBay Suggestions

The eBay community continues to grow by leaps and bounds. One reason it remains a popular site is because many of its features began as suggestions from people like you. Therefore, eBay offers you a way to send suggestions for how eBay can improve its services. If you have a suggestion, send it by e-mail to suggest@ebay.com. Because of the volume of e-mail it receives, eBay cannot promise that you will receive a personal reply to your message.

About eBay

When you visit the "About eBay" page from the community listings, you'll see links to information about eBay Inc., including press releases, a company overview, information about the eBay Community, the eBay Foundation, eBay in the news, investor relations, and job offerings. If you want to dig deep into how eBay works, this is the site to visit. Through the press releases, you can find out how eBay is looking toward the future by seeing what alliances it is forming with other companies. You can read about how the company started and wade through all of the legal mumbo-jumbo in the company's public financial records. Maybe you'll find out that you want to buy some eBay stock. If you're interested in finding a job (and want to live near San Jose or Salt Lake City), then you can see what's available and send your resume by e-mail to jobs@ebay.com.

MANAGING YOUR eBAY ACCOUNT

When you became a registered eBay user, you selected a User ID and password, but there may come a time when you'll want to modify something about your account. For example, suppose your original eBay User ID was "iambeaniecollector." After a while you get tired of typing in that long name. You want to change your User ID. eBay provides a way. Select the Change My User ID link in the "My eBay" section of the "Services" list on the site map page. Simply type in your old User ID and password and your new User ID and the change is made. However, when you change your User ID, eBay will give you a pair of "shades" 👓 to help you tell other eBay users about your new look. The "Shades" icon will appear after your User ID for 30 days. During this time, your old User ID will be "embargoed." No one else will be able to use your old User ID until the 30-day period has expired. All of your current auctions, and any other eBay activity, will be immediately updated to reflect your new User ID. You may only change your User ID once every 30 days.

Also under "Services" you can change your password and your e-mail address. Since anyone knowing your password can bid on an auction that obligates you to spend money, you should keep it a secret. If you ever suspect someone knows your password, you should change it immediately.

SUMMARY

eBay is alive with people. Not only are the auctions busy and active—the whole community is talking. If you really want to learn more about the items you buy and sell, jump onto one of the eBay forums and discuss your ideas, ask questions, learn from others, and make new friends.

Chapter

6

Selling Your
Own Merchandise

O nce the auction bug has bitten you, it doesn't take long until you
get the urge to sell as well as buy. Fortunately, several Internet
auction sites have made selling so easy that literally hundreds of
thousands of people are doing it every day. Unfortunately, because it's so
easy, many of these sellers place their items in auctions without considering how to make their items stand out and sell. That is why a third of all
items placed on Internet auctions never receive even one bid. The next
few chapters will show you how to decide what you should sell, how to
place your items up for sale in an auction, how to maximize your profits,
and how to successfully conclude the sale.

WHY SELL YOUR ITEMS AT AUCTION?

Every weekend across America people drag their unwanted items out of
the garage, put up "Garage Sale" signs around the neighborhood, and sit
for hours selling their goods for pennies on the dollar. Forget garage sales!
The Internet is making them a relic of the past. They are just too ineffi-
cient. For example, suppose you have a few Cabbage Patch dolls to sell.
At a garage sale you may get a dozen people to look at them and only a
few will be really interested in buying one. Chances are slim that a customer who is willing to pay top dollar for your dolls will come by. Therefore, if you want to sell them, you'll have to price them at a bargain. Now,

suppose you put these same dolls up for sale on an auction web site where a thousand people will see them. Don't you think this would give you a chance of making a better profit? Yes! Plus, the auction format frees you from having to price your dolls at a discount—the price is set by the market itself, and it goes up as more people become interested in your item. Those buyers interested in your dolls will have to bid against one another until the one who is willing to pay the most wins the privilege of buying the doll. You get a great price for your doll and the customer who really wants the doll gets it at a price she's set herself. It's a win-win situation! It's the free market at its finest!

Here's one of the primary reasons that Internet auctions are so popular with sellers: It allows individuals to sell merchandise at close to a retail price. Why is that important? If you're a collector who's ever tried to liquidate your collection, you know how difficult it is to sell it at anywhere near its real value. Professional dealers will usually offer you *less than half* of what a price guide book tells you your collection is worth. That's understandable. They have to resell it at full price to make their profit. However, the result is that *you* take a loss so someone else can make a profit. It's a hard fact that collectors have had to face for years.

Now something new has come along giving individuals an advantage they've never had before. Internet auction sites put you on the same playing field as the professional dealer! Now you can get close to (or sometimes above) the guide book price by selling your items directly to another collector through an Internet auction. Suddenly, Internet auctions have *doubled* the real value of your items!

Remember those collections you stashed away years ago? Go ahead and dig through your attic and find those old coins, stamps, Pez dispensers, magazines, toys, comics, sports cards, and anything else that has value. Chances are good that you can sell it on an Internet auction. However, don't think that Internet auctions are only good for selling collectibles. It's also a great place to sell antiques, electronic equipment (both new and used), books, music, videos, jewelry, office supplies, art, automobiles, boats, lake property, and just about anything else.

Although there are no iron-clad guarantees, for many goods (unique items, popular collectibles, and antiques in particular), the price you'll get at auction is usually much more than you'd get selling them at a garage sale or at a flea market—and more than you'd get wholesaling them to a retail dealer. However, there are some items that are not well suited to be sold on Internet auctions. Chapter 7, "Deciding What to Sell," discusses the specifics of how to select items that will bring you the most profit at auction.

PREPARING TO SELL ITEMS AT AUCTION

It is wise to gain experience selling on Internet auction using items you already own or that you can initially get in small quantities. Don't go out and buy a thousand widgets thinking that you'll make a killing selling them on eBay. Experiment first. For example, if you're a collector, you probably have duplicates. Perhaps you make jewelry or paint landscapes. Try to sell a few and see what you get. Do you already operate a retail store full of merchandise? Do you have access to a wholesaler where you can purchase popular items at half-off their retail value? Do you live near a factory that would allow you to purchase items at a deeply discounted price? Use merchandise you can get easily to gain experience selling at auction. As you gain experience, you may find a particular line of products that you can sell consistently at a worthwhile profit.

Selling items on Internet auctions makes you a part of the American Dream—you're starting your own business! Okay, it may be a very small business. Nevertheless, if you go beyond selling a few items, you're going to have to consider what it will mean to you financially and legally to operate this Internet auction enterprise.

LEGAL AND TAX OBLIGATIONS

Without getting into the details of the tax code, how you handle the act of selling merchandise can provide you with tax benefits or cost you additional taxes. If your buying and selling is classified as a *hobby* by the Internal Revenue Service, you'll receive few tax benefits but you'll be obligated to pay taxes on any revenue you receive from sales. If you operate as a business, then you'll have more tax deductions. Specifically, the 1999 IRS code has this comment about "activity not for profit":

> You must include on your return income from an activity from which you do not expect to make a profit. An example of this type of activity would be a hobby or a farm you operate mostly for recreation and pleasure. Enter this income on line 21 of Form 1040. Deductions for expenses related to the activity are limited. They cannot total more than the income you report, and can be taken only if you itemize deductions on Schedule A (Form 1040).

Hobby An activity which produces income but for which you do not expect to make a profit. You are obligated to report the income to the IRS, but you can only take limited deductions.

For more information from the IRS, check their web site at www.irs.ustreas.gov. Generally, if you intend to sell regularly on Internet auctions, it may serve you well to become an "official" business. In most states, this requires that you go to your county seat, fill out a *DBA* (Doing Business As) form, and pay a nominal fee (usually less than $20). Once you've become a business, you should keep financial records of all purchases and sales related to the business. You should also start a separate bank account so as not to mingle your personal funds with your business funds.

DBA When you operate a business that is not in your own name, you must generally file with your state or county for a "Doing Business As" designation that tells the county the name of your business and who owns it.

There are advantages to starting your own business. Once you've received a tax number and have a business checking account, you can usually begin purchasing merchandise from wholesalers. If you can purchase items that sell well on Internet auctions, you may be able to create a nice income from buying at wholesale prices and selling at retail. Having a tax number also allows you to purchase merchandise without paying sales tax. Of course, once you sell the item you may be obligated to collect sales tax and turn it back to your state's treasury. Consult your local and state tax guidelines to determine your own sales tax obligations.

Since every state is different, it is impossible to give specific information about what kinds of legal and tax obligations you may have once you start your own business. However, almost every state has printed guidelines that will help you wade through the process. Other resources include the United States Small Business Administration, your local Chamber of Commerce, *SCORE* (The Service Corps of Retired Executives), and local college business courses. SCORE is a volunteer organization of retired business men and women who offer free advice for people starting up their own business. You can usually get in contact with SCORE through your local Small Business Administration (SBA) office. If record keeping and accounting overwhelms you, consult an accountant to help you set up your books.

> **SCORE** The Service Corps of Retired Executives is a volunteer organization of retired business men and women who offer free advice for people starting up their own business. You can usually get in contact with SCORE through your local Small Business Administration (SBA) office.

Must You Collect Sales Tax?

One of the most confusing aspects of doing business across state lines is the question of sales tax. Even Congress has been discussing how they might tap into the vast arena of Internet sales to raise more revenue through taxation. To get specific answers about your state's requirements, you should consult a local CPA or your state government's tax office. For many states, the current obligation of the seller is to collect state sales tax whenever a sale is made to a buyer in the same state. This is why you'll often see auction ads that mention something like "Texas residents add 8.25 percent sales tax to your winning bid." The seller collects the tax, then pays it to the state. If you're operating as a business within your state, you will receive a state tax certificate and instructions on how to collect and turn over the taxes to the government. If you operate as a business and fail to collect and pay taxes you may be exposing yourself to legal problems. Better be safe and make sure you know your state's requirements before you turn your hobby into a business.

ACTING LIKE A BUSINESS

Even though Internet auctions are designed to allow individuals to sell person-to-person, many buyers expect you to act like a real business. They want quick answers to questions, quick turnaround on their purchase, a pleasant purchasing experience followed by a nice "thank you," and assurance that what they'll receive is exactly what they paid for. Increasingly, buyers want to be able to pay by credit card and have a money back guarantee.

If you're a crotchety old stick-in-the-mud, you may have a problem providing this level of service to your customers. However, if you enjoy corresponding with people and helping them feel good about their transaction then you'll do well.

Anyone who's spent time in sales knows that pleasing customers is not all that difficult. It's mostly common sense. Just adopt the same guideline that James Cash Penney used when he opened his first department stores—originally called the Golden Rule Stores and now known as JCPenney. *Treat other people the way you want to be treated.* This simple rule has helped many businesses achieve and maintain success. For more information on how to successfully operate your Internet auction sales as a business, refer to Chapter 11, "Managing Your Auction."

The Golden Rule "Treat other people the way you want to be treated." This rule has been the common sense basis for superior customer service in many successful businesses.

WHY SHOULDN'T I SELL?

A pessimist may tell you that "every silver cloud has a dark lining." He will look hard to find reasons to *not* become involved in selling in Internet auctions. He will easily find a few. There *are* some reasons you should consider before you get involved. Some of the most obvious problems that surround an auction business include time and record keeping commitments, dealing with customer problems, and avoiding risks.

Selling requires commitment. When you begin an auction, you've obligated yourself to complete the auction in an honest and timely manner—representing that the merchandise you offer to sell is genuine, corresponding with your high bidder within a reasonable amount of time, and delivering the goods you promise on time and in good condition. If you're unable to follow through on the details required to complete an auction, you will disappoint the buyer and cause yourself grief and frustration. If you've never balanced your checkbook and can't keep your bills paid on time, what makes you think you'll be able to keep up with the numerous details involved in seeing through every auction to its completion? Don't disappoint yourself and the customers. If you don't have these skills, then either find a partner with the required detail abilities or choose some other way to make money.

Selling also requires people skills. If you spend much time in the eBay chat rooms you'll find that there are plenty of frustrated buyers who can't understand the antics of some incompetent sellers. Almost every buyer complaint is based on miscommunication or a seller's unbending attitude. For example, there was a recent tiff between a seller who refused to accept a check for payment and a customer who would only pay by check. The seller claimed that he didn't want to get stuck with a bad check (which is reasonable), but the buyer had no problem waiting until the check cleared. The seller still refused. Other sellers in the chat room chided the seller for being so unreasonable, but he would not change his position. Forget the old adage, "The customer is always right." There would be no compromise! It was a matter of principle! If this is the kind of seller you intend to become, you're going to experience a lot of frustration.

On the other hand, if you're a pushover you may find yourself losing more money than you make. Some buyers will try to get you to ship them the merchandise before a check clears. Unless you know the buyer or have good evidence of her honesty, shipping before getting payment is an open road to loss. Once your merchandise is shipped a thousand miles away, you'll have a hard time getting it back. Be wary of buyers who want to pay half now and half when they receive the package. (Suggest that they use an escrow service.) Also, keep an eye out for bidding scams. If you think you've been defrauded, you should contact your auction host immediately. It's one matter to be accommodating to a genuine customer, but there's no reason to pull your punches when someone is out to steal money or merchandise from you.

Only you can determine if the risks and troubles associated with selling are worth your effort. If you're committed to keeping your customers happy by reasonable compromise and are willing to take the time to make sure every transaction is handled quickly and smoothly, then you'll do okay and you'll enjoy the benefits of operating a successful Internet auction business.

eBAY SELLER RESOURCES

You are not alone. Once you decide that you want to sell your merchandise on eBay or other Internet auctions, you'll be in good company. Besides the tips and resources in this book, there are a number of places on the Web where you can get hints and answers to questions. On eBay there are two major areas for getting help on selling your items: eBay seller services and chat rooms.

To access seller services on eBay, click on the <u>Site Map</u> link at the top of any eBay page. Under the "Sell" and "Services" headings, you'll find a number of other links that will help you set up an auction:

✔ **Sell Your Item Form**   This link under the "Sell" heading displays a form that you can fill out to tell eBay all of the particulars about placing your item up for auction. Chapter 8, "Creating a Winning Ad," describes the steps you'll take to fill out this form.

✔ **Manage My Items for Sale**   A series of links under this heading in the "Services" category allows you to correct problems with your ad, revise your ad, select ways to promote your auction, end your auction early, and create many auction descriptions at a time. Details about how to manage your auctions are described in Chapter 11, "Managing Your Auction."

✔ **Powersellers**   If you reach the level of selling over $2,000 in merchandise every month and have a feedback rating of at least 100, you can become an eBay *Powerseller*. These sellers gain additional privileges, promotion, and attention from eBay. Chapter 14, "Making a Living on Internet Auctions," discusses what it takes to reach this level of sales.

✔ **Seller Accounts**   eBay is not free. If you sell merchandise on eBay you'll pay them a fee. Therefore, eBay gives you a way to keep up with your account in the <u>Seller Account</u> links under "Services." Detailed information about your Seller Account is discussed in Chapter 11, "Managing Your Auction."

Powerseller   An eBay seller who auctions over $2,000 in merchandise every month and has a feedback rating of at least 100.

Other valuable resources for sellers are the help forums and chat rooms. eBay can't document a solution to every possible problem you'll encounter. Therefore, when you run across situations where you can't find an answer, go to a help forum or chat room. From any eBay page, click on the <u>Site Map</u> link, then find the <u>General Support Q&A Board</u>

link under the "Help" listing. This board allows you to ask questions 24 hours a day, 7 days a week. You'll usually get an answer back from a person knowledgeable about your situation. Check this board out even if you don't have a question. From reading the questions and answers you'll quickly learn a lot about how transactions proceed, what problems people encounter, and how they might be best solved. The other main resource for answers is the eBay chat rooms. (These chat rooms have been previously described in Chapter 1, "Starting Out.") The chat room where you'll find the most experienced sellers is in the "eBay Café." Utilize these resources when you come across a problem you can't seem to get resolved any other way.

SUMMARY

Internet auctions are a fantastic way to sell your merchandise with very little start-up costs. It is a great way to dip your big toe into a giant ocean to decide if you're willing to jump in for a swim. If you choose to make the commitment to be a seller, the next few chapters will show you how to select merchandise to sell, how to create a winning ad, and how to manage your auctions.

Chapter

7

Deciding What to Sell

W hen you place an item for sale on an Internet auction, you hope it will sell at a good price. However, a surprising number of auctions either receive no bids at all or end up with a winning bid that is lower than the seller had hoped for. Unsuccessful auctions cost the seller time and money. Therefore, as a seller you'll want to select items to sell that will attract lots of bidders and realize winning bids that maximize your profits. You probably began your selling experience by simply auctioning off dusty trinkets from your attic. Since you likely don't remember what you paid for these items to begin with, the price you receive for them is almost like pure profit. However, this well of "free" merchandise will soon run dry.

Eventually, every seller who wants to make a continuous stream of revenue on Internet auctions has to find a source for new merchandise. Just as in any retail business, you've got to figure out what merchandise you can acquire inexpensively to sell for more than what you paid for it.

CHOOSING WHAT TO SELL

Most people have some idea of what they want to sell when they begin looking at Internet auctions. It's reasonable to assume that you'd do best at selling merchandise you know something about. For example, if you've been a coin collector for twenty years, you'll probably want to sell coins. If you're an avid camera buff, you might want to buy and sell photography equipment. If you operate an antique store, you'll probably want to sell antiques.

Suppose you decide to sell coins. You should ask yourself, "Which coins sell best at auction? Which are in the most demand?" To find answers to these questions, you must do a little research. Your research may help you discover that auctions for United States coins are usually more successful than auctions for foreign coins. Or, you may discover that auctions for coins from 1800 to 1900 result in completed sales more often than auctions for contemporary coins. Once you find out what's in demand, you need to look at supply. Can you get a supply of the coins you want at a discount price? Is the demand high enough that you can sell the coins for more than you paid for them?

Just as in any market, Internet auction prices are based on *supply and demand.* The law of supply and demand says that the price for a good will rise when demand is high and supply is low. Therefore, when you select what you want to sell, it's best to find an item that is in demand. Then, if you can acquire this item for less than it normally sells for in the market, you have a chance to make a profit by selling it to those who want it.

Supply and Demand   An economics law that states that the price for a good will rise when demand is high and supply is low.

WHAT'S IN DEMAND?

If you were going to open a retail store, you'd probably browse through other successful stores first to find out what they're selling. You wouldn't want to open a store full of merchandise that no one wants! In the same way, when you decide what items to sell in Internet auctions you should use the same logic. Study the marketplace. Fortunately, eBay gives you just the tool you need—the completed auction search. Using this search method you can plainly examine completed auctions to determine if they ended with a successful sale or not.

For example, suppose you decide to sell United States coins. To find out which United States coins are in demand, use the completed auction search. Here's how you do it. From the main eBay page, under the "Categories" listing, click on the <u>Coins & Stamps</u> link. You'll see a list of links that begins like this:

Coins (39669)

    US (28296)

        General (1329)

        Cents (3850)

        Nickels (1499)

        Dimes (1817)

        Quarters (2003)

        Halves (3152)

        Dollars (4630)

        Errors (428)

        Collections, Lots (682)

        Mint, Proof Sets (2122)

        Gold (1290)

        Colonial (143)

        Commemorative (1012)

        Currency (2651)

        Certificates (1180)

You may first be tempted to look at the number of coins for sale in each category to determine demand. This is a mistake. It only tells you what coins are most *offered* for sale, not how many actually ended up with a successful sale. As you'll see in the following analysis, the number of auctions available for a coin type does not necessarily correlate with the probability of a sale.

To determine which categories are the best sellers you must examine how many auctions *within* a particular category end in a successful sale. To examine a category's sales, click on a category name, say "General," then click on the <u>Completed</u> link at the head of the listing. A list of the most recently completed auctions will be displayed. There will often be several pages of completed sales listed, with fifty auctions listed per page. You can easily count how many of the auctions received bids. For example, 70 of 100 (70 percent) general coin auctions recently resulted in bids. Although some of these may not have ended in sales because a reserve was not met, this figure will give you a good comparison by which you can judge how one category's sales compare to another.

As you examine the list you'll notice that some auctions received only one bid while others received two or more bids and still others may have received dozens of bids. Generally, if an auction receives only one bid, it means that the item was not in high demand. The seller probably didn't realize as much profit as he wanted from that auction. However, when an auction receives multiple bids it means that demand is high for that item and bidders are competing against one another. When bidders compete with one another the auction price goes up. This kind of auction produces the best profit for the seller. Therefore, you'll want to know what kinds of auctions attract the most bids. Table 7.1 looks at a sample of auction results for U.S. coins. Notice the three columns. The first column shows what percent of auctions resulted in at least one bid. The second column shows the percent that received two or more (multiple) bids and the third column shows those that received five or more bids.

As you can see from this analysis, some coin auction categories result in sales more often than others. If you're trying to decide what kind of coins to sell, you can use this analysis to focus in on the coins that are most in demand. The most popular coins are those that received the

TABLE 7.1 Sample Auction Results for U.S. Coins			
Coin Type	Percent with Bids	Multiple Bids	5 or More Bids
General	70%	55%	30%
Cents	80%	66%	34%
Nickels	72%	46%	26%
Dimes	76%	61%	27%
Quarters	69%	57%	29%
Halves	83%	65%	35%
Dollars	86%	80%	58%
Errors	68%	36%	16%
Collections, Lots	83%	68%	44%
Mint, Proof Sets	90%	78%	42%
Gold	87%	78%	61%
Colonial	87%	79%	50%
Commemorative	73%	60%	37%
Currency	76%	65%	41%
Certificates	66%	43%	13%

strongest showing as reported in the five or more bids category. This analysis indicates that auctions for U.S. gold, dollars, colonial, collections, and mint sets are the most in demand. The items in least demand are certificates and error coins.

This kind of analysis can get you started in finding items to sell, but it is not foolproof. There may be subcategories within these larger categories that vary in demand. For example, within the mint and proof set category you might find that proof sets are much more saleable than mint sets. To find this out you'll have to analyze the completed sales more closely and pull out the specific items you want to compare. Your own expertise in an area will help you understand what subcategories may be worth analyzing further.

Because there are well over a thousand categories it would be too much to analyze every one in detail. Therefore, you should consider first looking at broad categories where you have some interest or expertise. Table 7.2 gives an overview of the kinds of completed auction results you'll find in a representative selection of eBay categories. Remember that within each of these categories there may be some subcategory that will sell better or worse than the overall category.

From this table you can determine what kind of auction results to expect within these broad categories. For example, if you're trying to reach the Powerseller level in eBay, then children's software would not be the category you'd choose as your main product offering, since only about 13 percent of these auctions receive five or more bids.

To determine what items sell well on eBay, begin examining those categories that have high demand. You might notice some trends. For example, many of the collectible items in demand are from the era when Baby Boomers were children—Barbie dolls, Madam Alexander dolls, old-fashioned writing pens, Lionel Rail Roads, Vintage Fiesta pottery, and classic board games. Another group of items in great demand are computer and high-tech products such as computers, games, and digital cameras. Mull over the list yourself and see if you can detect a trend that could help you target your auctions toward those buyers who have the money and initiative to make bids.

As you look over this list, or perform your own analysis, remember that the supply and demand for products rises and falls. The Furby doll was very hot (and in short supply) for a while during Christmas of 1998. Now the supply is larger, and although it is still selling well, the price it brings is less than half of what it was fetching in its heyday. Be careful not to jump onto a hot toy bandwagon at its peak. A number of people paid close to $100 for Furbys when they were in short supply.

TABLE 7.2 Overview of eBay Auction Results

Category	Percent with Bids	Multiple Bids	5 or More Bids
Antiques/General	66%	49%	29%
Antiques/Books	67%	41%	24%
Antiques/Prints	45%	18%	8%
Books/Child/Golden	67%	47%	18%
Books/Computer	55%	31%	16%
Books/Rare	61%	44%	27%
Videos/Horror	41%	15%	10%
Videos/Children	64%	46%	24%
Music/CD/POP	67%	51%	35%
Magazine/Sports	62%	37%	14%
Magazine/Technical	53%	19%	6%
Coins/England	65%	43%	12%
Stamps/US/Airmail	72%	56%	33%
Stamps/US/Duck	76%	61%	43%
Ads/Auto/Chevy	45%	17%	5%
Ads/Soda/Coke	47%	24%	12%
Art/Amateur	59%	41%	20%
Art/Fine	38%	30%	12%
Autographs/Movie	68%	59%	32%
Bears/Boyd	60%	39%	17%
Bottles/Avon	30%	14%	2%
Watch/Pocket	83%	73%	48%
Plates/Franklin Mint	67%	58%	32%
Comics/Superhero	73%	66%	39%
Crafts/Cross Stitch	61%	37%	12%
Decorative/Hummel	76%	52%	33%
Ephemera	62%	45%	17%
Fraternal/Masonic	82%	65%	27%
Hallmark/Ornaments	37%	26%	17%
Kitchen/Small Appliances	63%	43%	22%
Metal Lunchboxes	69%	55%	38%
Movie Props	70%	57%	33%

(Continued)

94

Category	Percent with Bids	Multiple Bids	5 or More Bids
Military/WW II	58%	38%	17%
Pez	72%	52%	35%
Phonographs (vintage)	79%	69%	51%
RR Models/Lionel	84%	79%	61%
Collectable/Writing/Pens	86%	72%	61%
Digital Cameras	91%	83%	77%
Computers/PC	67%	61%	50%
Computers/Mac	87%	79%	59%
Software/Children	59%	33%	13%
Games/Nintendo	88%	80%	60%
Dolls/M.Alexander	87%	79%	59%
Barbie/Vintage	89%	83%	62%
Jewelry/Fine	57%	45%	27%
Glass/Swarovski	74%	68%	52%
Porcelain/Lenox	69%	50%	29%
Pottery/Vintage Fiesta	93%	87%	58%
Memorabilia/NASCAR	52%	25%	7%
Trading Cards/Baseball	71%	51%	30%
Action Figure/GI Joe	85%	69%	43%
Action Figure/Star Wars	73%	57%	27%
Ty Beanies	70%	51%	33%
Toys/McDonalds	65%	51%	33%
Toys/Furby	81%	66%	48%
Toys/Lego	92%	81%	56%
Toys/My Little Pony	84%	68%	25%
Vintage Tin Wind-Ups	79%	71%	53%
Real Estate	57%	49%	40%
Automobiles	55%	50%	41%

TABLE 7.2 (Continued)

When the supply increased and the price of the Furby fell below $50, these speculators who didn't auction off their items before the fall in price lost a lot of money.

Once you've discovered areas of high demand, you'll need to determine how to get a supply of the items at discounted prices. No matter how hot an item is, if you can't get it at a discount price, you can't make any money.

HOW TO OBTAIN PRODUCTS TO SELL

Your local retailer makes a living by selling merchandise for more than she pays for it. In the same way, if you're going to make a profit, you'll have to sell your merchandise for more than *you* paid for it. That means that you have to somehow acquire your merchandise at a discounted price—or even for free. How can you do that? Following are a few ideas to help get you started.

Purchase Directly from a Local Wholesaler

If you live in a large city there are likely several *wholesalers* available to you. A wholesale company is a business that sells products to retailers at a substantial discount off the normal retail price. Most wholesalers specialize in a particular type of merchandise such as electronics, books, music, or candy, to name a few. Retailers can usually purchase goods from a wholesaler at 30 to 50 percent discounts off the normal retail price. Occasionally wholesalers will liquidate a line and sell the remainders for up to a 90 percent discount.

Wholesaler A business that sells products to retailers at a substantial discount off the normal retail price. Most wholesalers specialize in a particular type of merchandise such as electronics, books, music, or candy, to name a few. Retailers can usually purchase goods from a wholesaler at 30 to 50 percent discounts off the normal retail price.

Check in your Yellow Pages for wholesalers in your area. Wholesalers are usually located in a warehouse district, and you must usually apply for permission to be one of their customers. Most will require that you have a state sales tax number and pay with a company check. You must also often have to purchase in quantity or purchase a minimum amount of merchandise to qualify for a discount. Many wholesalers require that you prove to them that you have a storefront before they will sell you goods. If you don't have a storefront, you may have to arrange a partnership with a local merchant to gain access to the wholesaler. Select a wholesaler that carries the type of merchandise you think you'll be able to sell at auction at a reasonable profit. Once you gain access to the wholesaler you can purchase goods, place them at auction, and repeat the process as many times as the market will bear.

Some of the items you might be able to purchase from a wholesaler and resale on an Internet auction include expendable office supplies such as ink cartridges, specialty paper (photographic), computer supplies, computer components, and the like.

Purchase Goods from Auctions in Large Lots

Local live auctions can be a substantial resource for merchandise you can resell. Check any large city newspaper and you will probably find a number of auctions held every week. These auctions will usually include stores or manufacturers liquidating stock, unclaimed freight, city auctions for unclaimed stolen goods, and even private estate auctions. In these types of auctions you will often *not* find individual items being sold. It is common for items to be sold in large lots. An *auction lot* is usually a large number of similar items being auctioned as one item. For example, a lot may include a truckload of computer laptops, a hundred unused military mess kits, a dozen adding machines, or a pallet full of folding chairs. Carefully examine the auction lots and determine if you can resell the items individually at a profit. On many of these auctions you may have to purchase a dozen, a hundred, or even a thousand items. However, you'll often be able to get them for pennies on the dollar.

One way you can increase the value of items you buy at auction is to refurbish what you buy. For example, if you're computer savvy, you might be able to purchase pallets of computer components and software then put them back together to create useable computer systems.

Auction Lot   Usually a large number of similar items being auctioned as one item. For example, a lot may include a truckload of computer laptops, a hundred unused military mess kits, a dozen adding machines, or a pallet full of folding chairs.

Purchase from Discount Stores

One successful eBay seller purchases deeply discounted books from a local bookstore and then resells them on eBay. She pays $5 for each book and sells them at an average bid price of $15. Thus, she gets an average $10 profit for each sale. Over a six-month period she sold several hundred books and made a tidy $6,000 profit. Check the outlet and factory stores around your city to see if you can find one that sells resaleable merchandise for a deep discount. Some communities have factory outlet stores or other kinds of liquidation stores. Just remember that you'll probably have to get *at least* a 50 percent discount to make a decent profit from an item—and that's only if the item will sell for 75 percent or more of its normal retail value.

Create Your Own Product

You might be able to create your own product to sell at auction. Several software authors have found that they can sell games, educational programs, and other software programs using Dutch Auctions at a reasonable profit on eBay. For example, if you have or can secure the rights to reproduce a software program, you can make CDs in quantities of a thousand or more for less than a dollar a copy. If you sell dozens of CDs at $5.95 each week, you can make a decent profit. However, don't try to copy and sell someone else's copyrighted program—unless you want to end up in court!

Other self-made items that are sold on eBay include painting, photography, cross stitch, and crafts. If you have talent you might be able to use eBay to sell your creations. Keep an eye on the profit you make per item. If it takes you five hours to create a product, and you sell it for a $10 profit, you've only made $2 an hour for your work. You might as well flip hamburgers.

Repackage a Product

Some clever eBayers have discovered that they can repackage bulk products and resell them at a nice profit. For example, one eBayer purchases inkjet photopaper in bulk. She then repackages it into sets of 10 pages each. At a retail store, a package of ten pieces of this type of paper sells for about $12. If you can bulk purchase the sheets at only ten cents a sheet, you can create your own sets of 10 sheets, charge $2.99, and make a $1.99 profit on each package you sell. To sell enough of these packages to make it worth your while, you'd want to sell them through a Dutch Auction. That way you can sell dozens or even hundreds of packages in a single auction.

In fact, browsing through the current list of Dutch Auctions is a good way to get ideas for other ways you might resell products. Look around your community for manufacturers who might be willing to sell you their products in bulk so you could repackage them generically and sell them yourself.

Another way to repackage a product is to *add value* to it. For example, suppose you purchased a thousand nice picture frames at a closeout. You might have a difficult time selling the empty frames. However, if you were to use the frames to create a nice display of some collectable item such as stamps, sports memorabilia, or antique postcards, you might be able to increase their value enough to sell them at auction. Another way to add value is to create sets from common items. For example, the new state quarters that have been recently released by the mint are by themselves not worth more than a quarter each. However, several sellers have collected the quarters into sets and are selling them for a profit.

Add Value   The process of taking items that may individually be worth little and add something to them or combine them in a unique way to create a product with more value than the individual components.

Resell Free Items

Keep your eyes open for free items that might be saleable. For example, you can sometimes get leftover manufacturer's samples or overstocks for free by offering to haul them away. Watch for stores that are closing or moving. They may have samples or old merchandise stored away that they'd be happy to give to you if you cleaned out their storage areas for them. If there is a large convention or show in your community, you might be able to get interesting leftover supplies or samples. Is there a yearly new car show in your community? New car brochures are collectable items. Although you may not find anyone who will buy this year's car brochure, if you collect them for several years, you'll find that they eventually become marketable. In fact, one rule of thumb for saving collectibles is to look at items most people throw away—such as programs from state fairs, political rallies, sporting events, or historical events.

Many of these items fall into the *ephemera* category. Ephemera are defined as short-lived paper items of current and passing interest. This category includes newspapers, magazines, posters, printed programs, and the like. Some ephemera may be of instant value—such as programs from the Olympics or the Superbowl. Other items require several years before they become valuable enough to sell—newspapers describing historical events or product brochures, for example. It's often the case that at the time an event takes place, few people consider a free paper item related to it of any importance, and it is thrown away. Later, when people understand the significance of the event, material associated with it becomes valuable. Did you know that many of the free maps given out at the Disney and Six Flags theme parks in years past are now fetching handsome prices—sometimes as much as $75 each?

Ephemera   Short-lived paper items of current and passing interest, including newspapers, magazines, posters, printed programs, and the like.

Watch for events in your community, such as inaugurations, state fairs, sporting events, historical events, parades, and political rallies. If you can snap up leftover items that are destined for the trash can, you might be able to turn the trash into cash.

Buy Collections

Keep an eye on your newspaper's classified ads for garage sales, estate auctions, and offerings in the collectibles category. You'll often find that people sell their collections (or accumulations) when they need quick money, clean house, move, or have a death in the family. This can provide you with the material for many auctions. You could sell off individual pieces, or repackage and add value to the collection and resell it at a profit. Other ways you might be able to purchase collections and accumulations are in garage sales, church rummage sales (old children's Sunday School literature containing pictures are often very salable), and store closings. You might even consider placing your own "want ad" in your newspaper's classifieds to let people know you're willing to purchase their unwanted collections.

SUMMARY

If you want to sell on Internet auctions as a hobby, then just have fun buying and selling items within your own area of interest. However, if you want to expand your selling into a money-making proposition, then you'll have to give your selling strategy more thought. Research what is selling well on eBay and look around at your own resources to find out what you can buy cheap and sell at a premium.

8

Creating a Winning Ad

Are you fishing for fun or for food? That's the kind of question you should ask yourself when you decide to sell something in an Internet auction. If you're just in it for fun, you can bait your hook with whatever you have that's handy, but if you're in it to make some money, you'll want to fish with the best kinds of lures available in your tackle box. This chapter assumes that you want to make some money at auction. And even if you're just putting your line in the water to see what comes up, you can easily improve your chance of catching some fish by using just a few of the tricks mentioned here.

To place an ad on eBay you must complete its "Sell Your Item" form, describing how you want the auction to be held. Before filling out this form, you need to understand what kind of information will be required. The following sections describe how to put together your ad's wording and how to select certain required options to get your first eBay auction successfully launched.

UNDERSTANDING AD PREPARATION

Your success at selling an item in an Internet auction depends on how you present your treasure to potential buyers. Imagine for a moment that you're a typical customer searching through hundreds (or thousands) of items on an auction site. What will attract you to a particular auction? Initially, it will be the auction's one-line description. Follow this scenario:

A customer performs a search that produces a hundred or more possible auction listings on his screen. As he examines the listings, he'll be attracted to some one-line descriptions that contain the specific characteristics about the item he wants. Is this the right brand of glass doorknob? Is the Erector set in its original box? Is this a signed and numbered lithograph? Out of the hundreds of listings, he'll select a few to examine in more detail.

Will your auction be the one the customer chooses to look at more closely? That depends on how well you've created the one-line ad title for your product. Hopefully, the scenario above illustrates that the most visible part of your ad is often not the ad itself, but the one-line, 45-character description called the *ad title*. Without a good one-liner, shoppers will never step over the doorstep and into your main showroom—the long description. Therefore, your first task must be to create a good ad title for your product. After you've accomplished that, the next most important part of your ad is the description itself.

Ad Title A one-line, 45-character description of the product you're selling. This keyword description is by far the most important part of your ad *because without it you will not attract very many customers at all.*

Once you've created your one-line and full descriptions of your product, you're only a short way from beginning your first auction. The list of information you'll need to enter into the eBay auction preparation form to get a simple auction started includes:

✔ A concise one-line description
✔ An appealing and detailed description
✔ Fair and concise shipping options
✔ An appropriate auction category
✔ Length of auction
✔ Starting bid
✔ Location
✔ Your eBay User ID and Password

Once you know these pieces of information, you're ready to place your auction online. The remainder of this chapter shows how to come up with this information and place it into the eBay "Sell Your Item" auction form.

Creating a Concise One-Line Description

On most auction sites and particularly on eBay, the first encounter a customer will have with your auction is its one-line description, the ad title. Since most eBay searches are performed on the ad title, it is important that keywords for your product appear in this description. For example, suppose a customer is looking for an old Walt Disney Davy Crockett coonskin hat. If you're older than 40, you may remember how popular these hats were in the 1950s. (Sing along with me . . . "Davy, Davy Crockett, king of the wild frontier. . . . " To recapture a part of his youth, our Baby Boomer begins his quest by entering a few words into the auction search engine. The search engine examines the words entered by our would-be frontiersman and attempts to match them with words in millions of ad titles.

Is your ad title designed to help him find your coonskin cap? If his search words fail to match any words in your one-line item description, he'll never find your ad. Therefore, you must carefully consider what words you'll place in your title. Would the following description be an effective hook to bring customers to your coonskin hat ad?

Rare! Must see! Great old fur cap from the 50s! Neat!

The only word in the entire description that might match a customer's search is *fur*. Now think like the customer thinks, and write down words that you think he'd use to search for the item. For example:

Davy Crockett, Coon, Coonskin, Hat, and Walt Disney

Using this list you can construct an effective 45-character description, such as:

Walt Disney Davy Crockett Coonskin Hat Coon

Why use both *coonskin* and *coon*? Because your customer may use either of those as search words. Therefore, you'll want to be able to catch both possibilities.

When creating your one-line description you should keep in mind the special characters that eBay uses for searches. In particular, *never* use a dash (–) in your keyword descriptions. It is the excluder for eBay searches. Thus, if you used a keyword such as ACE-O-MATIC, users *will not* be able to search for it since it includes dashes. A search using ACE-O-MATIC would tell eBay to search descriptions for the keyword ACE, but not for O or MATIC. You should also avoid using of an asterisk (*) or a pound sign (#) in your descriptions. (See Chapter 2, "The Opening Bid," for specific information about eBay search syntax.)

To summarize, be as *specific* as possible in your one-line description. Use keywords in your brief description that your customer might associate with your item. If you can't fill up the entire 45 letters with obvious words, then you can use phrases such as *No Reserve, NR, Mint, Rare, Free Postage, Guaranteed, Click here*, and so on—words that will entice your potential customer to click on your brief description to see more details.

Writing an Appealing Ad

Now that your customer has noticed your hook and taken an initial bite by clicking on your ad title, it's time to offer your entire lure. But wait. Your customer is impatient. He has hundreds of ads to examine. You have only a few seconds to grab his attention or he'll click his browser's "Back" button and go on to the next match. How do you convince him to stay? How can you make your ad catch his eye?

You've probably already browsed through a number of ads on eBay and seen different styles ranging from ads with cryptic descriptions to glitzy ads containing flashing lights, animation, sound, and pages of description. Which of these two styles is best for your ad? Neither. You want your ad to be only as long as it takes to fully describe your offering and only fancy enough to present your item in its best light.

Cryptic ads are often filled with partial sentences, irregular punctuation, and misspelled words. This doesn't give potential customers a warm and fuzzy feeling about dealing with the seller. It's obvious that little thought went into the creation of this ad—maybe it means that the seller is sloppy or a slob. You wouldn't want to do business with him, would you?

On the other hand, super-flashy ads full of animations that take forever to load make you wonder if the seller is trying to sell you on the glitz rather than on the benefits of the item itself. Maybe he's trying to cover up the product's flaws by surrounding the description with distractions. Who does he think he is? I'm no fool. I'll move on to a seller I can trust.

Your ad should sell yourself as well as your product. Create ads that tell your customer in simple and catchy words that you have the product he wants—correctly and concisely described with a moderate amount of hype—but don't overdo it. Design the ad so it assures the bidder that you'll conduct the transaction in a professional and forthright manner. If your item is expensive or is a collector's item, the professionalism of your ad is even *more* important. Do you have to be a professional copywriter to produce such an ad? No. You simply need to follow a few simple suggestions.

Before you write your own ad, read ads from other sellers. Pay close attention to the ads that make you want to purchase an item. Print them out and study them. Also look at ads in mail-order catalogs such as *Land's End* and *Spencer Gifts* and study classified ads in the backs of magazines. Many of these ads have been developed through years of testing, market research, and trial and error.

All of this seriousness about wording your ad doesn't mean that it should be boring or dry. No! Ads should have personality! They must invite your bidder in to have a good time. The ad should be an invitation— stop here for just a minute and let me pour you a cup of coffee. And, by the way, look at this neat gizmo that I have for sale! Here's an inviting ad that begins with a little pizzazz:

> R2D2 Where Are You? Here he is. He's an official *Star Wars* Beanie Buddy . . . and now he can be your buddy too . . .

The beginning of this ad appeals to *Star Wars* fans and introduces the merchandise at the same time. It tells the buyer that the seller knows something about *Star Wars*. (The first phrase is a direct quote from the movie.) Collectors would rather buy from a fellow collector—someone who shares the same fantasies or dreams. On the other hand, an ad aimed at a coin collector should be much more detailed and to the point:

> PCGS Certified MS-65 1929-S Standing Liberty Quarter with full head visible and a light frosting on the reverse.

The beginning of this ad tells the buyer that the seller knows a thing or two about coins, and that this coin in particular includes a certified grade.

The first sentence or two of your ad is crucial. It must capture the eye and imagination of your customer and make them want to continue to read the remainder of your ad. Spend some time thinking about what your customer will want to know up front. Then, when you've captured his attention, go on to describe the important details of your item.

Pay Attention to Details

What details are important to describe? Everything you can think of. You want to leave no reason for your customer to pass up your offer. Answer every possible question. For example, give measurements of your item. Have a ruler handy whenever you're writing an ad. How tall is the item? How wide? How big around? You might also indicate how much it weighs if you think it's important. For collectibles, include information on tags or original boxes. Mention copyright dates, country of manufacturer, company, author, version, and so on. You never know what detail someone will be looking for. Also describe any flaws in your item. Does it have nicks? Is the paint faded? Is it scratched? It's better to give too much detail than to leave the bidder wondering. In fact, you may save yourself the frustration of having to deal with returns or unhappy customers by giving the most honest and complete description possible in your ad. Here's a checklist of some of the things you might include in your description:

- ✔ Brand, version, model
- ✔ Dimensions (height, width, etc.)
- ✔ Colors, fabrics, materials
- ✔ Copyright, trademarks, country of origin, manufacturer's marks, etc.
- ✔ Grade—if possible a certified grade. For commonly collected items such as stamps, coins, and baseball cards, make sure you use and understand the official grading system for that particular item.
- ✔ Flaws: nicks, scratches, bends, peeling paint, missing pieces, etc.
- ✔ Always be completely honest in your descriptions.

Of course, you don't want to spend hours coming up with an ad to sell a ten-dollar piece of merchandise. If you'll simply keep these guidelines in mind when you're writing your ad, you'll increase your chance of attracting customers and bids. However, if you're selling an expensive item or selling many items through a Dutch Auction, it may be worth your while to pay extra careful attention to how you word your ad. The more ads you write, the easier it will become.

Grading Your Collectibles

If you're selling collectibles then you must pay special attention to grading your item. In Chapter 5, "Participating in the Collector's Paradise," you were introduced to the eBay Library. This library contains numerous resources for you to use in grading and describing your collectibles. Since most collectors will be familiar with the specific terms used in grading, you should strictly use the appropriate terms for that type of collectible. For example, the word "good" has a specific meaning for coin collectors. When you say a Walking Liberty Half-Dollar coin is in *good condition* a knowledgeable collector will translate the word *good* into a specific meaning:

> The coin is heavily worn with the design and legend visible but faint in spots. The legend and date is weak but readable and the top of the date is worn flat. The rim is flat but nearly complete. The eagle on the reverse is nearly flat but its outline is completely visible. Lettering and motto on the reverse is worn but clearly visible.

Is that what you meant by good? That's what the collector will expect. You can see that simple words such as *good*, *very good*, and *fine* should not be used in ads for graded collectibles unless you know precisely what they mean. If you don't have a copy of the official grading book for your particular type of collectible, go to the eBay Library to see if it has the information you need.

By the way, never try to clean or repair collectibles unless you're very sure of what you're doing. For example, a cleaned coin is often worth *much less* than a coin in its original state. If you're not sure whether you should repair or clean an item before trying to sell it, ask someone in an appropriate chat room for an opinion.

Using Words that Sell

Some words sell better than others. There's a famous story about a mail-order company that experimented with the wording in one of its ads. The company sold a course that taught how to repair radios. (This was some years ago!) One version of the ad's title read something like *Learn How to Repair Radios*. Another identical ad used the title *Learn How to Fix Radios*. The ad that used the word *fix* rather than *repair* was by far more successful in getting prospective buyers to respond. In fact, changing that single word in the ad from *repair* to *fix* meant thousands of dollars of extra income for the mail-order company!

How can you use this information? You could run an experiment like this yourself if you repeat the same ad many times. However, most sellers will not have that kind of opportunity. Therefore, your next best option is to know some of the tricks mail-order sellers have used for years—how to use words that arouse good emotions in buyers and that are inviting without being threatening. In the radio example, it was determined that many people were intimidated by the word *repair*. It sounded too technical. However, most people thought they could *fix* a radio. People are emotional about what they want to buy. Therefore, your ad should appeal to our common emotions. One strategy used by ad copywriters is to appeal to one or more of the five most common emotional factors: love, pride, fear, guilt, and greed.

- ✔ *Love* Your wife will think you are Mr. Special when you present her with this lovely diamond ring.
- ✔ *Pride* "I pledge allegiance to the flag!" Be proud that you're an American. Purchase my July the Fourth flag and banner kit and display your colors this Independence Day.
- ✔ *Fear* Save your family! Don't let them be killed or maimed by the awesome and horrible force of a tornado. How can you save your family from ever having to worry about a tornado again? Purchase these easy-to-use, research-tested blueprints for creating a tornado-proof safe room in your existing home.
- ✔ *Guilt* Is your family slowly dying from drinking impure city water? Buy the ace-o-matic water purifier and your precious loved ones will be drinking the healthiest water on your block.
- ✔ *Greed* These rare purple porcupine beanie dolls will never be produced again and there are only 124 of them left in the entire world. Don't wait or you'll miss out on this once-in-a-lifetime opportunity. Get yours now before they are all gone!

Choose your words carefully. Select words that are appropriate to the item you're selling without misrepresenting your product. Give your buyers assurance by using words and phrases such as *guarantee, examine my reputation,* and *my iron-clad promise.* For a sports oriented product, you might want to use phrases such as *hit a home run, all-star service,* and *our product withstands in-your-face, teeth gritting, bone crushing torture.*

Keep your ad upbeat. Stay away from negative words. Avoid phrases that may give your customer a bad impression. Instead of saying "I flatly refuse to take CODs. If you send me a check, I will not send your item until my bank tells me it wasn't made of rubber," you might instead say, "No CODs please. If you pay by check, your item will be shipped promptly once your check clears." Which of these two sellers would you rather deal with?

Specifying Shipping Options

Before your customer bids, she's going to want to know how much it will cost to have the item shipped. Even if you've done a good job with your description, you can turn off a customer with a poorly conceived shipping policy. Of course most sellers charge the buyer for shipping, but some sellers attempt to make a bit of extra cash by charging too much for postage and handling. Informed customers notice and appreciate sellers who try to keep down the cost of shipping.

The best policy for shipping and handling is to charge the customer only for the actual cost of delivery. What are these delivery costs? They are determined by your location, the size and weight of your item, the speed of delivery desired, and any extra add-ons to shipping such as insurance and COD. In Chapter 4, I described a number of options for shipping goods. You may decide that you'll ship using first class postage, but what if a customer wants quicker delivery? A good policy is to offer your customer a few simple shipping options. For example, your ad might say:

> Shipping is $2.00 by regular mail or $3.20 for priority shipping. You choose.

Most buyers notice when a seller is willing to work with them to ship an item inexpensively. This is particularly important for items that sell for less than five dollars. For these items, the shipping may cost more than the item itself. Customers who realize this up front will be less likely to bid on your item.

Postage is usually easy to figure when you're shipping an item. The "handling" part can be more complicated. Some sellers want to charge their customers what it cost to buy a shipping box, packing paper, tape, and the gasoline to drive to the post office. This is not standard business practice. However, if a buyer requests some special and unusual services, then the seller might want to consider charging extra for these items. For example, some sellers charge a few dollars extra for COD since it requires a lot of paperwork.

Look for ways to minimize the cost of your mailing. The more money you save here, the better your profit. Using Priority Mail from the United States Post Office is popular since you can get free Priority Mail shipping envelopes and boxes. Similar boxes are available from UPS and FedEx. For times when you can't use these complimentary boxes, consider reusing other boxes that you can get from local retailers. Since stores are always getting in new supplies and merchandise, they're usually more than happy to give you their boxes. As a bonus, these boxes are often full of leftover packing material. Most sellers should never have to purchase boxes or packing materials. Recycle old boxes and packing peanuts. Use newspaper for packing when necessary but be careful not to use it on merchandise where the ink might rub off on the item and damage it.

End of Auction Assurances

Once you've thoroughly described your merchandise and shipping policies you'll need to describe to your buyer how you'll handle the end-of-auction transaction. Many Internet users have significant concerns about transacting business in e-commerce. Therefore, you need to overcome this fear factor by assuring your customer that her item will be delivered on time and in good condition. You can use several ways to do this:

- ✔ Mention your Feedback Rating (assuming you have a good one).
- ✔ Offer a guarantee. Chances are that if you've described your auction well you'll never have to refund any money. However, give your buyer the assurance that if things go wrong, you'll make them right.
- ✔ Make buying from you as easy as possible. Accept as many kinds of payments as you can. If possible, accept credit card payments.
- ✔ For expensive items, offer to use an escrow service to handle payment.

The way you give a potential buyer assurance is by clearly describing how you'll handle the transaction for the winning bidder. Here's some sample wording you could include at the end of your ad:

> Bid with confidence. Every item I sell is fully guaranteed to be as represented or I'll refund your bid. See my Feedback Rating. I'll ship your item to you promptly as soon as payment is received. (Checks must clear.) Visa and MasterCard payment is available. Thanks for your bid! Have a GREAT day!

Mail-order companies have known for years that you must make your sale as easy as possible for the buyer. The same situation exists for auctions. Take away any barriers to bidding and payment that you can imagine. Give a guarantee. Offer easy ways for payment to be made. Present yourself as a helpful friend. Make bidding fun.

STARTING AN AUCTION

You've thought about how you're going to word your ad and are now ready to start an auction. Hold your breath. This is the real thing! This section will show you how to place a simple auction on eBay by using the "Sell Your Item" auction form. First, click on the "Sell Your Item" icon on the main eBay page, or click on the "Sell" menu item, then "sell your item form." The top part of the "Sell Your Item" form is shown in Figure 8.1.

Filling Out the eBay Auction Form

Once the eBay "Sell Your Item" form appears on your computer screen you can begin filling out the form describing your auction. The first item to fill out is the one-line description. Remember that you want to include as many keywords in this description as you can. Type in your description into the text box provided. To display the next item in the form, scroll down the page using the scroll bars on the right side of the form window.

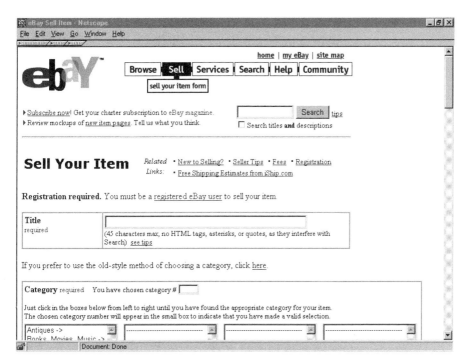

Figure 8.1 The eBay Sell Your Item Form.

Selecting the Auction Category

The second item on the form is the *auction category*. The auction category is the section within eBay where your auction item will be placed. There are more than 1500 categories available. Selecting the correct category for your item is an important decision since it gives your item exposure to the customers who do their searching within a narrow set of categories. If you place your item in an incorrect category, you may decrease your chance of getting the number and quality of bids you want. Your earlier research and experience in searching for similar products will tell you what category best fits your item. If you're unsure of the proper category, do a few searches for similar items and take note of where they are placed.

Auction Category The section within eBay where your auction will be placed. There are more than 1500 categories available. Selecting the correct category for your auction item is an important decision since it gives your item exposure to the customers who do their searching within a narrow set of categories.

Figure 8.2 shows the auction category selection item. To indicate a category, click on the general category selection in the first, leftmost box. In this example, "Photo & Electronics" is selected. Once you select a main category, eBay places a list of possible subcategories into the next list box. The second selection box in Figure 8.2 shows that the item "Photo Equipment" is selected. eBay then places a list of options for Photo Equipment in the third selection box. When you select "Subminiature," eBay fills in the "You have chosen category #" box with the number 709. This is the eBay number for the "Photo & Electronics/Photo Equipment/Subminiature" category.

In subsequent auction definitions, once you've determined a category number, you can simply enter the number in the "You have chosen category #" box without having to go through the selection box procedure. If you've created eBay auctions in the past and prefer the old style category selection method, you can click on the link indicated by the "If you prefer to use the old-style method of choosing a category, *click here*." option listed at the top of the category selection box to display the old style auction form.

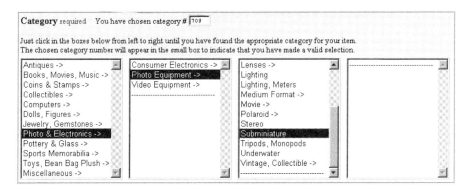

Figure 8.2 The eBay Category Selection Form.
(This material has been reproduced by John Wiley & Sons, Inc. with permission of eBay, Inc. Copyright © eBay, Inc. All rights reserved.)

Entering the Item Description

Below the item category is a large text box that allows you to type in your item description, as shown in Figure 8.3. Suggestions for wording your ad were given in the first part of this chapter. Now you're ready to put it all together. But before entering the ad text, notice the "hint" below the Item Description text box that tells you, "You can use basic HTML tags to spruce up your listing." *HTML* (Hypertext Markup Language) is a series of Web commands (also called tags) you can include in Web text that gives your browser instructions on how to display information on the viewer's screen. (Specific HTML commands are described in detail in Chapter 10, "Improving Your Presentation.")

HTML Hypertext Markup Language is a series of commands (also called tags) you can include in Web text that gives your browser instructions on how to display information on the viewer's screen.

For your first auction description you'll use a simple HTML command that displays your description in a more readable format. The command you'll use is <P>, which tells your browser to break the text into paragraphs. Examine the sample item description below to see how this command is used:

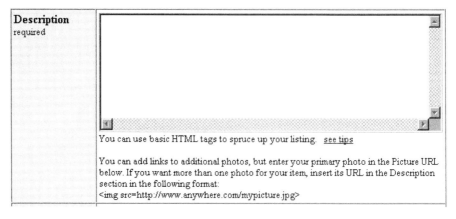

You can use basic HTML tags to spruce up your listing. see tips

You can add links to additional photos, but enter your primary photo in the Picture URL below. If you want more than one photo for your item, insert its URL in the Description section in the following format:
<img src=http://www.anywhere.com/mypicture.jpg>

Figure 8.3   The eBay Item Description Form.

(This material has been reproduced by John Wiley & Sons, Inc. with permission of eBay, Inc. Copyright © eBay, Inc. All rights reserved.)

R2D2 Where Are You? Here he is. He's an official STAR WARS Beanie Buddy . . . and now he can be your buddy too . . . This R2D2 plush doll is 5 1/2 inches tall and is the likeness of the robot in STAR WARS. He's made of a silver and blue fabric, is brand-new in mint condition and still contains the original STAR WARS tag. Information on tag is "For all ages, Created by Kenner, 1997, Copyright Hasbro." Inside tag is information on how to join the STAR WARS fan club.
<P>
Thanks for bidding on this auction. Good luck!
<P>
Successful bidder pays $3.20 for Priority Mail shipping anywhere in the U.S. Bid with confidence. Every item I sell is fully guaranteed to be as represented or I'll refund your bid. See my Feedback Rating.
<P>
I'll ship your item to you promptly as soon as payment is received. (Checks must clear.) Visa and MasterCard payment is available.
<P>
Have a GREAT day!

Notice that the <P> paragraph marker is placed between each paragraph in the item description. Case does not matter, so you could use <p> as well. On a standard keyboard, the "<" and ">" are shift characters located on the "," (comma) and "." (period) keys. A blank line *will not* separate paragraphs correctly. Therefore, if you do not include the <P> command to separate paragraphs, the description will be run together in one single long paragraph that will make the information hard to read. If you use the <P> paragraph commands as in the example above, the description will be displayed like this on a user's screen:

R2D2 Where Are You? Here he is. He's an official STAR WARS Beanie Buddy . . . and now he can be your buddy too . . . This R2D2 plush doll is 5 1/2 inches tall and is the likeness of the robot in STAR WARS. He's made of a silver and blue fabric, is brand-new in mint condition and still contains the original STAR WARS tag. Information on tag is "For all ages, Created by Kenner, 1997, Copyright Hasbro." Inside tag is information on how to join the STAR WARS fan club.

Thanks for bidding on this auction. Good luck!

Successful bidder pays $3.20 for Priority Mail shipping anywhere in the U.S. Bid with confidence. Every item I sell is fully guaranteed to be as represented or I'll refund your bid. See my Feedback Rating.

I'll ship your item to you promptly as soon as payment is received. (Checks must clear.) Visa and MasterCard payment is available.

Have a GREAT day!

However, if you do not use the <P> commands in your description, the ad text appears like this on the user's screen:

R2D2 Where Are You? Here he is. He's an official STAR WARS Beanie Buddy . . . and now he can be your buddy too . . . This R2D2 plush doll is 5 1/2 inches tall and is the likeness of the robot in STAR WARS. He's made of a silver and blue fabric, is brand-new in mint condition and still contains the original STAR WARS tag. Information on tag is "For all ages, Created by Kenner, 1997, Copyright Hasbro." Inside tag is information on how to join the STAR WARS fan club. Thanks for bidding on this auction. Good luck! Successful bidder pays $3.20 for Priority Mail shipping anywhere in the U.S. Bid with confidence. Every item I sell is fully guaranteed to be as represented or I'll refund your bid. See my Feedback Rating. I'll ship your item to you promptly as soon as payment is received. (Checks must clear.) Visa and MasterCard payment is available. Have a GREAT day!

The second version of the description is not as readable or eye pleasing as the paragraphed version. Since you're trying to make it as easy as possible for readers to get your message, you'll want to break up your text with the <P> command.

Selecting Other Auction Options

Following the item description, a number of other auction options are available for selection. (Most of these will be discussed in detail in Chapters 9 through 11.) For this first auction description, only the required items will be described.

Figure 8.4 shows the form item called "Item Location." In this section of the form you must indicate your item's location, a region, and your country. This information is important to the buyer because it may determine shipping costs. For the item location enter a city and state name such as Cedar Hill, Texas. Since there are a number of city names that are common to several states, be sure to include the state name. Also select a region and country name from the list boxes provided.

The next set of required items include "Quantity," "Minimum Bid," and "Duration." Quantity will always be one (1) unless you are using a Dutch Auction. The minimum bid is your choice for the lowest bid you

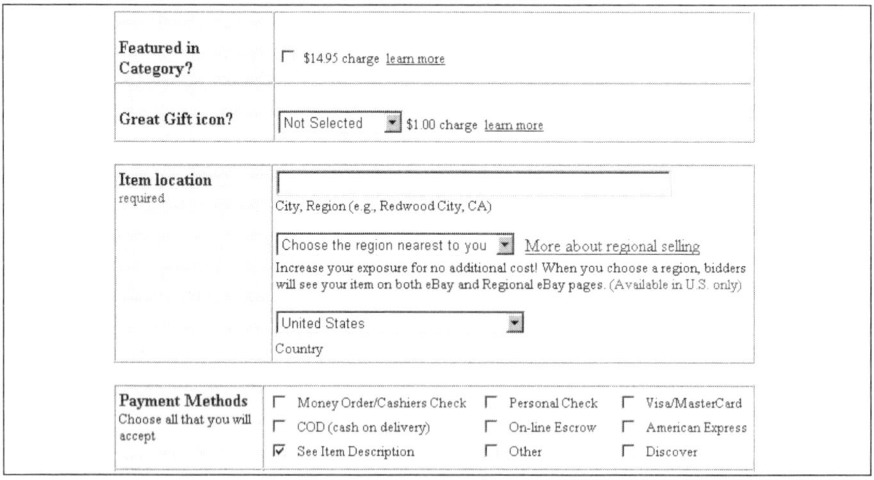

Figure 8.4 The eBay Item Location Form.

will accept for your item. This option allows you to avoid selling your merchandise for less than it is worth. However, many experienced sellers realize that if they begin an item at a low bid, say $1.00, the item will generate more interest and will attract more bidders. In the long run, this strategy often results in a higher ending bid than what would be realized if the opening bid were set higher. In fact, many auctions never receive any bids because the seller sets the opening bid too high. If you're selling many similar items, you should experiment with the opening bid price to see which one generates the most interest and highest ending bids.

Right below where you enter your minimum bid price is an option to enter a reserve price for your auction. Selecting a reserve price is another strategy open to you to protect your item from being sold below its value. In a _Reserve Auction_, you choose the lowest price you would be willing to take for your item. Then, you can set the opening price for your auction at $1.00 without having to worry about selling out too cheaply. If the bidding doesn't rise to your minimum reserved price, you are not obligated to sell your item to the highest bidder. Unless you mention what your reserve price is in your ad, the bidders won't know its amount. The only indication bidders have of the status of the reserve price is a note on the bid form that tells whether or not the current bid exceeds the reserve price. However, many bidders are wary of reserve auctions and will not bid on them at all. Therefore you have to choose how to set up your auction:

- ✔ Enter a high opening bid that protects your item from being sold at a low price.
- ✔ Enter a low opening bid and hope that you'll start a bidding war among bidders that will drive the price higher.
- ✔ Specify a reserve price.

Although low opening bids attract bidders, you open yourself up to the risk of selling your item at a bargain basement price. Only experience will teach you what items you can safely begin with a low bid.

The final option in this section of the form is the auction duration. Currently, eBay allows you to select three-, five-, seven-, or ten-day auctions. Seven-day auctions are the most common. Simply select the one you want from the pull-down box. Additional information about using Dutch Auctions, protecting your minimum acceptable bid using Reserve Auctions, and selecting your auction's duration is covered in Chapter 11, "Managing Your Auction."

Even though it's not a required item, take a look at the shipping

Reserve Auction   In this type of auction, you choose the lowest price you would be willing to take for your item. Then, you can set the opening price for your auction at $1.00 without having to worry about selling out too cheaply. If the bidding doesn't rise to your minimum reserved price, you are not obligated to sell your item to the highest bidder. Unless you mention what your reserve price is in your ad, the bidders won't know its amount. The only indication bidders have of the status of the reserve price is a note on the bid form that tells whether or not the current bid exceeds the reserve price. However, many bidders are wary of reserve auctions and will not bid on them at all.

options. Notice that for this auction you are specifying by default that the shipping information for the auction is in the text of this ad. This is the most common way to tell the buyer how shipping will be handled.

Reviewing Your Auction Description

The last required items in the form are your eBay User ID and Password. You must be a registered eBay user to begin an auction (refer back to Chapter 1 for registration information). Once you've entered your ID and Password, click on the "Review" button. eBay will display a page showing you a summary of all of the items you've selected. If you've omitted required information, an error page will be displayed. Figure 8.5 shows the eBay error notification page. Click on your browser's "Back" button to go back to the "Sell Your Item" auction form and correct the error. Click on the "Review" button again to display the summary page.

Figure 8.6 shows a sample auction summary page. Always review this page carefully; it is your last chance to make corrections in the auction before going live. Pay particular attention to the spelling on your one-line and detailed descriptions. It's critical that you have *no mistakes* in your descriptions and keywords since potential bidders who want to search for your item will use them. Also, check all of the other form items you've filled in. Are they all correct? Once you're satisfied with your auction description, click on the "Submit" button.

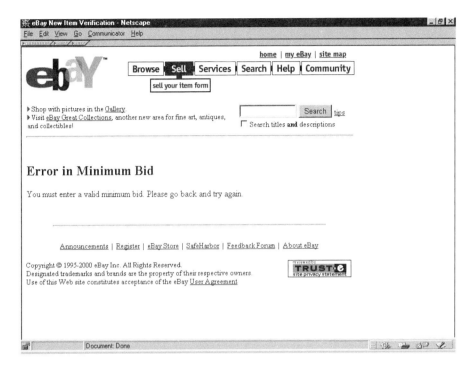

Figure 8.5 eBay Error Notification Form.
(This material has been reproduced by John Wiley & Sons, Inc. with permission of eBay, Inc. Copyright © eBay, Inc. All rights reserved.)

Taking Your Auction Live

When you click on the "Submit" button, you'll see a page similar to the one in Figure 8.7 telling your that you auction has begun. You've made it! Your auction is live!

It can take three to four hours for your auction to actually be available to eBay's search engine. However, you can immediately take a look at how your auction will be displayed by clicking on the link provided on the "Auction has begun!" page. It's a good idea to click on this link to verify that your auction is correct. Also, you might print out the auction page to document your auction. Staple the auction description to your auction checklist for future reference. Remember, you've just *begun* the auction process.

If you see an error in your auction, all is not lost. eBay provides a way to make changes to auctions even after they've begun. See Chapter 11, "Managing Your Auction," for more information on changing your auction.

Please verify your entry as it appears below. If there are any errors, please use the back button on your browser to go back and correct your entry. Once you are satisfied with the entry, please press the submit button.

Your User ID:	takethecake
The title of the item:	R2D2 Beanie buddy Star Wars Discontinued V/MC
Optional boldface title:	no
Featured auction:	no
Featured category auction:	no
Great Gift auction:	no
Optional Gallery:	no
Optional Featured Gallery:	no
The category of the item:	Toys, Bean Bag Plush:Action Figures:Star Wars:General
Optional reserve price:	no
Optional private auction:	no
Bidding starts at:	$1.00
Quantity being offered:	1
Auction duration in days:	7 days
Location of item:	Cedar Hill, TX
Region:	TX-Dallas-Fort Worth
Country of item located:	United States
Money order/Cashiers checks:	no
Personal checks:	no
Visa/MasterCard:	no
Discover:	no
American Express:	no
Other:	no
OnlineEscrow:	no
COD (collect on delivery):	no
Billpoint Online Payments:	no
Seller pays for shipping:	no
Buyer pays fixed amount for shipping:	no
Buyer pays actual shipping cost:	no
See item description for shipping costs:	yes
Will Ship Internationally:	no
The description of the item:	

R2D2 Where Are You? Here he is. He's an official Star Wars Beanie Buddy, and now he can be your buddy too. This R2D2 plush doll is 5 1/2 inchdes tall and is the likeness of the robot in Star Wars. He's made of a silver and blue fabric, is brand new in mint condition and still contains the original Star Wars tag. Information on tag is "For all ages, Created by Kenner, 1997, Copyright Hasbro." Inside tag is information on how to join the Star Wars fan club.

Thanks for bidding on this auction. Good luck!

Successful bidder pays $3.20 for Priority Mail shipping anywhere in the US. Bid with confidence. Every item I sell is fully guaranteed to be as represented or I'll refund your bid. See my feedback score.

I'll ship your item to you promptly as soon as payment is received. (Checks must clear.) Visa and MasterCard payment is available.

Have a GREAT day!

If this information is correct, please press the submit button to start the auction. Otherwise, please go back and correct it.

Fees:

• A non-refundable insertion fee of **$0.25** will apply to this listing immediately. This fee is due even if your item does not sell.

Total Fees: $0.25

If your item receives bids, you will be charged a final value fee based on the closing value of the auction. This fee is 5.0% of the value up to $25.00, 2.5% of the value from $25.00 up to $1,000.00, and 1.25% of the value above $1,000.00. Complete information is in the Fees and Credits page.

Click this button to submit your listing. Click here to cancel.

submit my listing

Figure 8.6   eBay Auction Item Summary.

(This material has been reproduced by John Wiley & Sons, Inc. with permission of eBay, Inc. Copyright © eBay, Inc. All rights reserved.)

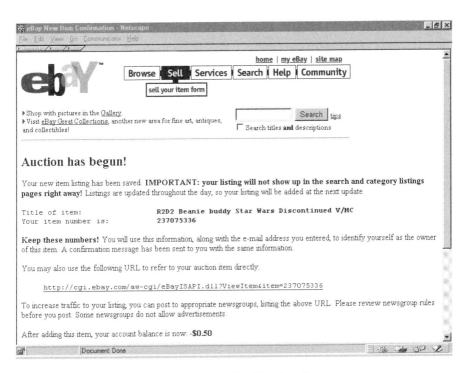

Figure 8.7 eBay Auction Has Begun Notification Form.

SUMMARY

You've started your first auction using a simple ad. If you've carefully selected the keywords for your one-line description then potential bidders will soon begin flocking to your auction. If you've entered an interesting and compelling description of your item, you're likely to begin getting bids. But, could you still improve your ad? The answer is yes, and the next chapter will show you how.

Chapter

Creating and Using Pictures in Your Ads

In the previous chapter you learned how to word your auction title and description so they would bring people to your auction and make them want to bid. But words alone may not be enough to sell your item. What else can you do? Adding a picture to your description will enhance the pulling power of your auction. This chapter describes how to include a picture in your ad and also covers some of the basics of using digital imagery effectively.

PLACING PICTURES IN YOUR ADS

If the wise Chinese philosopher Confucius were using Internet auctions today, he might create the saying "A picture is worth a higher bid." Why are pictures so important when selling merchandise on an Internet auction? Pictures help the bidder verify that he's bidding on the correct item. For complicated items, such as old collectibles, a picture can reassure the bidder of the condition of an item and show authentication markings. If an item has flaws, it may be important to include pictures that show the flaws—to prevent returns, unhappy buyers, and negative feedback.

There are two steps in making a picture available in your ad. First you must use a scanner or digital camera to capture a picture to your local computer's hard disk. This picture is stored in a file called a *digital image*. A digital image (also called a picture file or graphical image) is simply a computer file that contains information that tells your computer how to display a picture on the computer screen. Secondly, once you've placed a picture file on your local computer you can then use your Internet connection to upload the file to your *personal Web space*. Your personal Web space is actually part of a hard disk assigned to your Internet account where you can store personal files to make them available on the Web.

Digital Image   Also called a picture file or graphical image, a digital image is a computer file that contains information that tells your computer how to display a picture on the computer screen.

Personal Web Space   Part of a hard disk assigned to your Internet account where you can store personal files to make them available on the Web.

You've probably taken many pictures in your life but you may be new to digital photography and scanning. When you create digital pictures for Web use, there's more to it than just point-and-click. You must also be concerned about two other issues—the picture's *file type* and *file size*.

SELECTING THE BEST GRAPHIC FILE TYPE

Before you can use a picture file in your auction description, you have to make sure it is in the correct file format. A *graphics file format* is the method used to compress and store an image as an electronic file. Just as there are different sizes of batteries, different brands of cars, and different film sizes, competition has created a variety of picture file types. Whether Windows or Mac based, the two most commonly used picture file formats suitable for Internet use are the GIF and JPEG formats. Several other commonly used file formats for computers include BMP, TIFF, and PCX. Depending on what method you use to capture a picture (by scanning or by digital photography) you may find yourself with one of the file types that are not suitable for Web use. For example, if your scanner captures pictures in the BMP or PCX file format, you'll need to use a conversion program to convert the picture to an acceptable format (GIF or JPEG) before using it in your auction description. Specific information on how to convert files is described in "Editing and Converting Graphic Files" later in this chapter. Fortunately, most new scanners and digital cameras support JPEG or GIF, so you may not have to do any conversions. Check your user manual to see if your camera or scanner software supports GIF and/or JPEG formats.

Graphics File Format The method used to compress and store an image as an electronic file. Just as there are different sizes of batteries, different brands of cars, and different film sizes, competition has created a variety of picture file types. Whether Windows or Mac based, the two most commonly used picture file formats suitable for Internet use are the GIF and JPEG formats.

JPEG files are preferrable because they are generally smaller than GIF files. Therefore they can be sent faster across the Internet and thus displayed faster on your computer's screen. That doesn't mean you should never use GIF files. If you have a GIF file that isn't too large, go ahead and use it. However, if you have a choice, always select the JPEG option for capturing files when it's available. In fact, if you're considering purchasing a digital camera or scanner to use in creating ads for the Internet, make sure the product's software supports JPEG.

WHY IS PICTURE FILE SIZE IMPORTANT?

Each computer picture file contains information that tells the computer how to display the picture on the screen. High-resolution pictures contain a lot of detail, and therefore the file size for high-resolution pictures is large. Lower resolution pictures require less detail, and consequently their file sizes are smaller. Computer screens are only able to display pictures at 72 dpi (dots per inch) which is a fairly low resolution (compared to print media). If you use picture files that contain more than 72 dpi, then your files will be larger than necessary. Therefore it is best to create pictures at 72 dpi or less.

If you're personally using a fast Internet hookup (a fast modem or direct connection) then for you, pictures in auctions will display quickly. When you see pictures appear quickly, you may be deceived into thinking that they'll appear just as quickly for everyone else. However, there are a number of people—potential customers—connected to the Web who are using relatively slow connections. A user's *modem speed* dictates how quickly files are downloaded from the Internet to the user's computer. Thus, a user with a slow modem will have to wait longer for an image to appear on his screen than a user with a faster modem. Today's modem speeds range from 14.4K (which is a slow Internet connection) to 56K and higher. To compensate for users with slow modems, you should create pictures for your auctions which are small enough to be seen relatively quickly by all users.

Modem Speed   Dictates how quickly files are downloaded from the Internet to the user's computer. A user with a slow modem will have to wait longer for an image to appear on his screen than a user with a faster modem. Modem speeds range from 14.4K (which is a slow Internet connection) to 56K and higher.

How small of a *file size* should you use for your picture files? The size of a file is measured in bytes, where each byte is eight 0s or 1s (bits) of storage space. A byte is approximately one keystroke of information. Most graphic file sizes are reported in thousands of bytes. Thus, a file that is 30K contains about 30,000 bytes of information. To display the picture defined, this file means that 30,000 pieces of information (bytes) have to be transmitted across the Internet connection to your own computer. Thus, the speed of your Internet connection determines how fast the file will be displayed.

File Size   The size of a file is measured in bytes. Each byte is eight 0s or 1s (bits) of storage space. A byte is approximately one keystroke of information. Most graphic file sizes are reported in thousands of bytes. Thus, a file that is 30K contains about 30,000 bytes of information.

A 28.8K modem is able to receive about 1,900 bytes per second. Therefore, if you're displaying a 30K file using 28.8K modem, it will take about 16 seconds to display the picture. If your picture file is 174K bytes long, it will take your computer about a minute and a half to display the picture. That amount of time may be too long to hold a potential buyer's interest—unless your item is so unusual, desirable, or unique that it is worth the wait for the picture to appear.

Table 9.1 illustrates how file size and modem speed affect the time required to display a JPEG file. As a comparison, the same 30K JPEG file that took 16 seconds to display, when converted to GIF format is 66K in size and takes about 36 seconds to display. That's one of the main reasons to capture in JPEG format whenever possible.

As a rule of thumb, you should strive to keep graphics file sizes to 50K bytes or less, except in special circumstances.

Now that you know the basics about how images are displayed on the Internet, you're ready to capture your own images.

USING A SCANNER

One popular and relatively inexpensive method of acquiring pictures for the Internet is by using a *scanner*. A scanner is similar to a photocopy machine. However, instead of making a paper copy of the image, it stores a picture file of the image on your computer. If you sell items that are mostly two-dimensional and flat, a scanner may be your best method of creating picture files. Scanners work well with postcards, books, posters (small ones), trading cards, and so on. For three-dimensional items such as Beanie Babies, jewelry, pens, etc., scanning can be less effective than

TABLE 9.1 Modem Speed and File Size Effects on Time to Display for JPEG Files		
Modem Speed	File Size (JPEG)	Time to Display
14.4K	30K	30 seconds
28.8K	30K	16 seconds
56K Single ISDN	30K	7 seconds
14.4K	174K	185 seconds
28.8K	174K	95 seconds
56K Single ISDN	174K	47 seconds

digital photos. You may want to use a video camera capture or digital camera picture for these type of items, as discussed later.

Scanner A scanner is similar to a photocopy machine. However, instead of making a paper copy of the image, it stores a picture file of the image on your computer.

When purchasing a scanner, select the flatbed variety rather than the kind that feeds pages like a fax machine. Flatbed scanners allow you much more flexibility in the kinds of items you can scan. Plus, if you are scanning rare originals, you run the risk that the feed-through variety may damage your merchandise.

As with any image-capture device, when creating pictures with scanners you need to pay attention to resolution. In your scanner software there's a setting that allows you to select the resolution for your picture. If your software has a setting for "Web" pictures, that is probably the one you want to use. Usually, the "Web" setting will be for 72 dpi resolution. If the resolution setting has a choice for number of colors to capture—for example millions of colors, 256 colors, or 16 colors, or black and white—you'll want to select the lowest setting that adequately illustrates your item.

If your item cannot be placed directly on the scanner, you might still be able to use your scanner to capture its picture by taking a photograph of the item and then scanning the photograph. If you have an instant camera, you can quickly take a picture, then scan the photo within minutes. For inexpensive items, this method would not make practical sense since it could add significantly to the cost of the items you sell and cut into your profit.

When you scan your image, pay attention to how much of the picture is being included in the saved file. Most scanner software allows you to perform a test scan, then draw a rectangle around the area of the picture to cut off the sides of an image to make it the proper size and to remove, or *crop*, unwanted parts. If your scanner software allows you to do this, you'll probably not have to use a graphics editing program to get rid of extraneous information in your image.

Crop In computer graphics, cropping means to cut off the sides of an image to make it the proper size or to remove unwanted parts.

If your scanned image needs additional cropping or color adjustment, you can use a graphics program to fix it. Refer to the section titled "Editing and Converting Graphic Files" later in this chapter.

USING A DIGITAL CAMERA

If you want to become a serious and frequent Internet auction seller, you'll need a *digital camera*. A digital camera looks and operates like most handheld still cameras, but instead of capturing the image to film it captures the image into a computer memory chip or onto a computer disk file. It's by far the best single option to have for the creation of pictures for the Web—particularly if the item is three-dimensional.

If you don't already own a digital camera, there are a few features you should look for before you purchase one. For example, you need to consider what method will be used to move the images from the camera to your computer. Most digital cameras require that you install a cable on your computer that you can then attach to your camera to download the pictures. An alternative method on some digital cameras is to capture the images directly onto a standard 3.5″ computer diskette. After taking a picture with this type of camera, you can then place the diskette into your computer and copy the images directly onto your computer's hard drive. A third method is to capture the images to a flash memory chip, which can then be inserted into certain kinds of PCMCIA slots (used mostly in laptops). The easiest of these three methods is to capture the image directly to a diskette.

 Digital Camera   Looks and operates like most handheld still cameras, but instead of capturing the image to film, it captures the image into a computer memory chip or onto a computer disk file.

Another important feature to look for in a digital camera is what kind of file formats the camera supports. It's best if you use a camera that saves directly into the JPEG format. This saves time by not requiring you to convert the files before uploading them. Some cameras require that you transfer your images into a software "gallery," then resave them into a desired format. As this extra step will be time consuming, you should avoid cameras whose files are handled in this way.

Will you be taking close-up pictures? If you sell small items such as rare coins or stamps, you'll want to make sure your camera has a macro (close-up) lens, or is able to zoom down to the point where you can take clear photographs of small objects.

When using a digital camera, just as in the other capture methods, pay attention to the size of the file created by the picture. On many cameras, you can set the resolution before taking a picture. This is usually referred to as the e-mail or Internet mode and it is designed for electronic transmission. This setting is the preferable mode for an Internet auction picture. If you take your pictures in a low-resolution mode to begin with, then you may not have to use a secondary program to shrink the picture before loading it on the Web. If you're running Internet auctions for income, any time you can save gives you more time to spend on expanding or operating your business.

Just as in film photography, there are a few tips that can help you take better pictures. You're probably familiar with how portrait artists are concerned with lighting. Think of yourself as a photographer taking a *portrait* of your merchandise. For example, if you're taking your photograph indoors you may want to set up several sources of light around your item to reduce shadows. Many people prefer to take photographs outside or in a semishaded area using natural light. Usually, your best photographs will be those that rely on natural lighting (unless you have a professional setup). Serious sellers will set up a small photo studio with good lighting and a neutral (white, black, or gray) backdrop where photos can be taken quickly. To make sure your item shows up well in the photograph, follow these suggestions:

✔ Place your item on a solid background (if it is small). For example, use a poster board, sheet, or some other solid background. If your item is mostly white, use a dark background. Otherwise, use a light background. Do not use a patterned background.

✔ Frame the item as you take the picture in such a way that will eliminate any distracting background clutter. Remember that your customers are only interested in your merchandise, not the decorations in your bedroom.

✔ Affix the camera to a tripod to hold it steady.

If your photograph doesn't come out exactly right, you may need to fix the image with a graphics editing program. Refer to the section titled "Editing and Converting Graphic Files" later in this chapter.

USING VIDEO CAPTURE

If you don't have a digital camera, and you already own a video camera, there's another way to capture digital images. This method is called *video capture*. With this method you capture a video picture from a video camera or video player and transfer a digital still image into a computer file. The one piece of equipment you may not already have to perform this trick is a video capture device. The most popular video capture device is one called the Snappy from Play, Inc. Some Macs and PCs already have built-in video capture capabilities. You'll need to either have the built-in video capture capabilities or an external video capture device such as the Snappy to turn a video image into a picture file.

Video Capture   Taking a video picture from a video camera or video player and transferring the digital still image into a computer file.

Here are the items you'll need to undertake video capture:

✔ A video camera

✔ A video capture device (such as a Snappy or a built-in video capture connection)

✔ Video capture software (comes with Snappy and most video capture cards)

✔ Video cables (usually come with your video camera)

To use the Snappy image capture device, connect the video output from your video camera to the input of the Snappy device. Then, connect the Snappy to your computer's parallel (printer) port. If you've installed a video capture card in either a PC or a Mac, attach the video cables directly from the camera to the plug on the video card.

Set up the item to be photographed in a well-lighted place and turn on your video camera (you don't have to be taping). Frame the picture so as little of the background shows as possible. Using the Snappy software as an example, begin the video capture program and click on the Preview button. If you've installed everything correctly, you'll see the image from

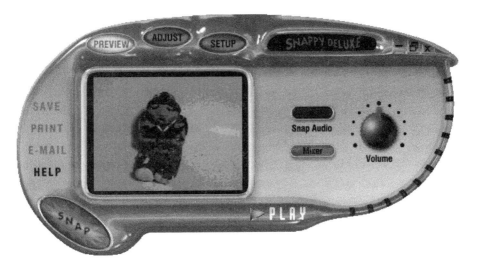

Figure 9.1 Snappy video capture preview mode.
(*Source:* Play Incorporated. Reprinted with permission.)

your video camera on the Snappy's Preview screen as shown in Figure 9.1. The image may look jerky and in a poorer resolution than what you see on your television set. This is normal. It may also be displayed in black and white, depending on how you have your Snappy set up—but the captured image will be in color. Using the Adjust and Setup buttons, select the settings on the video capture program so that the image will be captured in JPEG format and at a 320×240 resolution or lower.

Once you've set up the picture, click the Snap (capture) button. The full captured image will then appear on your computer screen. You can now review the picture to see if it shows off your item correctly. If not, reposition the item, change the lighting, or adjust the tripod and try again. Once you're satisfied with the image, save it to your hard disk. The final image is displayed in Figure 9.2.

Another way you can use the Snappy is to capture images from videotape. If your image is large or far away from your computer, you can videotape a picture of the item, then connect your video camera to the Snappy device, play the tape, and capture the image from the tape.

If you're unable to capture your picture just the way you want it, you can use a graphics editing program to fix the image. Refer to the section titled "Editing and Converting Graphic Files" later in this chapter.

Figure 9.2   A captured video image.

PLACING PICTURES ON THE INTERNET

Now that you've successfully created a picture file, you'll want to make it available for your auction description. Before your picture can be displayed in your ad, it must exist somewhere on the Internet. The usual procedure for placing your picture in your ad is:

1. Capture a picture to your computer's local hard disk.
2. Upload the picture to an *Internet Service Provider* (ISP).
3. Display the picture in your ad by entering its Internet address.

An Internet Service Provider (ISP) is a company that sells connections to the Internet. For a fee, they allow you to dial in to one of their computers, which allows your computer to gain access to all of the information on the Internet. Usually, your ISP also provides you with a limited amount of Internet disk space to which you can transfer files from your computer and make them accessible on the Web. Here's a list of the most common types of Internet Service Providers and what kind of storage space they provide:

- ✔ *General ISP*: If you have a dial-up or direct connect account that attaches you directly to the Internet using Netscape or Internet Explorer, then you are using a general ISP. Usually, your account includes some amount of disk space that you can use for your own personal Web files. Some of the more well-known general ISPs are Internet America, AT&T, and GTE.

- ✔ *Specialized ISP*: AOL (America Online) is an example of a specialized ISP, which has its own proprietary user interface. It provides limited Web space to each user for Web storage.

- ✔ *WebTV and MSN*: If you have this type of ISP, you're out of luck. You'll have to use some other Internet service for your pictures (see the other options in this list).

- ✔ *CompuServe and Prodigy*: Look for documentation at your host's web site on uploading files to your Web space.

- ✔ *Free space*: If you don't have any other way to save images on the Web, you might consider using one of the free image storage locations. See "Using Free Space for Image Storage" in the following pages.

ISP An Internet Service Provider is a company that sells connections to the Internet. For a fee, they allow you to dial in to one of their computers, which allows your computer to gain access to all of the information on the Internet. Usually, your ISP also provides you with a limited amount of Internet disk space to which you can transfer files from your computer and make them accessible on the Web.

You'll use the web site space provided to you by your ISP to store your auction picture files. What does a filename look like on the Internet? Just like all of the files on your local hard disk, every file on the Internet has a unique name. The name of a file on the Web is referred to as a Web address, an Internet address, or by its more formal name, a *Uniform Resource Locator* (URL). The URL is a filename syntax that is understood across the Internet that allows you to create and reference files from anywhere in the world. The URL filename syntax begins with the protocol type used such as "http://" plus the name of your web site (such as www.myisp.com) plus directories in the web site "mywebname/ebay" and a filename such as "mossrose.jpg." Sections of the name are separated by slashes (/). Thus, a full URL for a file could be something like http://www.myisp.com/mywebname/ebay/mossrose.jpg.

Uniform Resource Locator (URL)   This is a filename syntax that is understood across the Internet that allows you to create and reference files from anywhere in the world. The URL filename syntax begins with the protocol type used such as "http://" plus the name of your web site (such as www.myisp.com) plus directories in the web site "mywebname/ebay" and a filename such as "mossrosejpg." Sections of the name are separated by slashes (/). Thus, a full URL for a file could be something like http://www.myisp.com/mywebname/ebay/mossrose.jpg.

Once you place an auction image on the Web, you'll have to know its URL so you can display the image within your auction ad. The most common ways to place images on the web site are:

✔ Using a standard *File Transfer Protocol* (FTP) program
✔ Using your provider's specialized FTP method, such as with AOL
✔ Through a web site creation program such as Microsoft's Front-Page.

File Transfer Protocol (FTP) is a method two computers use to communicate with each other for the purpose of transferring a file from one computer to the other. The following sections describe how to upload pictures using FTP and other methods. How do you know which method to use? Ask your service provider. If you are using FrontPage to manage a web site, it may mean that FTP is not available to you. If your web site does NOT not have "FrontPage extensions" loaded, it usually means you will need to use FTP. When in doubt, call the support line at your Web host.

File Transfer Protocol (FTP) A method two computers use to communicate with each other for the purpose of transferring a file from one computer to the other.

UPLOADING IMAGES USING AN FTP PROGRAM

To upload images to your own Internet web site using FTP, you'll need a software program on your local computer that supports FTP transfers. There are a number of commercial and *shareware* programs available. Some of the most popular FTP programs are:

✔ WS_FTP Pro from IpSwitch (www.ipswitch.com). An evaluation version is available. This is the most widely used FTP program.

✔ CuteFTP is a simplified Windows-based File Transfer Protocol (FTP) program. Information about it is available at www.cute ftp.com. An evaluation version is also available at the web site.

✔ FTP Voyager is an FTP Client program for Windows 95/NT which allows you to perform FTP operations in the same way you normally perform file operations on your local machine. More information is available at www.ftpvoyager.com.

✔ Fetch is a user-friendly Macintosh FTP client; it allows point-and-click, drag-and-drop file transfers to and from any machine with an FTP server, over a TCP/IP network. Fetch is free to users affiliated with an educational institution or charitable nonprofit organization; all other users may purchase a license.

Before you can use any of these FTP programs you need to know the following information. (You may need to contact your Web provider to get this information.)

Shareware A marketing method that allows you to download and use programs for evaluation. If you decide to use the program on a regular basis, you purchase the program from the shareware company. This is also known as "try it before you buy it" software. To find shareware programs, visit web sites such as www.tucows.com or www.shareware.com.

✔ Your ISP's FTP address (usually something like ftp.nameof yourisp.com)

✔ Your service provider's host type ("Automatic Detection" is usually sufficient)

✔ Your User ID

✔ Your password

You also must have a connection to your host either through a dial-in modem hookup or a direct connection through your cable provider or some other system. The following example shows how to use FTP for file transfer using the WS_FTP program.

Before using WS_FTP for the first time, you must create a new profile for your connection using the information in the list above. An example of how that information will look is given in Figure 9.3. When you first begin the WS_FTP program, a "Sessions Properties" dialog box will be displayed. To create a new profile for your own ISP, click on the "New" button. The "Session Profile" dialog box will appear as illustrated below. Fill in the appropriate blanks with the information from your own ISP account. Once you've entered this information, click on the "Save" button. You'll only have to enter this information once. When you begin this program again, it will remember your ISP information, and you'll be able to connect by simply clicking "OK."

After you've filled in the information and saved it, click "OK" to connect to your personal disk space. If everything is correct in the Session Profile box, you should connect. If you don't connect, you may have an error in your modem setup. Check your modem's installation instructions and information from your ISP to make sure you've set up your modem correctly.

When you connect to your ISP, a new screen will appear that displays the names of files on your local hard disk in a panel on the left of your screen and names of files on your Internet web site on the right, as shown in Figure 9.4.

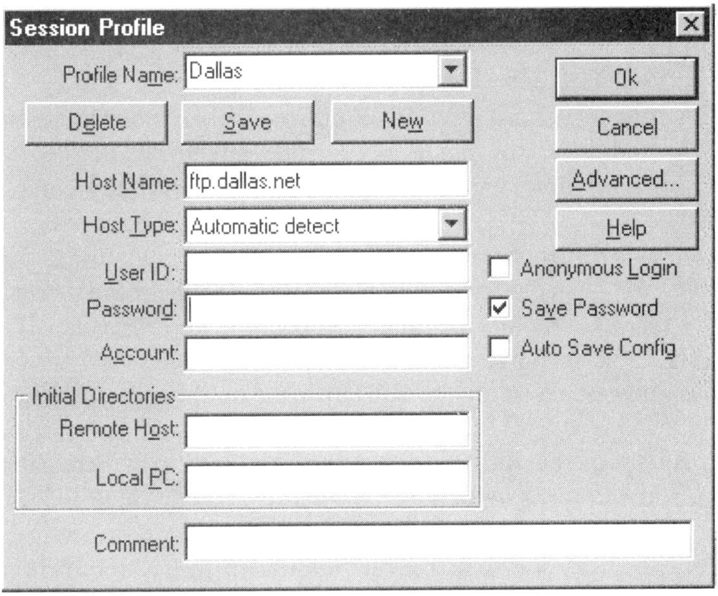

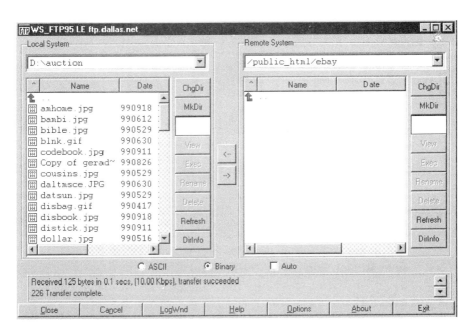

Figure 9.3 Creating an FTP session profile.
(*Source:* IpSwitch, Inc. Reprinted with permission.)

Figure 9.4 WS_FTP program.
(*Source:* IpSwitch, Inc. Reprinted with permission.)

For easy file management, you might want to create a directory on your hard disk to store your auction picture files as well as a similar directory on your ISP Web space. Use standard procedures to create a directory on your local hard disk. In Windows, display your drive window, right click, and enter the name of the new directory, such as auction. This will create a directory called D:\AUCTION (assuming you're using the D:\drive).

To create a directory on your Web account, first make sure you are in your public Web space. (This is often called the public_html directory). If you're not in this directory, but it is displayed in the right panel, double click on its name to move to that directory. To make a new directory to store your images, click on the MKDIR button and enter a new name, such as eBay. The new directory name will appear on the list of directories and files. By double clicking on the directory's name, you'll change to that directory. You can navigate between directories by clicking on a directory name to open it, or by clicking on the up-arrow icon to move up the directory tree. Before transferring files, you'll want to have your directories set up so your local directory and your Web directory are both open to the place where you store your auction images.

In Figure 9.4, notice that the panel on the left is showing files in the local folder called D:\AUCTION. These are files on your local hard disk. The panel on the right is in a network folder called /home/mywebname /public_html/ebay. In this illustration, there are currently no files in the eBay directory. To place an image from your hard drive into your web site follow these steps:

1. Begin the WS_FTP Program. Connect to your web site and change to your auction image directories on the web site (right panel) and on your local hard disk (left panel).

2. Click on the name of the image file on your hard disk. Then click on the arrow pointing to the right (between the right and left panels). This tells WS_FTP to copy the file from your hard disk into the Web directory. The transfer should take only a few seconds, and you should see the filename appear in the Web directory. Transfer as many files as you need during any one session. In fact, you can select multiple files to transfer by holding down on the "Ctrl" key while clicking on file names in your hard disk directory. Then, when you click on the right arrow, all of the selected files will be copied to your web site. Figure 9.5 shows the progress of copying a file from the local hard disk to the Web directory.

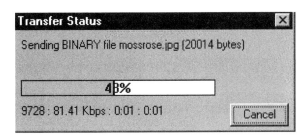

Figure 9.5 An FTP transfer in progress.
(*Source:* IpSwitch, Inc. Reprinted with permission.)

3. When you've finished copying all of the files to the Web directory, end the FTP program by clicking on the "End" button. Depending on how your communications software is set up, you
may also have to close down your connection program.

Once you've saved your images on your web site, you can access a
file from anywhere on the Internet, as long as you know its proper address
(URL). What is the Web address for your image? The Internet address for
the mossrose.jpg file becomes

http://www.myisp.net/mywebname/ebay/mossrose.jpg

How is this address constructed? The first part (http://www.myisp.net)
points to your ISP provider. This is followed by the name of your account,
which in this example is "mywebname." (Your account name is probably
a name you selected when you signed up for the service.) Following the
name of the account is the name of the directory created in the example
above, "eBay." Finally, the name of the file finishes out the complete Internet address.

If you have your own domain name (e.g., www.mydomain.com),
your image's address will be even simpler—something like:

http://www.mydomain.com/ebay/mossrose.jpg

Some web sites are sensitive to case, which means that a file named
MOSSFOSE.JPG is not the same as a file named mossrose.jpg. If you can't
seem to access your file across the Web, it may be that you'll need to pay
close attention to the case. You can easily check to see for yourself that
your image is available and active on the Web by going to your browser
(online) and entering the address for your image in the "Location"

textbox at the top of your Netscape browser or in the "Address" textbox in Internet Explorer. For example, entering the address:

http://www.myisp.net/mywebname/ebay/mossrose.jpg

displays the image in the browser as shown in Figure 9.6. (Of course, this name is made up for the example in this book, so don't expect it to really work.)

Once your image is available on the Web, it can be readily used in your auction description. For example, in the eBay "Sell Your Item" form (described in Chapter 8), you'll see an item called Picture URL. This is where you enter the address for your picture. For the Moss Rose plate, you'd enter http://www.myisp.net/mywebname/ebay/mossrose.jpg in the Picture URL text box.

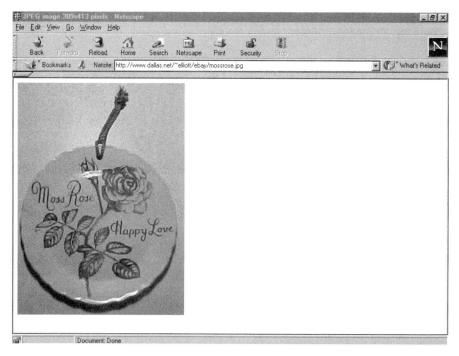

Figure 9.6   A graphic displayed in a broswer.
(*Source*: Netscape Communicator browser window © 1999 Netscape Communications Corporation. Used with permission.)

UPLOADING IMAGES TO AOL

Uploading images to AOL also uses the FTP protocol, but AOL has created its own unique method for transferring files. This method involves a number of screens and can be long and time consuming if you're using a slow connection. If you plan to upload quite a few files to the Internet, you might consider getting an ISP space and using the FTP method described earlier. Or, take a look at the section below called "Using Free Space for Image Storage." To upload a picture file to AOL, follow these instructions:

1. From the AOL main screen, click on <u>Keyword</u>, then enter <u>My Place</u> to go to the "My Place" window as shown in Figure 9.7.

2. On the "my ftp space" window, locate the spot called "See My FTP Space." When you click on this item, AOL displays a window called "members.aol.com/youraolname," shown in Figure 9.8. Notice the "Upload" button at the bottom of this window. This is the option you want to select to send a file from your hard disk to your private disk space on AOL.

3. Click on the "Upload" button in the members.aol.com window. A textbox appears called "Remote Filename." Enter the name of your graphic file (it must have a .gif or .jpg extension) as you want it to be on your AOL disk space. For example, you might enter something like mossrose.jpg. Click "Continue."

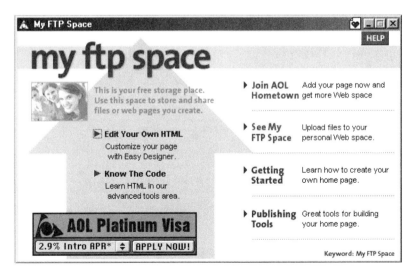

Figure 9.7 The AOL My Place window.
(*Source*: America Online. Reprinted with permission.)

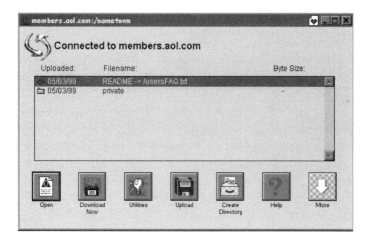

Figure 9.8 The AOL FTP upload window.
(*Source:* America Online. Reprinted with permission.)

4. A dialog box called "Upload File" is displayed, as shown in Figure 9.9. This is where you'll tell AOL which file on your hard disk you want to upload. If you know the name of the file, enter it in the textbox at the bottom of the dialog box. If you do not know the file name, click on the "Find File" button and find the file on your hard disk. Once you've entered the name of the file to upload, click on the "Send" button. AOL will then transfer the file from your hard disk to your AOL Web space.

5. When the file transfer is finished, click "OK."

You can test to see if your image was successfully transferred by going to your Web browser and entering the name of the file. For AOL, the name (for this example) will be:

http://members.aol.com/yourAOLname/mossrose.jpg

Once your image is available on the Web, it can be readily used in your auction description. For example, in the eBay "Sell Your Item" form, you'll see an item called Picture URL. This is where you place the address of your picture. For the Moss Rose plate picture, you'd enter http://members.aol.com/yourAOLname/mossrose.jpg in the Picture URL text box.

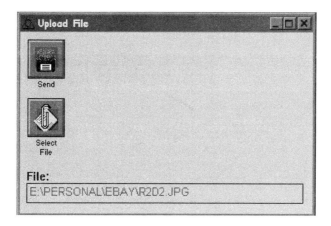

Figure 9.9   The AOL upload file window.
(*Source:* America Online. Reprinted with permission.)

UPLOADING IMAGES USING MICROSOFT FRONTPAGE

If you manage your web site using Microsoft FrontPage, you may not be able to use the FTP method for uploading files. In this case, you must use FrontPage to transfer your images to the Web. To upload a file from your local hard disk to your web site, follow these instructions:

1. Open your web site using FrontPage by connecting to your ISP. If you've never used FrontPage to open your Web page, consult your provider's instructions or contact your provider's support group.

2. Select the Folders view from the View menu, then select the directory where you want to place your image files. If you don't yet have an image directory, right click on the Folder list panel and enter the name of your new directory (such as eBay or Images).

3. From the FrontPage File menu, select "Import." A dialog box appears called "Import." Click on the "Add File" button.

4. A dialog box similar to an open box appears. Find and select the name of the file to upload from your hard disk. When you select a file, it will appear in the list of files to import. Select as many files as you want.

5. When you've finished selecting the files you want to import, click on the "OK" button on the "Import" dialog box. All of the files in the list will be copied from your hard disk to your remote Web location.

Once you've copied files to the Web, they are available for viewing or for inclusion in an ad. You can test and access your graphics file the same way as described in the "Uploading Images Using an FTP Program" section above.

USING FREE SPACE FOR IMAGE STORAGE

If you don't have a place to store your images on the Web, all is not lost. You can use one of the free web sites on the Internet. Some companies provide free Web pages just to increase the traffic at their web site. How can they do that? They make their living by advertising, and the more people they get to visit, the more advertising they can sell. Some of the currently popular sites are www.geocities.com, www.anglefire.com, and www.xoom.com.

Once you obtain your Web space, you can upload your images to it and then access the images within your auction ads. Before a web site will grant you use of their space, you typically have to register with them. However, you'll want to be careful to protect yourself and your e-mail address. Before signing up with a web site, make sure they offer these assurances:

✔ They won't resell your e-mail address to anyone (unless you request it and enjoy getting junk e-mail).

✔ They won't arbitrarily begin charging you for the Web space at some point in the future. Be wary if they ask you for a credit card number.

Since free Web space may come and go, you might want to check in the eBay Café to find out what Web space people are currently using and are satisfied with. Once you've decided to use free space, you'll generally be required to fill in a registration form, and then you'll be e-mailed instructions on how to upload to your new web site.

Most of the free web sites use standard FTP methods to upload files. Once you register, they provide you with the site address for FTP uploads (typically ftp.sitename.com, your member name, and a password). Then, you simply use your FTP software (such as WS_FTP) as described earlier to upload your images to the site. Free sites may offer anywhere from 2 megabytes of free storage or more. If you carefully delete files you no longer need, then one of these free sites should be sufficient to store a number of auction images.

EDITING AND CONVERTING GRAPHIC FILES

If your scanner, camera, or other device insists on capturing a picture in a file format other than GIF or JPEG, or if your picture needs cropping or color adjustment, you'll need to convert or correct the image using a graphics software program. There are a number of graphics programs you can use to convert these files. Some of the commonly used programs (many available as shareware on the Web) include:

> **Microsoft Image Composer** This program comes as a part of Microsoft FrontPage (Windows and Mac) and the Microsoft Visual InterDev (Windows) Web development tool, so you might check to see if you already own it. This program allows you to open a picture image from a number of file formats, then save the image for use on the Web. Besides GIF and JPEG file formats supported by Image Composer include Windows bitmapped files (.BMP), Adobe Photoshop (.psd), Portable Network Graphics (.PNG), flashpic (.FPX), Microsoft Picture It (.MIX), Altamera Composer (.ACC), Microsoft Image Composer (.MIC) and tagged image file format (.TIF).

> **PhotoDeluxe** This is a Windows and Mac program from Adobe and is available in home and business editions. Complete information can be found at www.adobe.com. The program contains "Step-by-Step Guided Activities" that lead you through working with pictures. You can directly import pictures from a number of scanners and digital cameras.

> **Paint Shop Pro** Evaluation versions are available as shareware, and the home page for this program is www.jasc.com. Paint Shop Pro 5 includes professional-quality graphics and photo-editing tools, making it easy for you to enhance digital photographs. You can retouch and edit photos and images and import photos from scanners and digital cameras. The program is Web graphics-smart and supports more than 40 different graphics file formats.

CONVERTING AND EDITING PICTURES IN IMAGE COMPOSER

One program you can use to correct problems with your file is Microsoft's Image Composer for Windows. Other Windows and Mac programs contain similar features and can be used to perform the same image enhancements described here. This example will show how to use the program to take an existing graphic image file and prepare it for use on the Web. It assumes that you've already used one of the procedures above to create the image file.

Once you've begun the Microsoft Image Composer program, select File/Open to open the file that contains your image. Figure 9.10 shows Image Composer displaying an image of an American Indian Storytelling Doll. Looking at this image, notice that there are two items you might want to correct before saving it as a file for the Web. You'll want to crop the image to get rid of some of the white wasted space and perform color correction to make the image a little lighter.

To crop the image, click on "Tools/Arrange" to bring up the Arrange

Figure 9.10   A graphic file to be edited.
(*Source:* Microsoft Corporation.)

toolbox. The Crop/Extend tool is at the 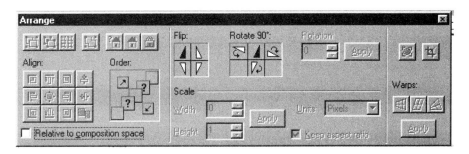 top right of this toolbox as shown in the Figure 9.11. Select the image by clicking once on it. Then click on the Crop/Extend tool. This will make the adjustment handles around the image turn to "Ts." Click and drag on the Ts to crop away the unneeded portions of the picture. (If you're using another graphics program, the procedure will be almost identical.) Also reset the picture boundaries to match the new size of your image. Once cropped, the image will look similar to the picture in Figure 9.12. Compare this image to the previous one.

To make color adjustments to the picture, close the Arrange toolbox and select Tools/Color Tuning from the pull-down menu. The Color Tuning toolbox with the Highlight/Shadows tab selected is shown in Figure 9.13.

This procedure is used to lighten or darken the image. Notice that the instructions on the dialog box tell you how to make certain adjustments in the color or shadows. For example, to lighten the entire picture a little, click on the bottom square handle on the highlight line and drag it a little to the left. You'll have to experiment with this procedure to become proficient in making corrections to your image. Click on the "Apply" button to see how your change will affect the picture. If you don't like what you've done, move the highlight adjustment handle and try again. Most graphics editing programs contain similar color and highlight adjustment capabilities.

Although you have many tools at your disposal to correct images, it is better to try to use the methods described in the previous sections to make any adjustments as you are taking the picture, and avoid having to make time consuming adjustments later.

Other changes you might want to make include rotating the image,

Figure 9.11 Graphic editing tools for MS Image Composer.
(*Source:* Microsoft Corporation.)

Figure 9.12 A cropped graphic image.

(*Source:* Microsoft Corporation.)

adding text to the image (maybe a copyright notice if you want to protect the picture), or creating one image file containing multiple pictures as described in the next section, "Using Multiple Pictures in Your Ads." Once you've made these changes, follow these steps to save the picture for the Web:

1. Select the "Save for the Web" option from the File pull-down menu. Usually, from the next dialog box that appears, you'll want to select to save "All sprites in the composition area." Click "Next."

2. The program will ask you to select if you want the image to be transparent to the Web page background or not. Select the option "Fill them with the background color," and click "Next."

3. For the "Select a fill in color" dialog box, choose the default and then click "Next."

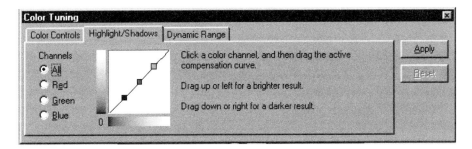

Figure 9.13 MS Image Composer Image Tuning toolbox.
(Source: Microsoft Corporation.)

4. The program builds several views of your image, as shown in Figure 9.14. The left panel (connection speed) tells you what modem speed is being used for the download time comparisons. In this example, a 28.8K modem speed is being used. The right panel contains a selection of partial images that shows what the image will look like when saved with a selection of GIF and JPEG resolutions. It reports the file size and approximate download time for each image. Which image resolution should you select? Look through the list and click on the JPEG image that represents your item adequately using the lowest amount of download time. Click "Next."

5. The program will display information about how the file will be saved. Click on the "Save" button and enter a filename.

The file is saved to your hard disk and is ready for you to upload it using one of the procedures described earlier in this chapter.

USING MULTIPLE PICTURES IN YOUR ADS

Since most auction sites, and eBay in particular, only allow you to specify one image on its ad form, you can get past this restriction by creating a single graphic that contains more than one picture. An example of a single image containing two pictures is shown in Figure 9.15.

In most graphics editing programs, you can insert two or more pictures, crop them to size, place them next to one another, and then save the combined picture as a single file. One of the advantages of this technique

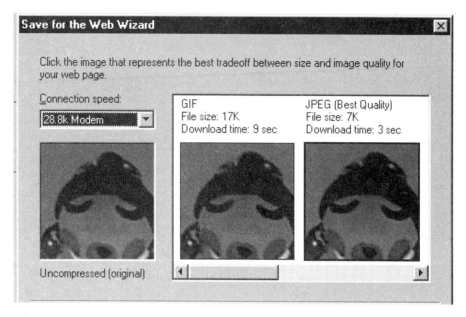

Figure 9.14 Saving a file for the Web.
(*Source:* Microsoft Corporation.)

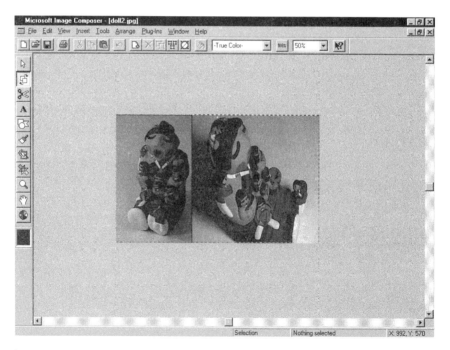

Figure 9.15 Multiple pictures in a single file.
(*Source:* Microsoft Corporation.)

is that it allows you to show a complete view of your merchandise as well as a close-up of important characteristics such as mint marks, copyrights, or flaws.

SUMMARY

If you're serious about selling merchandise in Internet auctions, pictures are an essential component to creating successful ads. If you're going to sell a lot of items, you'll need to make the picture-taking process as simple as possible. This means taking the picture once and avoiding the need to edit or correct the image. For expensive and detailed items, you'll want to have the capability to create a presentation of multiple images that will allow you to show off all of the important aspects of your merchandise. Want to make your ad even more attractive by using fancy graphics, colors, and even sound? These topics are discussed in the following chapter.

Chapter

Improving Your Presentation

W hen you browse through auction ads on the Internet you may begin to believe that the more gee-whiz colors, graphics, and sounds you can add, the better. This is not necessarily the case. Because *everything* you include in your ad makes it display slower, you must carefully consider what kinds of eye-candy in the ad will add real selling power. You'll want to have just enough without overdoing a good thing. Your goal is to capture the interest of that prospective customer who clicks on your ad description. You only have a few seconds to capture her interest or she will go to the next ad. This chapter shows you how you can improve the selling power of your auction by adding pictures, graphics, colors, sounds, highlights, and links to your ad.

ADDING PIZZAZZ TO YOUR AD

Auction ads should be fun and even entertaining. In an Internet auction you're not limited to the static black and white of a classified ad. You've got opportunities for highlighting, pictures, color, and even sound. Depending on the content of your ad, these enhancements can help you capture the imagination of your customers and entice them to bid more often. They take a little extra work on your part, but once you have the techniques down, you'll be able to spruce up your ads with little effort.

Using Simple HTML Commands

In Chapter 8, "Creating a Winning Ad," you were introduced to the term Hypertext Markup Language (HTML) and used the <P> tag in a simple ad description. However, that was only the tip of the iceberg! HTML is the primary language of the Net. Most of the pages you browse through on the Internet are written in HTML. That should give you an idea about what you can do with this language. Fortunately, by learning only a few of the HTML tags (like the <P> paragraph tag used earlier) you can quickly give your ad a face-lift. If you're simply too intimidated by HTML, just skip to the section in this chapter called "Using Ad Preparation Software" for a more automated approach to pizzazz.

In this section, you'll learn how to strategically place HTML tags directly into your ad text. As you saw earlier when you used the <P> tag, HTML tags are included in the body of your ad description when you type it into the ad description textbox. Tags can be placed anywhere in the text—they don't have to be on a separate line. Also, HTML commands are not case sensitive, so the command <P> is the same as the command <p>.

Using the <P> Paragraph Command

The <P> paragraph command tells the Internet browser to skip a line (create new paragraph). For example, enter this text into an ad description:

> Decorative Staffordshire plate with a picture of a crimson moss rose on the front and the message "Moss Rose, Happy Love."
> <P>
> Information stamped on the back of the plate says "Royal Staffordshire Ceramics/Made in England." The plate has a hanging hole at the top and comes with its original tassel. The date for this item is unknown but it appears to be quite old. The plate has no cracks or chips. It measures about 5⁵/₈ inches across.
> <P>
> Thanks for bidding on this auction. Good luck!

The <P> command will cause the description to place a blank line wherever the <P> is located. Use this command to separate paragraphs in your ad description to make it more readable.

Using the
 Break Command

The <BR> break command is similar to the <P> paragraph command except it does not skip a line—it only breaks the text to the next line. This command is handy for when you want to make a list of items, one line at a time. For example:

> Here's the most important information about this plate:
> <P>
> * Moss Rose, Happy Love message
> * Royal Staffordshire Ceramics, Made in England
> * Contains the original hanging tassel
> <P>
> The date for this item is unknown but it appears to be quite old. The plate has no cracks or chips. It measures about $5^5/_8$ inches across.

Here's how this text will appear:

> Here's the most important information about this plate:
>
> * Moss Rose, Happy Love message
>
> * Royal Staffordshire Ceramics, Made in England
>
> * Contains the original hanging tassel
>
> The date for this item is unknown but it appears to be quite old. The plate has no cracks or chips. it measures about $5^5/_8$ inches across.

Notice how the lines cut by the <BR> command do not contain an extra skipped line like those that used the <P> command.

Using the <B> Bold Command

To make some part of your description appear in bold type you can use the bold <B> and </B> HTML tags. The bold command requires two HTML tags. The <B> tag tells HTML to start displaying text in bold and the </B> tag turns the bold off. Thus, the following text:

> <B>Decorative Staffordshire plate</B> with a picture of a crimson moss rose on the front and the message <B>"Moss Rose, Happy Love."</B>

would produce the following results:

> **Decorative Staffordshire plate** with a picture of a crimson moss rose on the front and the message **"Moss Rose, Happy Love."**

Use the bold tags to emphasize important text in your auction ad.

Using the <I> Italics and <U> Underline Commands

To make some part of your description appear in italics type you can use the <I> and </I> HTML tags. Use the <U> and </U> commands to specify underlined text.

Here's an example:

<I>Decorative Staffordshire plate</I> with a picture of a crimson moss rose on the front and the message <U>"Moss Rose, Happy Love."</U>

would produce the following results:

Decorative Staffordshire plate with a picture of a crimson moss rose on the front and the message <u>"Moss Rose, Happy Love."</u>

Use the italics and underline tags to emphasize important text in your auction ad.

Using the <HR> Horizontal Line Command

The <HR> command stands for "horizontal rule." It places a horizontal line across the screen. Therefore the text:

Thanks for bidding on this auction. Good luck!
<HR>
Successful bidder pays $3.20 for Priority Mail shipping anywhere in the U.S. Bid with confidence. Every item I sell is fully guaranteed to be as represented or I'll refund your bid. See my Feedback Rating.

will appear as:

Thanks for bidding on this auction. Good luck!

Successful bidder pays $3.20 for Priority Mail shipping anywhere in the U.S. Bid with confidence. Every item I sell is fully guaranteed to be as represented or I'll refund your bid. See my Feedback Rating.

Use the horizontal line to break up your ad into sections, such as the description of the merchandise followed by all of the ad shipping and payment options.

Using the <H#> Font Size Commands

the <H#> command allows you to specify a font to be used for a heading. The "#" is a number from 1 to 6 with 1 indicating the largest font and 6 representing the smallest. For example,

> <H1>Moss Rose, Happy Love Plate</H1>
> <P>
> Here's the most important information about this plate:
> <P>
> <H5>* Moss Rose, Happy Love message
> * Royal Staffordshire Ceramics, Made in England
> * Contains the original hanging tassel
> <P></H5>
> The date for this item is unknown but it appears to be quite old. The plate has no cracks or chips. It measures about $5^5/_8$ inches across.

would create the following text:

Moss Rose, Happy Love Plate

Here's the most important information about this plate:

* Moss Rose, Happy Love message
* Royal Staffordshire Ceramics, Made in England
* Contains the original hanging tassel

The date for this item is unknown but it appears to be quite old. The plate has no cracks or chips. It measures about $5^5/_8$ inches across.

Notice how the header commands begin with <H#> and end with </H#>. Headings do not let you select an exact font because the definition of the fonts used in headings differs for different browsers. However, headings will usually be in a bold font. Therefore, they are good at creating emphasized text.

Using the <CENTER> Command

The <center> and </center> commands can be used to center text on your screen.

For example, the text:

<CENTER><H1>Moss Rose, Happy Love Plate</H1></CENTER>
<P>
Here's the most important information about this plate:
<P>
<H5>* Moss Rose, Happy Love message
* Royal Staffordshire Ceramics, Made in England
* Contains the original hanging tassel
<P></H5>
The date for this item is unknown but it appears to be quite old. The plate has no cracks or chips. It measures about $5^5/_8$ inches across.

will produce the following results:

Moss Rose, Happy Love Plate

Here's the most important information about this plate:

* Moss Rose, Happy Love message
* Royal Staffordshire Ceramics, Made in England
* Contains the original hanging tassel

The date for this item is unknown but it appears to be quite old. The plate has no cracks or chips. It measures about $5^5/_8$ inches across.

Use the center command along with other font enhancement commands to create titles for your auction ads.

Using the <FONT COLOR> Command

To catch your customer's attention, you might use the <FONT COLOR> command to make some of your text stand out in color. This command uses the syntax <FONT COLOR=colorname> and </FONT COLOR>. For example:

<FONT COLOR=RED><H1>Moss Rose, Happy Love Plate</H1>
</FONT COLOR>
<P>
Here's the most important information about this plate:
<P>
<H5>* Moss Rose, Happy Love message
* Royal Staffordshire Ceramics, Made in England

* Contains the original hanging tassel
<P></H5>
The date for this item is unknown but it appears to be quite old. The plate has no cracks or chips. It measures about $5\frac{5}{8}$ inches across.

would cause the title Moss Rose, Happy Love Plate to appear red on screen. Colors you can use in this way are aqua, black, blue, fuchsia, gray, green, lime, maroon, navy, olive, purple, red, silver, teal, yellow, and white.

Using the <table> Command

As you browse through eBay auctions, you'll notice some whose text appears inside a box. This effect is created with the <table> command. This command can become rather complicated, but the simplest use of it is to create a table with one entry, and to place the rest of your ad copy within that table. To do this, place the following commands at the top of your ad text:

```
<table border=1 bgcolor=lawngreen><tr><td>
```

and place this command at the end of your ad text:

```
</td></tr></table>
```

The <table . . . > command begins the table and defines a border (border=1) and a background color (bgcolor=). The commands <tr> and <td> create a single table row and a single table cell. The background color can be chosen from hundreds of possible colors. A sample of these colors that work well as backgrounds include beige, peachpuff, lightpink, pink, lightsalmon, cornsilk, khaki, yellow, gold, lavender, lavenderblush, palegreen, lawngreen, lime, lemonchiffon, lightblue, lightcoral, lightcyan, aquamarine, orange, orangered, orchid, palegoldenrod, paleturquoise, palevioletred, papayawhip, lightblue, plum, royalblue, hotpink, pink, and teal.

The following example places the moss rose plate ad inside a box:

```
<table border=1 bgcolor=lawngreen><tr><td>

<H1>Moss Rose, Happy Love Plate</H1>
<P>
```

Here's the most important information about this plate:
<P>
<H5>* Moss Rose, Happy Love message
* Royal Staffordshire Ceramics, Made in England
* Contains the original hanging tassel
<P></H5>
The date for this item is unknown but it appears to be quite old. The plate has no cracks or chips. It measures about $5^5/_8$ inches across.

</td></tr></table>

These series of commands will produce the following ad (with a green background):

Moss Rose, Happy Love Plate

Here's the most important information about this plate:

* Moss Rose, Happy Love message
* Royal Staffordshire Ceramics, Made in England
* Contains the original hanging tassel

The date for this item is unknown but it appears to be quite old. The plate has no cracks or chips. It measures about $5^5/_8$ inches across.

Experiment with boxes and colors until you find a style you like.

Displaying an Image or Animation within Your Text

eBay normally only allows you to specify one picture file in your ad description, as described in Chapter 9. However, by using the HTML <IMG SRC=> command, you can place an image anywhere in your description. The syntax for this command is <IMG SRC="URL">. As you may recall from the previous chapter, the URL is the Internet address of a file. Therefore, if you have a graphic on the Web at www.myisp.com/ebay/moss rose.jpg, you can use the following command to place that image anywhere in your description:

<img src= "http://www.myisp.com/ebay/mossrose.jpg">

Use this command to place as many images as you need to convey the information about your merchandise. You can also use it to display a personal logo or a cute eye-catching animation. There are thousands of small animated GIF files available in CD collections that you can use as eye-catchers in your ads, or if you're artistic, you can use any number of graphics programs to create your own logos. Just be careful not to include too many images in your description since they can slow down the time it takes for your auction to appear on the user's screen.

Adding Links to Your Description

If you operate a business or if you want to provide additional information about a product you're selling, you might want to include a link to another site within your ad description. To include a link in your auction description use the command

<A HREF = "URL">some text</A>

For example, you might include this text in your ad:

For a biography of the illustrator whose works are offered, <A HREF = "http://www.yoursite.com">click here</A>

This will appear on screen as

For a biography of the illustrator whose works are offered, <u>click here</u>.

When a user clicks on the <u>click here</u> link, his browser will display the information on the Internet page defined by the HREF = statement. eBay has limitations in your user agreement about what you can link to from your auction ad that includes links to unauthorized sites. Review your eBay user agreement if you are unsure about what you might be able to include in a link.

Using Sounds

A few sellers have experimented with sounds within ad descriptions. Before you place a sound in your ad you might want to consider how it will be used. A background sound sometimes startles users when it suddenly comes out of the computer's speakers. If your potential customer is browsing eBay from his office cubicle (yes, people do browse through eBay at work!) and he hears sound coming from your ad, he'll quickly exit your description and hope that no one in the office noticed. Also, sound will work on some computers and not on others. Occasionally, sounds have been known to crash a computer. With that warning in mind, here's information on how to include a *midi sound file* in your ads. A midi sound file is one of a number of files that contain information that your computer can interpret into music or sounds. Midi files can be recorded by you on your own computer, can be purchased on sound CDs, or may often be found free on the Web. These files usually have a ".mid" file extension (filename.mid). To include a background sound in your ad using a midi file, use the command:

<embed hidden= true autostart= true volume=max src="URL">

This version of the command starts the sound file in the background so there is no interaction from the user (and no way for him to stop the sound). The URL is the location of the sound file on the Internet, such as "http://www.myisp.com/mysound.mid." An alternate method of using the embed command is

<embed hidden= false volume=max src="URL">

In this version of the command a button appears allowing the user to select whether or not to play the sound.

Another popular type of sound file is the *wave file* (filename.wav). To play a wave file sound in background, use the command:

<bgsound src="URL" loop="#">

where the number in the loop option is the number of times to play the wave file, such as loop="3."

Do not include a sound file in your ad unless it is critical to your ad. If you must include a sound file, such as an excerpt from a talk or song, either select the option that allows the user to optionally play the sound, or include a link within your ad that takes your prospective buyer to another Web page that contains the sound file. That way the user can choose to listen to the sound instead of having it thrust on him without his knowledge.

Midi and Wave Sound Files Two types of files that contain information that your computer can interpret into music or sounds. Sound files can be recorded by you on your own computer, can be purchased on sound CDs, or may be often found free on the Web. Midi files usually have a ".mid" file extension and wave files usually have the extension ".wav."

Putting It All Together

Once you've developed an ad style, save the HTML code into a file (using Word, Write, etc.). Then, when you get ready to create a new ad, don't enter the HTML code from scratch, use the old ad you saved as a template and change the appropriate parts of the ad to fit the current merchandise you're selling. Simply copy the HTML code from your file then paste it into the description box of the auction ad form.

The tags discussed here are only a small part of the HTML language. Some of the other commands you might want to look into using include bulleted lists, numbered lists, backgrounds, borders, and other font options. Although there are too many HTML commands to cover in this quick lesson, there are a number of HTML tutorials available on the Internet where you can learn some additional tricks. For example, to display the eBay HTML tutorial, select the <u>Help</u> link at the top of any eBay page, then select the <u>Images/HTML board</u> link. Another source of tutorials for HTML and other eBay related ad preparation information is at www.pongo.com.

USING AD PREPARATION SOFTWARE

You're not stuck with having to know HTML to create fancy ads. The popularity of eBay has stimulated several software authors to create programs that help you create and place your ads on eBay. These *ad preparation software programs* allow you to simplify the ad creation process by automating some of the repetitive tasks (such as specifying your shipping policies) and by making some of the more confusing procedures (such as FTPing image files) simpler and more automated.

Following are a few of the programs available:

✔ **AuctionAssistant** allows you to create auction listings without having to know HTML. It will also automatically FTP your images to the Web, fill in the eBay forms required for listing your items, and retrieve information from eBay to help you keep track of your auctions. AuctionAssistant is published by Blackthorne Software. A trial version is available for download at www.blackthornesw.com.

✔ **Virtual Auction Ad Pro** is designed for making auction ads for popular auction sites including eBay, Amazon, Aaands, Auction-Universe, NuAuction, and Yahoo! In this program you create your ad by filling in the blanks on an on-screen form and the program builds the ad for you, creating the necessary HTML code. You then paste the created code into the auction ad form. An evaluation copy of this software is available from Virtual Notions at www.virtualnotions.com.

✔ **The Auction Wizard** was developed specifically for use with eBay. It includes an HTML template editor to help you create your ads plus a database to help you keep track of your auctions. A trial version of the Auction Wizard is downloadable from Standing Wave Software, Inc. at www.standingwavesoftware.com.

Ad Preparation Software Programs   These programs allow you to simplify the ad creation process by automating some of the repetitive tasks (such as specifying your shipping policies) and by making some of the more confusing procedures (such as FTPing image files) simpler and more automated.

There's a learning curve involved in using any of these programs, but if you're going to be listing a number of ads, it might be worthwhile to use one of them to streamline your auction ad creation and uploading processes.

For example, suppose you're creating an auction ad using AuctionAssistant. The program's dialog box used to create an ad is shown in Figure 10.1. In this dialog box you merely fill in all of the information

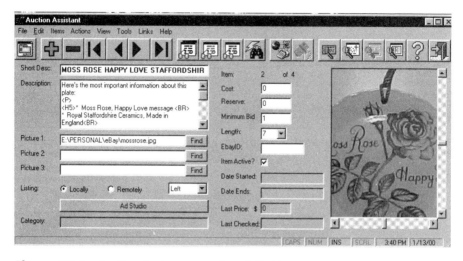

Figure 10.1 AuctionAssistant auction definition screen.
(*Source:* Blackthorne Software. Copyright © 1998, 1999 Blackthorne Software. Reprinted with permission.)

about the ad such as the ad title, description, minimum bid, length of auction, and so on. You can also select up to three pictures to include in the ad. Your own standard wording for shipping, taxes, and other notices as well as color options are selected by clicking on the Ad Studio button. Once you've defined these values, you don't have to reenter them for subsequent ads.

Notice that in the Description textbox, you're still allowed to use HTML. Although AuctionAssistant will provide most of the major HTML code needed to fashion your ad into a professional looking auction, you can still spruce up the ad a little by including a few of your own HTML touches. For example, if you want your paragraphs to be separated by a line, you'll need to place a <P> HTML tag between them.

Once you've filled in information about your ad, you can preview your ad before uploading it. When you're satisfied with your creation, AuctionAssistant will upload your images and will fill in the eBay auction form for you. AuctionAssistant will open your Internet browser at the eBay auction form with all of the information you've specified already filled in. This allows you to double-check everything by reviewing the ad (just as you did in Chapter 8) before actually taking the auction live. Figure 10.2 shows the moss rose ad created by AuctionAssistant. Once you've begun the auction you can also use AuctionAssistant to keep track of your ads and manage your correspondence with the winner.

MOSS ROSE HAPPY LOVE STAFFORDSHIRE

Here's the most important information about this plate:

* Moss Rose, Happy Love message
* Royal Staffordshire Ceramics, Made in England
* Contains the original hanging tassel

The date for this item is unknown but it appears to be quite old. The plate has no cracks or chips. It measures about 5 5/8 inches across.

Thanks for bidding on this auction. Good luck!

Successful bidder pays $3.20 for Priority Mail shipping in U.S.. Buy with confidence. Every item I sell is fully guaranteed to be as represented or I'll refund your bid. See my Feedback Rating.

NO RESERVE!

Buyer pays s&h and insurance if desired. Please allow time for personal check to clear or send m.o. for quick shipping.

Please check out the other auctions we currently have running on eBay.

Figure 10.2   An auction ad created by AuctionAssistant.
(*Source:* Blackthorne Software. Copyright © 1998, 1999 Blackthorne Software. Reprinted with permission.)

SUMMARY

With a little practice, you can make your ads look as professional as any on the Web. If you're a hands-on kind of person, then you might want to create your own HTML template using the commands described in this chapter and then use it to create your ads. If HTML is a little too much for you to learn, then the ad creation programs can help you create your ads easily and quickly. Once you've gotten down the process of creating exciting and appealing ads for your products, you're ready to tackle the job of managing your auction business. That's the topic of the next chapter.

Chapter

11

Managing Your Auction

F rom fast food restaurants to brokerage firms, the most successful businesses are those that have learned to do important sales-related tasks efficiently and consistently. They don't reinvent their business every time they make a sale and you shouldn't reinvent the auction process every time you start an auction. With a little knowledge, experience, and planning, you can operate your auctions in such a way that you'll *maximize* your profits with a *minimum* amount of effort. This chapter helps you select the best options for running your own auctions.

STARTING YOUR AUCTION WITH SUCCESS IN MIND

The purpose of your ad is to attract customers and convince them to bid. When you begin an auction, you must decide what kind of auction is best for your particular product. eBay (and most other auction sites) offers these general kinds of auctions:

- ✔ Standard Auction
- ✔ Reserve Price Auction
- ✔ Private Auction
- ✔ Dutch Auction

A general description of these auctions was given in Chapter 1, "Starting Out." This discussion will look at these auctions from a seller's point of view.

Choosing Between a Standard and Reserve Price Auction

The two most common types of auctions are the Standard and Reserve Auctions; the main difference between them is the ability to protect you against selling for a low winning bid. Which should you choose? Knowing a little about customer psychology and facts about bidding patterns can help you understand the pros and cons of each auction type.

When you start your auction by filling out the auction form, an important entry to consider is your *opening bid* amount. The opening bid is the lowest bid a buyer can make on your auction. Users are more likely to be attracted to auctions with low opening bids than to those with high bids. If you examine auctions on Internet sites such as Egghead and uBid, you'll see that opening bids for even expensive items often begin as low as $1. These companies have learned that low opening bids attract customers. In the same way, you should consider opening your auction with a low bid. People want bargains. If they see a product priced at a bargain price, they're more likely to bid. Then, once they've broken the ice, they are more likely to continue bidding on your item as the price escalates.

Opening Bid   The lowest bid a buyer can make on your auction. Users are more likely to be attracted to auctions with low opening bids than to those with high opening bids.

If you attract several bidders, then you'll start a little bidding war. When a bidder discovers that someone else is interested in your item, his belief that your item is desirable is validated. Now the bidding becomes a game. Each bidder wants to get this desirable item, and as the bids rise it just convinces each one of them that the item is even more valuable. The bidder who wants the item most wins, but in the long run you win as well. In fact, it's not unusual for an item that may normally sell for $50 to sell for much more than that if a bidding war is involved.

However, if an item is worth $50 and you begin the bidding at $50 you'll either attract no bids at all, or if you attract the single $50 bid you're not likely to have it raised beyond that amount. If you're able to sell your item, you'll only get your minimum acceptable price and not the maximum price a bidding market could create.

The drawback to setting a low opening bid in a Standard Auction is that it *may not* attract bidders. Some auctions don't even attract bidders with an opening bid of one cent! Therefore, a low opening bid is a risk. If you use low bids in a Standard Auction and get few bidders, you'll end up selling your wares at low prices (or not at all). That's not being very successful. How can you know when to use low opening bids? You should only use low opening bids on items that are sure to attract customers. How can you tell if your item is attractive? There are two ways. First, if your item is similar to others that are being sold, do a search on completed auctions to see what prices the other items have obtained. If similar items consistently sell after attracting multiple bids, then you can be reasonably sure that your item will also attract bidders. The second way to know if your item will attract bids is by experience. If you specialize in a particular kind of item, you'll know how popular it is and if it is likely to attract bids. If you sell the same standard item all the time, you have the opportunity to experiment with opening bids to determine how they affect your final prices. Seasoned sellers often find that even though they occasionally end up selling a few items at bargain prices because of low opening bids, it's worth using them because they tend to drive up final prices for most items.

You can protect yourself against low winning bids by using a *Reserve Price Auction*. In a Reserve Price Auction you can set the opening bid very low, but you're not required to sell your item unless the bid reaches a certain level set by you at the beginning of the auction. In a Reserve Price Auction, bidders know there's a reserve price, but they do not know what it is. In order to win the auction, a bidder must meet or exceed the reserve price and have the highest bid. If no bidder meets the reserve price, the seller does not have to sell his item to the highest bidder.

Reserve Price Auction   The seller may set the opening bid very low, but is not required to sell the item unless the bid reaches a certain amount. In a Reserve Price Auction, bidders know there's a reserve price, but they do not know what it is. In order to win the auction, a bidder must meet or exceed the reserve price and have the highest bid. If no bidder meets the reserve price, the seller does not have to sell his item to the highest bidder.

However, Reserve Price Auctions have a tarnished reputation. One reason they're unpopular with some bidders is because a few sellers put very high reserves on the auction to see how high the bidding will go. This gives the seller a cheap appraisal of how much his item is worth, but he never really intends to sell it. Bidders who want the item can't understand why their high bid isn't enough. Still other unscrupulous sellers have been known to put up high reserves, and when the bidding never reaches the reserve level, they try to force the high bidder to buy the item anyway. Of course, the buyer is not obligated to make the purchase and may have moved on to some other auction. These situations have often led to angry e-mails, complaints to eBay, and bad feelings that have often resulted in negative feedback for both parties. Don't ruin your own reputation by making this kind of mistake. Always make your reserve price the lowest price you'd still be willing to sell your item.

Which type of auction, the Standard or Reserve Price, is best to use? If you're confident that your item will be popular among bidders, the low opening bid Standard Auction is the best choice. If you don't know if your item is popular, or if you'll simply not sell it under a certain price, then you must use the higher opening bid or Reserve Price Auction to protect yourself.

When Should You Use a Private Auction?

A footnote to the decision between a Standard and Reserve Price Auction is whether to also make your auction a *Private Auction*. A Private Auction may be operated as either a Standard or Reserve Price Auction, but without revealing the identities of the bidders. Relatively few auctions are held as Private Auctions. Most sellers will tell you that Private Auctions usually contain pornography or offensive material. In reality, you'll see auctions for Beanie Babies, watches, and items in almost any category being sold in Private Auctions. The only explanation for this is that some sellers don't realize what the option means when they're setting up their auction.

Private Auction   May be operated as either a Standard or Reserve Price Auction, but without revealing the identities of the bidders.

The purpose of the Private Auction is to shield bidders against embarrassment or identification. If you're selling something that potential bidders may be reluctant to bid on if they know their User ID will be revealed to the public, then you should select the Private Auction option.

Using Dutch Auctions

Dutch Auctions are a valuable tool to the serious seller. They allow her to sell many items within a single auction. To sell the same number of items in individual auctions would increase her auction fees, paperwork, and make her miss out on buyers who might be willing to buy multiple copies of a product. If you have several (or many) identical items to sell, consider using the Dutch Auction format. (A general description of the Dutch Auction was given in Chapter 1, "Starting Out.")

What are the main differences between a Dutch Auction and a Standard Auction from the seller's point of view? In a Dutch Auction, a bidder not only bids on the item, he also indicates how many of the items he wants. Depending on the number of items available, there can be as many winners as there are items to sell. Plus, all winning bidders pay the same price, which is the *lowest successful* bid amount. Proxy bidding (the process where eBay will raise your bid for you up to a chosen limit) is not used in Dutch Auctions.

> **Dutch Auction**   The bidder indicates how many of the items he wants at his bid price. Depending on the number of items available, there can be as many winners as there are items to sell. Plus, all winning bidders pay the same price, which is the lowest successful bid amount. Proxy bidding is not used in Dutch Auctions.

When you create a Dutch Auction, your opening price strategy is different than on a Standard or Reserve Price Auction. Most Dutch Auctions have an opening price that is the lowest price the seller is willing to accept. When a seller has a thousand items available, he's probably not going to sell them all, thus he's really selling the item at a fixed price—what he's designated as the opening price. If you can make sufficient profit from the opening price, then you can repeat a Dutch Auction on a regular basis as long as there are bidders ready to bid. If you browse through the Featured Auctions on a regular basis, you'll recognize the same Dutch Auctions being held over and over again each week.

If you're selling a limited number of items in a Dutch Auction, then you stand a chance of having enough bidders to raise the winning bid beyond the opening price. There are two ways for bidders to win in a Dutch Auction. If a customer bids the opening price and there are enough of the items to satisfy all bidders, then he wins. However, once there are enough bidders to take up all of the available items at the original opening price, then a bidder must raise the bid in order to go to the top of the list and become a potential winner.

Before you can create a Dutch Auction on eBay, you must have a Feedback Rating of 10 or above and be a member of eBay for 60 days or more. These restrictions were put into place after some unscrupulous fly-by-night sellers began using Dutch Auctions to get payments and run.

When Should Your Auction End?

Timing the end of your auction may help you get more bids. Do you want your auction to end at 2 A.M. when there are few bidders awake, or at 9 P.M. on a Saturday night when a million people are browsing on eBay? Since many auctions attract last-minute bidders, you'll probably want your auction to end at a popular time of day. Of course, if you're selling an herbal cure for insomnia you might want to have your auction end at 2 A.M. when your potential customers are looking for relief.

Therefore, when you place your items up for auction, pay close attention to when the auction will end. Use some common sense about when people will be online. The busiest days of the week for auctions are on Friday, Saturday, and Sunday. However, there are also significant numbers of customers online most weeknights as well. The busiest times for auctions to end are in the evenings between about 6 P.M. and 11:00 P.M. (Pacific Standard or Pacific Daylight Time). The slowest times for auctions are early in the morning, from about 2 A.M. to 7 A.M. Adjust these times according to what time zone you're in. Also, consider what times your customers are likely to be on the Internet. Retirees and homemakers may be online during midday and not as much at night whereas middle-aged workers (the Baby Boomers) will do most of their Web browsing after work. Some sellers know that buyers on one coast or another are their best potential bidders and they will schedule their auctions to end at an optimal time for each coast.

eBay gives you limited options for what time your auction will end. Your only choice is to select the number of days the auction will last: either three, five, seven, or ten days. Therefore, if you want a seven-day auction to end at a particular time of day, you need to enter your auction information on the same day of the week and at the same time you want it to end. If you want your auction to end on a weekend, and you're beginning the auction on a Wednesday or Thursday, then you can select a three-day or ten-day auction so that the auction will end on Saturday or Sunday.

Some sellers believe that selecting a ten-day auction will always give the best chance at maximizing their bid. The more days the better, right? Not necessarily. Most auctions actually don't receive many bids until they are down to their last day or two. And some bidders will be reluctant to bid on an auction that will take so long to end. People want quick results. In a recent experiment where the same item was sold at different auction lengths and times, there was no difference in highest bids for auctions of three or seven days. It is more important *when* your auction ends than how long it is. Of course, no general rule can be made for every type of auction item. You should experiment within your own category to find out what works best for you.

Does Time of Year Make a Difference?

Most retailers know the peaks and valleys of the retail year. Of course, seasons differ for different types of products. Swimsuits and lawnmowers may not sell well from September to December, but for many other products it's the best time of the year. What is the best season for your category of product?

The biggest general peak season in auction (and retail) sales is just before Christmas. Anything that can be given as a gift will sell better from September to December than at any other time of the year. If you're selling collectibles, toys, jewelry, or any other potential gift item, you should consider concentrating your sales during that time. However, you shouldn't limit your sales only to a single season. For many items, sales are strong all year long.

Other sales cycles you might consider are seasonal and event-oriented. For example, hiking gear may sell well in the spring when people are getting the urge to walk in the great outdoors. Snow skiing gear, on the other hand, may sell well from fall to spring. Spooky items sell best prior to Halloween, romantic items sell best prior to Valentine's day, and certain baseball collectibles have a sales peak around the World Series. In anticipation for the release of *Star Wars Episode I* many old *Star Wars* collectibles rose in value. Then, after the movie had been out a while and the new collectibles were creating interest, some of the old collectibles slumped in value. A seller is just like a surfer—you've got to go after the wave when it's at its peak, otherwise your ride will not be as satisfying.

What other calendar-oriented factors influence sales? Since many of the items sold in Internet auctions are purchased from *disposable income*, you need to be aware of its impact on bidders. Disposable income is the amount of money you have to spend after the necessities of life have been purchased. There are several times during the year when normally disposable income is diverted to other uses. For example, families tend to purchase back-to-school clothes and school supplies in August. This may influence sales of items that normally appeal to customers in the 30 to 40 age range but it probably has no effect on items that appeal to senior citizens.

The income tax season may either help or hinder sales. For some families, tax season is a time for belt tightening, but for those that receive an income tax refund, it's an opportunity to make a major purchase. That's why appliance and automobile dealers have sales from February to April.

Therefore, if your first experience in selling at auction is during August, don't be disappointed if your sales aren't up to what you expected. Just wait a month. In September, the Christmas season begins! You may suddenly see an increase both in the number and size of bids. And when Christmas is over, don't take a breather. The buying exuberance usually lasts well into January.

Disposable Income   The amount of money you have to spend after the necessities of life have been purchased.

What else might affect auction sales? The consumer's willingness to bid and purchase is also governed by the general state of the economy. If there's a downturn or a recession, people begin to save more and spend less on frills. A major strike, a war, or a national catastrophe may dampen the mood of the buying public. On the other hand, bad winter weather may cause sales to increase since people are stuck inside and spending more time online.

If you specialize in a particular kind of merchandise, you'll soon be able to tell what cycles favor your sales. In fact, if you can also specialize in products with an opposite cycle, you might be able to smooth out your sales over the year to prevent having boom and bust months. On the other hand, you might want to sell your products only during your best season and sunbathe on the beach in Florida (or ski in the Colorado mountains) the rest of the year.

What Auction Options Should You Use?

Why are grocery store check-out lines surrounded by racks of magazines and candies? These are impulse items—stuff you might pick up and buy while you're waiting to check out. In the same way, eBay offers you an array of impulse items you can add on to your auction while you're getting it ready to go live. Here's a brief description of these add-ons and some information about when you might want to use one or more of them. The prices quoted may change, so check with eBay's current pricing to verify these amounts:

✔ *Adding your auction's picture to the Gallery ($0.25).* When a user clicks on the thumbnail-sized Gallery picture of your item, your auction ad will be displayed. Enticing pictures might attract some additional customers to your ad. However, there are so many pictures that unless a customer uses a search to narrow down his options, your auction will get lost in the thousands of other Gallery pictures.

✔ *Feature your item in the Gallery ($19.95).* This means that in addition to appearing in the Gallery listing pages, your item will also randomly appear at the top of the Gallery listing pages in a larger size.

✔ *The Boldface Title ($2.00).* This option makes your auction title appear in bold type to help attract customers.

✔ *Featured Auctions ($99.95).* Items listed in eBay's Featured Auctions are just a click away on a link that is prominently highlighted in the center of eBay's main page. In addition, eBay also randomly lists some of the Featured Auction titles on its main page, although eBay does not guarantee that a specific auction will be highlighted in this way.

✔ *Featured in Category ($14.95).* These items are listed prominently in a specific category listing.

✔ *Gift Icon ($1.00).* A gift icon can be selected to tell browsers that your auction is specifically targeted toward some event or holiday. You can select icons that highlight events such as anniversaries, babies, birthdays, Christmas, Easter, and so on.

You have to decide if the cost of any of these extras will enhance your ad sufficiently to pay for their cost. Don't just choose them because they're available. To justify spending $99.95 for Featured Auction status, you must expect well over a hundred dollars profit for the item (or items if it is a Dutch Auction). One way to emphasize your ad without paying extra is to capitalize all of the words in your title. It has the same overall effect as bold type, but doesn't cost you anything.

It's impossible to list which specific items will benefit from featured status, a Gallery listing, or special icons. You'll find seasoned dealers who argue both for using the extras and for not using them. Your best bet is to experiment with your own items to see if any of the available options increases your bids enough to justify the cost.

MAKING CHANGES TO YOUR AUCTION

Occasionally when you start an auction, you suddenly become aware of an error in your ad. Yikes! Perhaps you left out an important piece of information or you misspelled a key word in the title. If no one has bid on the ad, you have the opportunity to easily change it and correct the error. To make this change, display the ad in your browser and look for the "Update Item" label on the auction screen along with the sentence that states:

Seller: If this item has received no bids, you may revise it.

Click on the revise link, enter your eBay User ID and Password, and a screen titled "Update Your Item Information" will be displayed, as shown in Figure 11.1. When you revise an item, you can change item titles, modify descriptions, select a different category, add or change images, update payment options, and change shipping options. Once you've started your auction it's a good idea to review it immediately. Sometimes errors or omissions are not obvious until you see the live auction on the screen. If you can catch these errors before bids are made, then you can quickly change them by updating your description.

Items you cannot change in an ad include the item number, location, minimum bid, reserve price, auction duration, or any special listing features. If your ad contains significant errors other than those that can be revised, you may need to cancel your ad altogether by ending your auction early. See "Ending an Auction Early" later in this chapter.

Adding to Your Auction Listing

Even after your auction has begun receiving bids, you can still add to your auction description. Suppose you're selling an old transistor radio. In your ad you show a picture of the radio from the front. However, during the auction a bidder e-mails you with a question. What does the radio look like on

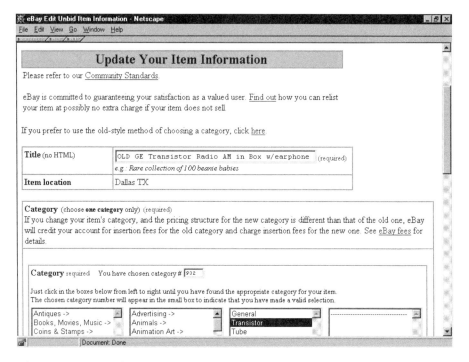

Figure 11.1 Updating an auction item.

the inside? You decide that you want to let all potential bidders see the inside of your radio, so you add an additional picture to the auction description.

To add to a current auction, click on the Services link at the top of any eBay page, then click on the Add to my item description link under the "Buying and Selling Tools" listing. A screen titled "Adding to your item description" will be displayed as shown in Figure 11.2. Once you indicate the item number, your eBay User ID, and your Password, you can enter additional information into a textbox. Since this box accepts HTML tags, you can also add graphics, links, and formatted descriptions as described in Chapter 10, "Improving Your Presentation." For example, you could enter the following information into the description textbox:

Here's a view of the inside of the radio:
<P>
<img src=http://www.myisp.com/mypicture.jpg>

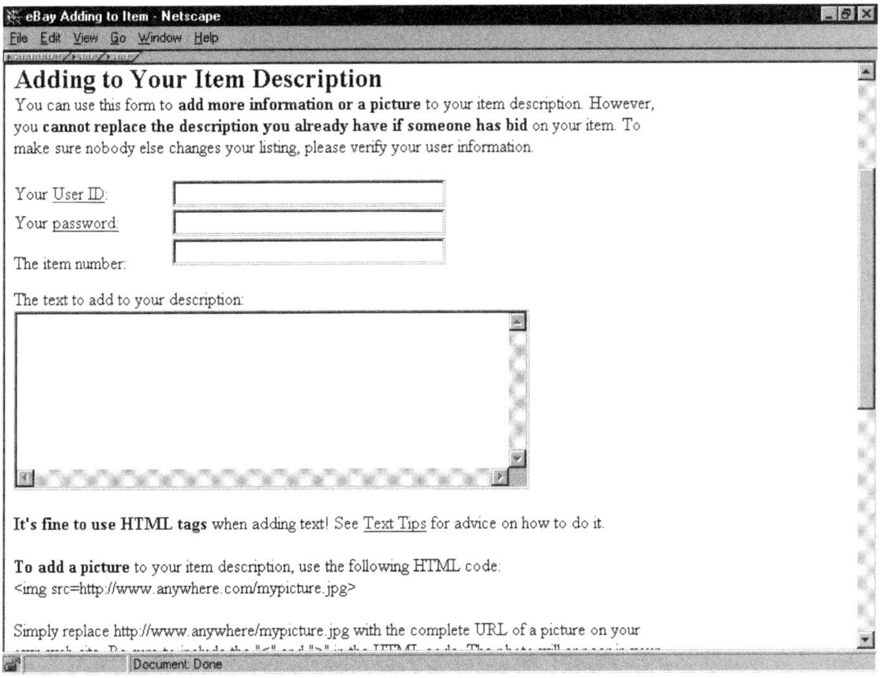

Figure 11.2 Adding to your item description.
(This material has been reproduced by John Wiley & Sons, Inc. with permission of eBay, Inc. Copyright © eBay, Inc. All rights reserved.)

Click on the "Review" button to see how your new information will look; if it is okay, then click on the "Add to Description" button to submit the change.

Once you've added new information to your ad, eBay will add a message in your ad that reads something like this "On 09/26/99 at 10:34:19 PDT, seller added the following information." The information you added in the textbox will appear immediately below this message. Figure 11.3 shows an ad with revised information.

Changing Your Auction Category

If your auction isn't receiving the bids you anticipated, it might be because you've placed your item in the wrong category. Or, perhaps your item could easily fit into more than one category. After it's had a few days in one category, you might want to change it to another. eBay allows you to change an auction category in midstream, whether or not your auction has received any bids. To make the change, click on the Services link at the top of any eBay page, then click on the Change my items category link under the

On 08/26/99 at 10:34:19 PDT, seller added the following information:

Here's a view of the insides of the radio.

Figure 11.3 An ad with revised information.

"Buying and Selling Tools" listing. Figure 11.4 shows the "Change the Category of Your Item" screen. Enter your eBay User ID, Password, and the auction number. Then select a new category for the item and click on the "Change Category" button at the bottom of the screen.

Canceling User Bids

Why would you ever want to cancel someone's bid? eBay suggests the following legitimate reasons:

✔ A bidder contacts you to back out of the bid and you agree to allow it.

✔ You cannot verify the identity of the bidder, after trying all reasonable means of contact.

✔ You want to end your auction early because you no longer want to sell your item. In this case you must cancel all bids before ending the auction.

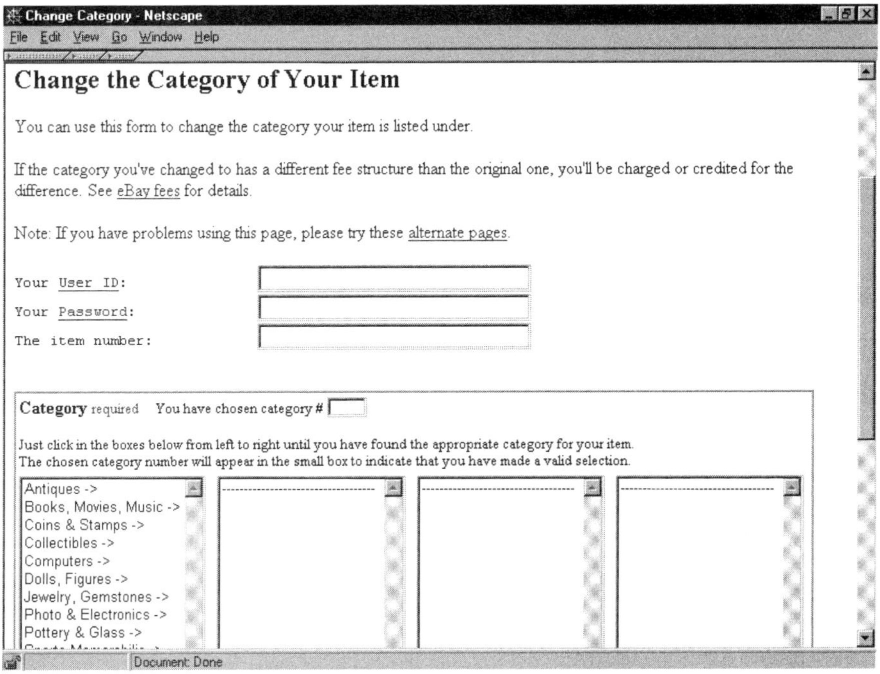

Figure 11.4 Changing an item's category.
(This material has been reproduced by John Wiley & Sons, Inc. with permission of eBay, Inc. Copyright © eBay, Inc. All rights reserved.)

As you become savvier in the ways of auctions, you might be able to identify bidders who are questionable. Perhaps you have an expensive auction going on and notice that the high bidder has zero (0) feedback. Does this bidder know what's going on? Is this the first time he's bid? You may want to check him out and see what else he's bid on recently. (You can do a bidder search by clicking on the Search link at the top of any eBay page, then enter the bidder's ID into the Bidder Search option.) If he has negatives in his Feedback score, you might get worried. Since every eBay user has to reveal his e-mail address, you can write a polite note to the bidder to find out his intentions. If you can't get a good answer, then you have a legitimate reason to cancel the bid.

Another problem to watch out for is a scam involving protected bids. In this scam, three partners work together. One will make a low bid on a new auction item and the other two will quickly bid against each other to raise the high bid up to a point where no one else will bid. Then, at the last moment, the two highest bidders cancel their bids, leaving the low bidder as the winner. In order for you to be aware of this potential scam you'll have to pay attention to the early bidders on your auction. If your auction bids shoot up quickly to an astronomical bid then you might suspect a scam. Research the two high bidders and if you're convinced that they are trying to pull a fast one, then cancel their bids. You should also contact your auction's security (safeharbor@ebay.com) and make them aware of the situation.

Another reason to cancel a bid is when the bidder contacts you and requests it. You'll have to be your own judge of the bidder's intent. Did he have a sudden financial downturn? A family sickness? Or perhaps the bidder misunderstood the ad and made a bid before checking out the facts. The bottom line is when you have a bidder unwilling to follow through on the auction. If there's still plenty of time left in the auction you may not suffer any consequences in letting him off the hook. If the auction is nearing an end, then canceling the high bidder may cause you to accept a lower final bid. In this case you might want to cancel all bids and end the auction, then relist it.

If you decide to end an auction early, then you must either accept the current high bidder's amount or cancel all bids before ending the auction. You should have a good reason (for example, your Picasso turned out to be a fake) and correspond with your bidders to let them know what's happening. (See "Ending an Auction Early," below.)

To cancel a bid, click on the <u>Services</u> link at the top of any eBay page, then click on the <u>Go directly</u> to More Buying and Selling Tools link under the "Buying and Selling Tools" listing, then click on the <u>Cancel bids on my item</u> link. Enter your User ID, Password, the item number, the User ID of the bidder whose bid you're canceling, and an explanation of up to 80 characters. Click on the <u>Cancel Bid</u> button to submit the cancellation.

Ending an Auction Early

Oh no! After you put your Catnip Beanie up for auction, the dog attacked it and tore it to shreds. What can you do? Unless you have a duplicate Catnip, your only real choice is to end the auction. You can't sell something you don't have! If no one has bid on your auction, ending it is simple. Click on the <u>Services</u> link at the top of any eBay page, then click on the <u>Go Directly</u> to More Buying and Selling Tools link under the "Buying and Selling Tools" listing, then click on the <u>End my auction early</u> link. Figure 11.5 shows the screen used to end your auction.

What if there are already bidders? If you have current bidders on your auction, then you'll have to cancel all bids before ending the auction. (See the section above titled "Canceling User Bids.") You should, of

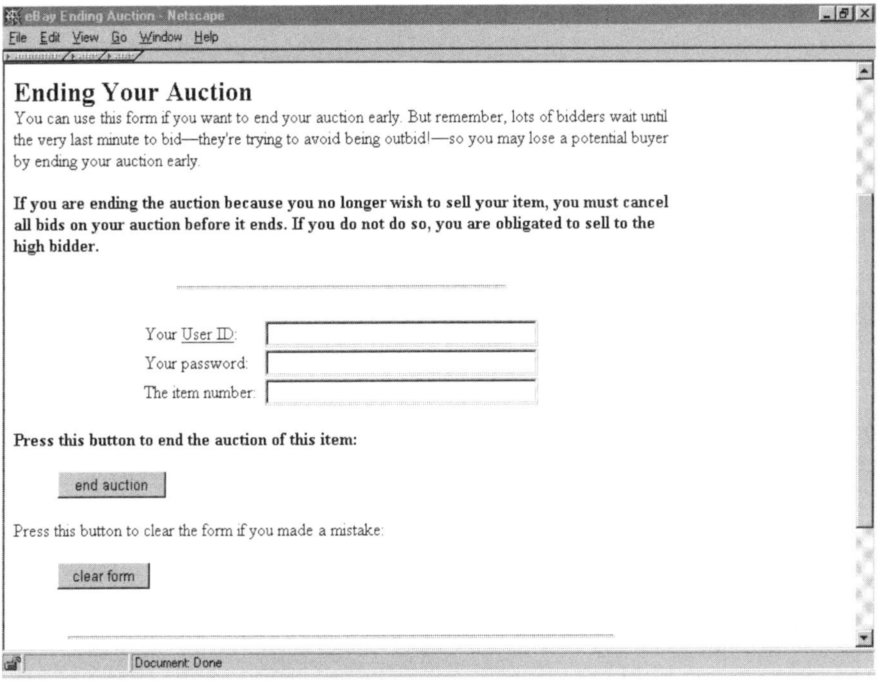
eBay Ending Auction - Netscape
File Edit View Go Window Help
Ending Your Auction
You can use this form if you want to end your auction early. But remember, lots of bidders wait until the very last minute to bid—they're trying to avoid being outbid!—so you may lose a potential buyer by ending your auction early.
If you are ending the auction because you no longer wish to sell your item, you must cancel all bids on your auction before it ends. If you do not do so, you are obligated to sell to the high bidder.
Your User ID:
Your password:
The item number:
Press this button to end the auction of this item:
end auction
Press this button to clear the form if you made a mistake:
clear form
Document: Done

Figure 11.5 Ending your auction early.
(This material has been reproduced by John Wiley & Sons, Inc. with permission of eBay, Inc. Copyright © eBay, Inc. All rights reserved.)

course, tell the high bidder why you are ending the auction. Otherwise you may be setting yourself up for negative feedback. Once you've canceled bids, then you can end the auction.

What happens to the auction fees when you cancel an auction? If you cancel the auction before any bids are received, then you can relist the auction, and your insertion fee will be adjusted accordingly. However, any special options you've chosen such as a bold title or inclusion in the Gallery are not refundable. (See the section titled "Relisting an Item," below.) If bids were received on the auction, then you cannot relist it and recover any fees. You'll have to begin it as a new auction if you want to run it again.

There are other reasons you might want to end an auction early. Maybe you're just tired of waiting. Or you've been contacted by your high bidder offering to make a final offer if you end the auction. He's in a hurry and wants your gizmo now! It's your decision. If you cancel the auction early without canceling the bidders first then your current high bidder rightfully wins the auction. When you end an auction that has bidders, eBay will send e-mail to the high bidder notifying him that the auction was ended.

Relisting an Item

If your auction doesn't attract any bidders, you can relist your item. Perhaps your ad title was too vague. Maybe your opening bid price scared away potential bidders. Or perhaps your reserve price was too high. eBay recognizes that there are times when one more try might do the trick, so it allows you to relist an item a second time for free under certain conditions. Then if your item sells the second time around, you'll get the insertion fee for the second listing back. If it doesn't sell the second time either, you'll be charged the normal insertion fee for the listing. Here are the conditions under which you can relist your item:

- ✔ You didn't receive any bids on your listed item for a regular auction.
- ✔ You are relisting the same item within 30 days of the closing date of the first auction.
- ✔ You didn't get any bids that met or exceeded your reserve price (for a Reserve Price Auction).
- ✔ You are relisting the item with the same or lower reserve price.

If your auction meets these criteria, then display the old auction by clicking on the My eBay link at the top of any eBay page. In the option "Days worth of ended auctions you want shown," specify enough days so that the auction of interest is displayed. Then enter your eBay User ID and Password. A list of your recent auctions will be displayed. Select the auction you want to relist, then find the following statement on your auction listing just under the Payment and Shipping statements:

Seller: Didn't sell your item the first time? eBay will refund your relisting fee if it sells the second time around. Relist this item.

Click on the Relist this item link and a page containing hints on how to improve your listing will appear. Click on the relist button and the standard ad insertion form will appear containing all of the information from your old ad. From this form you can make changes to improve the ad and resubmit the ad just as if it were a new auction.

UPLOADING MANY ADS AT A TIME

Entering new auctions by hand on the eBay auction form can become tedious fast. If you're creating a number of auctions on a regular basis, you'll want to streamline the process. You can use a program such as AuctionAssistant (described in the previous chapter) or you can use eBay's own bulk auction upload process called *Mister Lister*. Using Mister Lister you create a file that contains information about several auctions, then e-mail that description file to eBay. You can review how each auction will look online before taking it live. Briefly, here are the steps used to upload auctions using Mister Lister:

1. Create a collection of auction descriptions on your local computer. (You don't need to be connected to the Internet or on eBay to do this step.)
2. You send the batch by e-mail to eBay.
3. eBay sends you an e-mail telling you that your batch has been received in good order.
4. You go to eBay to review and start your auctions.

Mister Lister   A feature of eBay that allows you to quickly start several auctions at a time. Using Mister Lister you create a file that contains information about several auctions, then e-mail that description file to eBay. You can review how each auction will look online before taking it live.

To compile a collection of several auctions you can use the Mister Lister software program that is free and downloadable from eBay. Using this program you can define your auctions off-line by entering your auction information into a auction form. Usually this is much faster than doing it online since you do not have to wait for a response across the Internet. Once you've defined a collection of auctions, you send the information to eBay by clicking on the "Send this Collection" button. This e-mails your list of auctions to eBay. (You must be connected to the Internet to do this step.) Within a few minutes, eBay responds to you by e-mail and tells you if there are any errors in the submission. If errors are reported, you must fix the problems and resend the information. Once you have a clean submission, eBay allows you to review your auctions online and take them live.

To register for Mister Lister, click on the <u>Services</u> link at the top of an eBay page, then click on the <u>Go Directly</u> to Buying and Selling Tools link under the "Buying and Selling Tools" listing and choose the <u>Mister Lister bulk upload</u> link. From this page you can register to become a Mister Lister user, and download your own personal copy of the Mister Lister software program.

MAXIMIZE YOUR PROFIT AND MINIMIZE YOUR COST

There are two basic strategies any business can use to make more profit: increase revenues and decrease costs. This section presents the information you need to know to help you minimize your costs. For an Internet auction business, your largest ongoing costs (beyond the cost of goods sold) are usually the fees you pay to your auction host such as eBay, Amazon, or Yahoo! Therefore, to control your costs you need to keep an eye on these fees.

Calculating Your Selling Fees

There are several fees involved in running an auction: the insertion fee, additional options fees, and Final Value Fees. The fees described here were accurate at the time of this book's publication. However, these eBay fees may change periodically, so you should check with eBay to review their current fee structure.

When you place an ad in eBay, you will be charged a nonrefundable insertion fee. Fees vary by the type of auction you're using. For Standard and Reserve Price Auctions, the fees are as follows:

Opening Value or Reserve Price	Insertion Fee
$0.01 to $9.99	$0.25
$10.00 to $24.99	$0.50
$25.00 to $49.00	$1.00
$50.00 and up	$2.00
Cars (including classics), Trucks, and RVs	$25.00 fixed
Real Estate	$50.00 fixed

In addition, eBay recently instituted an additional fee for Reserve Price Auctions. A fee of $0.50 is charged for auctions with reserve prices from

$0.01 to $24.99 and a fee of $1.00 is charged for auctions with reserve prices from $25.00 and up. If the item sells, this fee is refunded. The purpose of this fee is to discourage people from placing auctions with artificially high reserve prices.

For a Dutch Auction, the insertion fee is based upon the opening value or minimum bid of the item you list for sale multiplied by the quantity of items you offer.

Fees for additional options such as a bold title, featured auctions, and so on, were listed earlier in this chapter in the section titled, "What Options Should You Use." Care must be taken when selecting these options because they can quickly eat up your profit. Only use options that you are sure enhance the effectiveness of your auction.

The *Final Value Fee* is an extra fee you pay to eBay based on the final results of your auction. The better you do, the higher the fee. For Regular and Reserve Auctions (when the reserve has been met) the final value is the closing bid. For Dutch Auctions the final value is the lowest successful bid, multiplied by the quantity of items sold.

Final Value For Regular and Reserve Auctions (when the reserve has been met) the final value is the closing bid. For Dutch Auctions the final value is the lowest successful bid, multiplied by the quantity of items you sold.

Final Value Fee An extra fee you pay to eBay based on the final results of your auction.

Once you know the final value for an auction you can calculate the Final Value Fee. Here's how you calculate your Final Value Fee (other than for real estate or vehicles):

1. Take the first $25 of your final value, and calculate 5 percent of that. If your item sold for $25 or less, this is your Final Value Fee.

2. If your final value was more than $25, take the additional amount, from $25.01 to $1,000, and calculate 2.5 percent of that.

3. If your final value was more than $1,000, take that additional amount and calculate 1.25 percent of the remaining amount.

4. Add these amounts together and you have your Final Value Fee.

For example, suppose you sold an item for $100 that had an opening bid of $1.00. Your insertion fee would be $0.25. The final value for the auction is $100. Five percent of the first $25 is $1.25. For the remaining $75, 2.5 percent would be $1.88. Thus your total fees for this auction would be $0.25 + $1.25 + $1.88 = $3.38.

The Final Value Fee for selling a car, RV, or truck is $25. If your vehicle does not sell, then there is no Final Value Fee. For selling real estate, there is no Final Value Fee. Your cost is only the original insertion cost.

You will not be charged a Final Value Fee if there were no bids on your item or if there were no bids that met your reserve price for your Reserve Price Auction. However, if you do have bids, then your Final Value Fee will be assessed whether you consummate the sale with the buyer or not.

You can pay your eBay fees automatically by credit card or by making periodic payments. To examine your payment options, click on the Services link at the top of any eBay page then click on the Go Directly to Buying and Selling Tools link under the "Buying and Selling Tools" heading. A listing of Seller Account options on this page includes a link to set up automatic credit card payments, print a coupon to make a payment on your account, view your current account status, request a refund for certain fees, and cash out your account if you have a credit balance.

How does eBay's fee structure compare to other auctions? Amazon's auction fee structure is very similar to eBay's and most items match eBay cent for cent. Amazon sometimes offers a lower insertion fee, but this fee is subject to change. Currently, placing an auction on Yahoo! and Excite (as well as a number of other smaller auctions) is free. However, there are also no opportunities for enhancing your auction with bold titles, featured status, or other options and the number of customers on these auctions is less. For more comparisons of auctions, see Chapter 15, "Other Auction Resources." If you're able to find a free auction that has the pulling power of eBay for your particular product, then you'll be able to save money on auction fees. However, don't be "penny wise and pound foolish." Before switching your ads to the free auctions, be sure you're able to sell your items with the same frequency and high winning bids you can get in eBay.

Receiving Credit on Fees

Although some fees on eBay are not refundable, you can recover some of your auction fees under certain circumstances. However, these credits are not automatic. You can request a full Final Value Fee credit if:

✔ The high bidder did not respond after you attempted to contact him. Allow at least seven days for the high bidder to respond.

✔ The high bidder "backed out" and did not buy the item.

✔ The high bidder's check bounced or he placed a stop payment on it.

✔ The high bidder returned the item and you issued a refund.

✔ The high bidder could not complete the auction due to family or financial emergency.

✔ The high bidder claimed terms were unacceptable.

The seller may request a partial credit for the Final Value Fee under these circumstances:

✔ The sale price was actually lower than highest bid.

✔ The high bidder backed out and you sold your item to a lower bidder at a lower price.

✔ One or more of your Dutch Auction bidders backed out of the sale.

If your auction results in any of the circumstances listed above you may contact eBay to request a Final Value Fee credit. To display information and forms necessary for receiving credit, click on the <u>Services</u> link at the top of any eBay page then click on the <u>Go Directly</u> to Buying and Selling Tools link under the "Buying and Selling Tools" heading. From the "Buying and Selling Tools" page, select the <u>Request Final Value Fee credit</u> link. Follow these instructions:

1. Wait at least seven business days for a bidder to respond to your attempts to contact him or her.

2. Fill out the Final Value Fee Credit Request Form within 60 days of the end of your auction. The link for this online form is on the "Buying and Selling Tools" page.

3. eBay will normally apply credits to your account within seven to ten business days.

4. If eBay has any questions about your Final Value Fee credit request they will contact you.

5. Be sure your credit claim is accurate and valid. Sellers who file false claims will have their eBay privileges suspended.

6. Information provided in your credit request will be used to identify Nonpaying Bidders—bidders who win auctions but don't follow through with the transaction. For more details, review eBay's Nonpaying Bidder Policy.

Your credit will be applied to your eBay fees, which you can review by clicking on the <u>Check my seller account status</u> link on the "Buyer and Sellers Tools" page.

SUMMARY

Any successful business requires some degree of management. In the Internet auction business, paying close attention to the details gives you a better chance at maximizing your profits. Your knowledge and experience in the game will give you a good chance of winning well-earned profits and a steady income. However, there is still one more set of responsibilities involved in bringing the auction to completion, and those tasks are covered in the next chapter.

Chapter **12**

Completing the Auction

Paperwork: there's no way around it. Once your auction has run its course, you've still got work to do. Fortunately, this work will bring money directly into your mailbox! All you have to do is communicate with the buyer, make sure he pays, keep track of checks, calculate postage, pack up the merchandise, and ship it. Oops, there are those details again. You can't get around the fact that you'll have to keep records. And don't think that hit-or-miss scribbles on yellow sticky notes will do the trick. But you don't need to be overwhelmed. With some simple strategies, checklists, and record keeping, you can make your auctions run like clockwork, and in time, they will bring more and more money into your banking account.

BE PREPARED WHEN THE AUCTION ENDS

Now that the auction has ended, what next? As the seller, the ball is in your court to carry the auction through to its end. However, before you start plowing ahead without a plan, take a look at the whole picture. You're going to need to keep track of the transaction and the best way to do that is to create a checklist. This checklist can either be on paper or on the computer, but it should at least contain the following information:

- ✔ Item description
- ✔ Date auction began

✔ Date auction ended

✔ Winning bid

✔ Winning bidder

✔ Date you contacted bidder

✔ Date payment received

✔ Payment type

✔ Amount of tax collected

✔ Has payment cleared?

✔ Date you sent merchandise

✔ Date you left feedback

You may also want to collect other information such as how much you paid for the item originally, how much postage cost, and so on. Keep the information you think is necessary for you to operate your business, including information for tax purposes. Then, use the information to make sure you follow through on each auction. Although most auctions will proceed without problems, you'll find that others will be plagued with missing payments, lost e-mails, and poor communication. If you don't keep accurate records, you're likely to find yourself with unhappy customers and negative feedback.

A simple way to keep your checklist is to create a list on paper, then photocopy a number of pages so you can attach all relevant information to the checklist as you gather it. Figure 12.1 shows a sample checklist you could use to keep track of your auction.

Einstein once said that you should keep things as simple as possible, but no simpler. Using that adage, you should make sure you collect and record all information about each auction, but do it as simply as possible. For example, print out the auction page as it appears on the Internet. Then, staple any correspondence about that auction (your e-mail messages to the winner, messages you receive from the winner, etc.) to that original page and make any notes about the transaction directly on the page. Keep the packet in an active auction file until everything has cleared, then file the bundle away. If you keep financial records on the computer, you can enter the pertinent information from the checklist into the computer once the transaction is complete.

Another way to simplify the end-of-auction process is to prepare the item for shipping before you receive payment. Then, when payment arrives, you can quickly paste on a mailing label and get the item in the mail. Your customer will appreciate your fast turnaround.

End of Auction Checklist
(Attach this to the copy of the auction information & correspondence)

Auction item: _____   Number: _____

Auction ended: _____   Winning Bid: $_____

❑ Check if no winner, or reserve price not met. Notes: _____

❑ Contact winner within 24 hours of end of auction Contact Date:_____

❑ Check if winner responds to the contact by e-mail. Date of reply:_____
(Attach copies of correspondence to this sheet.)

Total price: _____

Shipping   _____   How to ship? (Priority, etc.) '_____

Insurance   _____   How much? _____

Texas Tax   _____

Other   _____   What? "_____

TOTAL $_____

When was payment received? '_____

By ❑ Personal check ❑ Cash ❑ MO ❑ Charged ❑ Other? _____

If payment by check, has it cleared? '_____

Note any problems with payment (e.g., wrong amount, check bounced):

Date item was shipped to winner: _____

By ❑ Post Office ❑ UPS ❑ FedEx   Actual cost of postage: _____

Notes:

Original cost of item $ _____
Date you left feedback _____

Figure 12.1 A sample End of Auction checklist.

Corresponding with the Winning Bidder

When the auction ends you'll receive an e-mail from eBay giving you the high bidder's e-mail address. You should immediately send the buyer an e-mail telling her that she's a winner, and specifying how she should send you payment. It's best to have a standard letter already prepared that you can paste into your e-mail program, enter a few facts about the auction, and send it off. When you're holding fifty or more auctions per week, you'll appreciate any kind of automation you can use to speed up every process of the transaction. Figure 12.2 shows a sample letter template you can use over and over again by just modifying it slightly to match the current auction.

Building a Great Reputation

To encourage positive feedback, include a "please give me positive feedback" note in every package you mail. This note should contain a "thank-you" to the customer as well as instructions on how to leave positive feedback. Here's the text of a sample letter you could send to your customers:

> Dear Customer,
>
> Thanks for your purchase. We're continually putting up new auctions for 1950s toys, so please take a look every week for what we have to offer.
>
> We always leave positive feedback for our valuable customers. We'd appreciate it if you'd also leave feedback for us. To leave feedback, click on the <u>Feedback Forum</u> link at the bottom of the eBay home page, then select the item called <u>Leave Feedback about an Ebay User</u>. Our eBay User ID is "imanebay-seller." Thanks for your positive feedback and comments.
>
> Should there be any way we can improve our service, please let us know. Have a great day!
>
> Sincerely,
>
> Ima Seller

Just copy this letter on a half-sheet of paper and include it in all packages you send out. Don't leave it to individuals to think about leaving you feedback. It is true that your best customers will leave feedback automatically, but most customers need prodding. Since many users have

Dear

Congratulations! You're the winner of the auction for

Item:
Winning bid: $
(Texas residents add 8.25% sales tax) _____

Shipping: _____

Subtotal:

Total payment sent: $_____

(If you want to add insurance, let me know and I'll find out the cost.)

You may make payment by credit card, money order, or check by sending payment to:

Imanebayseller
PO Box 1169
Cedar Hill TX 75106

If you pay by credit card, please fill out the credit card information below. (For faster turnaround you can fax the payment info to 555-123-4567 or reply to this message.)

Please print this message (or your eBay notification) and include it with your payment so I can tell which auction you won. Thanks.

Thanks for bidding on this item. I hope you enjoy it. I'll ship it to you promptly when I receive your payment (or when your check clears).

eBay ID: imanebayseller   email: imaseller@dallas.net

SHIP ITEM TO: (Enter your address here)

If paying by credit card, include the following information:

Credit card type: ___ Visa ___ MC ___ American Express

Card number: _____

Exp Date: _____

Name on Card: _____

Signature: _____

Figure 12.2 Winner notification letter.

never left feedback before, these simple instructions will increase your chance of getting good feedback.

What Happens When You Can't Contact the Winner?

Occasionally your winner will give you the silent treatment. You'll send your congratulations about being a winner and you'll get no reply. What should you do? Occasionally, e-mail gets lost in cyberspace. If your winner doesn't contact you within a day or two of your initial message, send the message out again. You might tack a note on the front of your standard winner's notice.

> I tried to contact you on xx/xx/xx, but didn't receive a reply. Please let me know when you receive this notice. Thanks.

Wait a few more days for a reply. You might check out the bidder's feedback score. If he has a good score with no negatives, then he might be having some special difficulty. Perhaps he had to go on an unexpected trip. If the user has a zero score or a pattern of negatives or neutrals, your chance of seeing him honor his bid may be slim. If three more days go by and no message, send another notice with a message something like this:

> This is the third message notifying you that you were the winner on auction number #######. Please respond by xx/xx/xx to let me know if you intend to follow through on this auction. If there has been some reason you've been unable to correspond, please let me know. I would still like to close this deal with you. However, if I do not hear from you by xx/xx/xx, then I'll assume that you will not honor your bid.

You should give your customer a minimum of seven days from the end of the auction to respond to you. If after this third notice you do not hear from the bidder by the time limit you've specified then you probably have a *deadbeat bidder*. This is a bidder that has no intention to honor his bid. He may have gotten in over his head with winning bids, decided he didn't want what he won, or thinks he's having fun ruining other people's auctions. You're not going to get any money out of him, so you'd best move on to more worthwhile customers. Once you decide your bidder is a deadbeat, you have several options. If the next bidder in line had an acceptable bid you can contact him to see if he'd like the item at that price. Or, you can opt to relist the auction and claim a refund on the Final Value Fee as outlined in the previous chapter.

Deadbeat Bidder A bidder that has no intention to honor his bid. He may have gotten in over his head with winning bids, decided he didn't want what he won, or thinks he's having fun ruining other people's auctions. You're not going to get any money out of him, so you'd best move on to more worthwhile customers.

Whatever you do, don't spend hours worrying over how to handle these deadbeat bidders. They exist and you're going to get your share of them. Have a procedure in place and follow it, then move on. After giving the buyer adequate chance to respond, you have every right to leave negative feedback describing the fact that the bidder did not honor his bid. Perhaps this will save your fellow sellers from having to deal with this deadbeat.

Handling Payments

It's wonderful to see your mailbox full of payments. When you begin receiving money, you'll find that it will come in a variety of forms:

✔ **Cash** Even though no one recommends sending cash payment through the mail, you're still going to get your share of it, particularly for small items. Most people don't want to take the time to go to a store to purchase a money order and they don't want to have to wait for the check to clear for you to send them their merchandise. When you receive a cash payment, immediately count it and write down the amount on your checklist for that auction.

✔ **Money orders** Money orders are good for the seller and buyer alike. They are the ideal payment type. You can deposit them into your bank account, or if they are postal money orders you can cash them at the Post Office. For the buyer, the payment is assured so the merchandise can be sent out immediately. For the seller, the money order is cash in hand. However, if you sell items overseas you need to be wary of foreign money orders. Your bank may charge you a hefty fee to cash foreign money orders. Some banks charge $15 or more! Always insist that foreign money orders be that country's *official post office money orders* and denominated in United States funds. Since governments have mutual agreements for postal money orders, you can usually cash a foreign postal money order at a United States Post Office without paying any fee.

✔ **Cashier's check** These are checks written by a bank with the amount guaranteed. They are very reliable and you can deposit them into your checking account just as though they were normal checks. The payment will be promptly posted into your checking account, so there is no need to wait for the check to clear before sending out the merchandise.

✔ **Personal checks** Because people hate to spend their time and money buying money orders, you'll receive a number of payments by personal check. When you receive a personal check you should deposit it into your bank account *but do not ship the merchandise.* Hopefully you mentioned in your auction that the item would not be sent until payment has cleared. Therefore, you should wait until you're sure that the check payment is legitimate. You can verify that a check has cleared in several ways. If you use online banking you can check the status of the check on your computer. Some ATM machines allow you to print a statement that will tell you what checks have cleared. You can also check with the bank in person or on the phone to verify that a check has cleared. Once you've verified that the check has cleared, you can ship the merchandise.

✔ **Credit card payments** Of course a buyer can only pay by credit card if you have the ability to accept it. Credit card payments are an attractive payment option to many bidders and offering it will increase your chances of getting bids. Credit card payments usually give you quick access to your money when you deposit them into your banking account. The drawback of credit card payments is that you'll usually have to pay a fee to the credit card company for each transaction. These fees vary, but are usually in the neighborhood of 5 percent. How do you get the ability to accept credit cards? If you have a business checking account, you can apply through your bank. In fact, once you start selling on eBay you'll probably begin receiving offers from banks on how to apply for a credit card account. Watch the fees required for these accounts, since they can easily siphon off much of your profit.

✔ **CODs** Cash on Delivery is a process used by the United States Post Office that allows you to ship the merchandise without first receiving payment. The post office or your postal carrier collects the payment from the buyer and then sends you the payment by mail. CODs are no fun to use because they usually require you to make a visit to the Post Office and fill out several forms. Some sellers charge extra for CODs.

✔ **Escrow services** Another way the buyer may pay is by using an escrow service. In this case, the escrow company holds on to the payment until the buyer verifies that he's received the merchandise. Then the payment is forwarded on to the seller. Escrow services are mostly used when the transaction involves a large amount of money. (See Chapter 4, "Money Matters," for additional information on escrow services.)

You should always keep track of payments for each sale. Record cash amounts, check numbers, and keep copies of credit card transactions. These items may be important if there is a future problem with the merchandise.

What if the payment you receive is not correct? Sometimes the buyer will forget to include shipping in the total. Or perhaps you're supposed to collect sales tax and the customer left that out. Since you have the buyer's e-mail address, you should contact them immediately and request the missing amount. Have a standard e-mail letter ready to use so you won't have to write a unique letter each time. Here's some wording you could use:

Dear

Thanks for sending the payment for the eBay auction item: _____. The full payment required was $_____ ($_____ bid amount plus $_____ postage) and you sent $_____ making an outstanding difference of $_____. We've got your item ready to mail out as soon as we receive the remainder of the payment. Thanks for your prompt attention to this matter.

Sincerely,

Imaseller

Sometimes payments come to odd amounts, such as $15.12. If your buyer sends you $15 in cash, then the best course may be to forget the twelve cents and send the merchandise without further action. You'll have to make the decision about what amount of money is important enough to spend the time trying to collect it.

A harder problem to resolve is when you receive a payment in the mail with no explanation of which auction it's for. Although this sounds bizarre, it is in fact fairly common. You'll receive an envelope with a twenty-dollar bill and a note that says "Thanks." The amount won't match any particular auction and the return address doesn't even have a name. There's no way you can match the payment to an auction. What do you do? Have a standard letter ready to send such as:

Dear

Thank you for the payment of $_____, which we received on _____. We assume that this payment was for an auction you've won. However, since we process a number of auctions each week, we're unable to tell which auction your payment is for.

Please send us the following information (just fill in the blanks on this page and mail it back to us):

    Auction item: _____

    Auction number: _____

    Your name: _____

    Your e-mail address: _____

    Street address: _____

    City/State/Zip _____

With this information we will be able to determine which auction you won. We'll ship your merchandise promptly after we receive this information.

Sincerely,

Imaseller

Dealing with customer problems like this in a standard way will help you save time so you can move on to more important matters.

Shipping the Merchandise

The package you mail is the ambassador of your reputation. What you mail doesn't have to be a pretty package, but it should be sturdy. If you're using the United States Post Office's *Priority Mail* you can usually get free boxes and envelopes from them. Priority Mail is the choice for many sellers because boxes are free and delivery is usually within two days. Currently, a standard Priority Mail package that can carry up to two pounds is $3.20. This package is sufficient for many Internet auction purchases.

If you're just starting out in the "mail order" business, you may not be aware of the punishment a package can go through from your door to the buyer's. You should always package your items in boxes that seem too big. That gives you plenty of space to put packing around your item. If you're shipping a delicate item, you might consider the box-in-a-box packaging technique. That is, pack the item in a single box. Then pack that box inside a larger box—with at least an inch of packing material surrounding the inside box. Once you package your item, take a moment and shake the box. If your item shakes, it can be damaged. Try again. Giving your attention to careful packing can save you and your customer time and money.

Priority Mail   The choice shipping option for many sellers because boxes are free and delivery is usually within two days. Currently, a standard Priority Mail package that can carry up to two pounds is $3.20.

What About Insurance?

Insurance is usually offered as an option to buyers and is discussed from the buyer's point of view in Chapter 4, "Money Matters." Should it matter to you if your customer opts for insurance? What if the item is damaged on the way from your Post Office to their house? Whose fault is it? If sloppy packaging caused the item to be damaged, are you responsible for offering a refund? Most customers expect that the item is not truly theirs until it arrives in sound condition. If your item is damaged in transit you'll probably have to offer a refund. Therefore, insurance helps you as well as the buyer. If you're selling fragile merchandise or merchandise that is expensive you should strongly recommend that the buyer pay for insurance or you should build insurance into the price of shipping. For items insured for $100 or more, the United States Postal Service also offers restricted delivery and a return receipt to verify that the package arrived safely. This can also protect you against unscrupulous buyers who might try to claim damage that never occurred.

Dealing with Problem Customers

Customers come in a variety of flavors. Mostly, you'll find pleasant people who will like you and appreciate what you've sold to them. However, a small percentage of your customers will not be happy. Perhaps this problem customer does not like what you sent him. It was the wrong shade of blue or the scratch in the side was bigger than he expected. Whatever the reason, he'll want his money back, and his e-mails to you may be threatening and full of anger. Before you blow a fuse, try to evaluate his situation to see if he's got a good cause for his unhappiness. Successful business people will tell you that in the long run, if a customer is unhappy for *any* reason, then you should offer an immediate refund once the merchandise is returned. Don't try to match threat for threat. That will only escalate the problem and take away your valuable time from other matters that can help you make money. You're going to lose a little money on this situation so minimize its impact quickly and get it over with.

On rare occasions, your problem customer will be an outright criminal. His complaint will be trumped up. For example, he may have purchased a Superman comic book in mint condition. Now he claims it is not as described and he wants his money back. You offer him a refund but when you get the comic book back it is in much poorer condition than when you sent it out. What happened? It's the old switcharoo trick. He's sending you a different copy back for a refund expecting that he can keep the good mint condition copy for himself. How can you prove him wrong? It's always an excellent idea to keep a detailed photograph or photocopy of your merchandise (particularly if it is a collectible) just in case something like this happens. In fact, since you've probably already taken one or more pictures of your item for use in the auction, you should have something to compare with what he sent back. If possible, keep serial numbers of items you send out. If it will not damage the item, you can even place a small mark on the item that could be used to identify it in the future. For example, there are pens available that will write with ink that can only be read in ultraviolet light. If you mark your merchandise in this way, you can identify it easily if it is returned. Just be sure your security measures don't damage the merchandise. If your merchandise is returned, you should be able to identify it positively with your marks or with a photograph.

If you feel that a customer is committing fraud, you should contact your postmaster. The customer may have committed a federal offense, and your action may be able to prevent this criminal from stealing money or merchandise from other sellers. (For more information on auction frauds, see Chapter 13, "Controlling Risks.")

USING AUCTIONS TO
INCREASE YOUR OTHER BUSINESS

If you have an ongoing retail business where you sell items similar to what you sell at auction, then you should promote your retail business to your Internet customers. Do you have a printed catalog or price list? It should be placed in every package you send out. If you have a web site selling your products, then you should use every piece of correspondence, whether e-mail or regular mail, to advertise your site. Depending on the restrictions of the auction site, you can even place a link directly from your auction to information on your web site. Although eBay allows you to place links on your auctions, there are some restrictions. You are not allowed to have links to:

✔ other auction sites

✔ sites offering the same merchandise for the same or lower price

✔ sites offering merchandise prohibited on eBay

As long as you meet these requirements you can allow users to know that you offer similar merchandise at your normal web site by placing a link to it on all of your auctions. Even if you don't have a web site, you can still provide information about yourself and your business on your personal eBay "About Me" page. Place instructions in your auction ad that tell users how to click on the **me** ("About Me") icon for more information. (Refer to Chapter 1, "Getting Started," for instructions on creating a personal page.)

Most mail-order houses consider their *customer database* their biggest asset. It is a list that can always be used to create sales. What exactly is a customer database? It is a collection of customer names, addresses, and buying interests. You can use this database to target future sales to people who are already proven to be willing mail-order customers. Once you sell to a customer, he will recognize your business and may be willing to order from you again. Therefore, you should keep a list of all of your customers and store their e-mail addresses and postal addresses in a database. Then you can use this information periodically to promote future sales.

Customer Database   A collection of customer names, addresses, and buying interests. Sellers use this database to target future sales to people who are already proven to be willing mail-order customers.

SUMMARY

Plan ahead and have procedures ready for all of the tasks you'll need to perform at the end of the auction. A little preparation will make the process go smoothly and quickly and will allow you to spend more time creating more auctions. The result of your work will be money in your mailbox. In an ideal world that would be all there is to operating an Internet auction business. However, in today's world, you have to be aware of problems that may arise and threaten to take a bite out of your profit. The next chapter will help you identify and avoid many of these risks.

Chapter

Controlling Risks

I nternet commerce exploded onto the business scene so fast that no one could have been prepared for its impact. This new industry is changing quickly as it grows. It's bubbling over with opportunity, but it's also chock full of risk. Not only have entrepreneurs been lured by the Internet's possibilities, every charlatan, swindler, and con artist in the world (it seems) is looking for ways to use the Web to defraud you out of your money. Some of these crooks are professionals who've moved their mail and telephone fraud activity onto the Internet. Others are amateurs who think they can apply their shoplifting skills to a new venue. Your best protection against the wily ways of these scoundrels is to know what kinds of cons to expect and to have a defense against them.

TOP TEN FRAUDS FOR BUYERS TO AVOID

Most Internet auction sellers are honest. However, you've got to watch out for the few swindlers whose main goal is to cheat you out of your hard-earned cash. Here's a list of the top ten frauds that buyers should watch out for. If you believe one of these events is happening to you, report the activity to your auction's security department (for example, safe harbor@ebay.com).

10. **Shilling** In this scam, a seller works with a coconspirator to get the most out of your proxy bid. For example, suppose you

place a $100 bid on an item whose current high bid is at $35. If no one else bids on this item, you'd win it for the $35. However, if the seller suspects that you've placed a higher (proxy) bid, then he'll have his coconspirator bid up the price little by little until he outbids your limit. Then the coconspirator will retract his last bid making your bid of $100 the high bid. You've had $65 stolen out of your pocket! Keep a close watch on the auctions you're bidding on. If you see your proxy bid going up and up until you are outbid—only to find out that you're *still* the top bidder, then suspect shilling. If there's time before the end of the auction, you may also want to retract your own bid.

9. **Internet pickpockets** When an auction ends and you're the winning bidder, you'll typically get an e-mail from the seller telling you how you can pay. Some sly criminals have come up with the idea to beat the legitimate seller to the punch and to send you a fake message telling you to send your money to them instead. If you send your cash or money order to the wrong person, it may be hard to get your money back. Look at the return e-mail address from the seller to make sure it isn't from some other person trying to pull a fast one on you.

8. **Staged bidding wars** In this version of bid inflation, a buyer has one or two other accomplices try to begin a bidding war. If the buyer finds a willing participant, he and his accomplices will continue to escalate the price until the legitimate buyer (you) no longer raises his bid. Then the fake bidders will retract their high bids leaving you as the high bidder.

7. **Counterfeit feedback** It's fairly easy for a group of chums to give each other positive feedback to build up reputations. While you're examining a seller's feedback, look to see if those leaving positive feedback are all from the same e-mail host such as something@hotmail.com. This is a clue that the feedback may have been faked. If a seller is faking his feedback, then he's likely up to no good with what he's selling.

6. **Misrepresented merchandise** Many collectibles are valued according to their condition. If an item contains damage, it can severely decrease its value. Honest sellers will describe damage in detail and may even include pictures of the damage within the ad. You should keep a copy of the auction ad, including pictures, to compare to what you receive. If your merchandise in-

cludes damage that was not described, then you should ask for a refund.

5. **Dutch Auction bid inflation** Dutch Auctions are a little hard to understand and some sellers use this to their advantage. Suppose you bid $15 in a Dutch Auction and end up being one of several winners. The lowest winning bid on the auction is $12. However, the seller sends you a notice telling you that you won the auction for $15. He's trying to get an extra $3 of your money. In a Dutch Auction, every winner pays the same amount—the lowest winning bid.

4. **Imitations and incorrect grading** Watch out for fakes in every type of merchandise—coins, art, toys, watches, clothing, autographs, and so on. The most common frauds you'll see are reproductions being sold as the real thing, altered merchandise, and incorrectly graded collectibles. For example, a rare coin that is reported to be an MS-70 grade when it is actually an MS-65 can be overvalued by hundreds of dollars. Fortunately, in coin collecting you can get a definitive answer about a coin's true grade from a professional grading organization (PCGS: Professional Coin Grading Service). However, since grading is usually subjective, dishonest sellers will tend to inflate the value of their merchandise by overgrading it. Always look for some reliable source that can help you prove that what you're purchasing is real. If you have no proof, then you must base your belief on the honesty of the seller (and she may have been duped earlier into believing the item is real). If possible, arrange for an independent opinion of the authenticity of the item before finalizing the deal. The best defense against this problem is to know your seller, pay attention to her feedback, and get a second opinion about the grade of the item.

3. **A wolf in sheep's clothing** The picture looked good and the ad was appealing but when your merchandise arrives it's not what you thought it would be. Some unscrupulous sellers will put a picture of a brand-new item in their auction ad when the item they are actually selling is used. These sellers realize that most people will not bother to return merchandise even if they're dissatisfied with it. However, if you feel that you've been sent fraudulent merchandise you should contact the seller for a refund. If he will not cooperate, you should report the incident to

your auction's security and consider leaving negative feedback for the seller.

2. **Vaporware products** In this scheme the seller never really has possession of the item he's advertising for sale. Typically he'll be holding an auction for some very popular item such as a rare Ty Beanie Baby or the latest and hottest Christmas toy. Bidders are too excited about getting the product to notice that the seller has no track record. You send your money and get nothing in return. When you try to contact the seller you find that he has a very low or negative feedback score, he's no longer at his stated location, and he's left no forwarding address. Kiss your money good-bye.

1. **Creative Shipping Charges** Before you bid on any auction, pay close attention to shipping and handling charges. Sometimes these charges can be greater than the value of the merchandise itself. Honest sellers will quote a flat price for delivery or at least a price range. If the seller doesn't specify shipping charges, you may wind up being billed for postage, box, packing materials, ad insertion fee, labor, and so on. If you think you're being overcharged for postage and handling, try to negotiate shipping charges to postage only. In the vast majority of cases, charges beyond postage should never be over a dollar unless the buyer asks for special services, such as COD or insurance.

If you're concerned about a seller, you should check him out thoroughly. Look at his feedback. Send him an e-mail and ask about his product. Does he have proof of its authenticity? Is there any additional damage not shown in the pictures? If he's a serious seller, then he should answer promptly. If he doesn't answer at all, then pass up the item. If he does answer, evaluate what he says. Is he being honest and straightforward, or is he dancing around your questions? If you feel uncomfortable about the seller, avoid his auctions. If you end up purchasing a valuable item from a buyer you don't fully trust, you can protect yourself by paying for the item through an escrow service. (These services were discussed in Chapter 4, "Money Matters.")

Some auction sites are concerned enough about fraud that they are beginning to offer buyer's insurance. Amazon.com protects buyers from fraudulent sellers with an Auctions Guarantee program for all items under $250. If a buyer pays for an item and it is never delivered, or it is materially different from the one advertised, they will refund the buyer's money.

eBay guarantees purchases up to $200 in value (with a $25 deductible) through its SafeHarbor insurance system.

TOP TEN FRAUDS FOR SELLERS TO AVOID

Buyers aren't the only potential victims in Internet auctions. Just like retailers have to protect themselves against shoplifters, auction sellers need to protect themselves against sneaky criminals who try to defraud them out of their profits. Here's a list of the top ten frauds that sellers should watch out for.

10. **Switch and return** A buyer returns an item to you claiming dissatisfaction and wanting a refund. However, the item returned is not the exact item you sent to the buyer. The returned item might be a similar product with damage, a coin of a lesser grade, or a Ty Beanie Baby missing its tag. If you have no way to positively identify the returned item, you'll have a hard time justifying not providing a refund. Always keep detailed photos and records of every item you sell.

9. **Bid protection** This scam requires three players. One person will place a low bid on an item and will be quickly followed by two partners who place large bids on the item. You get excited because your auction is about to make more money than you could have imagined. Then, just seconds before the auction ends, the high bidders retract their bids, leaving the old low bid as the new high bid. The auction ends and you are stuck having to sell your item for a very low winning bid.

8. **Stopped payments** It's always wise to wait until a buyer's check clears before sending out his merchandise. Otherwise, the buyer can cancel his check, leaving you with no payment. Or, the check could be bogus in the first place. In either case you're likely to never see your money.

7. **Credit card fraud** In your exuberance to accept credit cards, always remember that they are not like money in the bank. You should always call your credit card provider to verify purchases before you send out the merchandise. If you wait for a few days and check the card only after you've sent out the merchandise, then you've set yourself up for a problem. What if the credit card is no good or stolen? Another potential problem to be aware of is that unhappy buyers have the ability to cancel a

charge. Check with your agreement to see what your remedies and responsibilities are if this happens.

6. **Purloined packages** What happens when a buyer calls you up a week after you've sent off her item and she says she's never received it? You're in a pickle if you don't have any proof that you sent the merchandise in the first place. Some sellers insist that anything over a certain value (such as $50) be sent with insurance that requires a signature. When your package requires that the buyer sign before taking delivery, then you have proof that the merchandise arrived.

5. **Used and returned** Beware of selling products that can be copied and used, then returned. CDs (music and software) and some videos can be copied. Some tickets, phone cards, and other cards with information on a magnetic strip can be used and then returned—either with a claim that they weren't used or with a claim that they didn't contain what you promised. Sometimes these cards have serial numbers on them; if you think you sold a legitimate card that was used and returned, you might be able to get the issuing company to give you records of when the card was last used.

4. **The hurry-up ploy** If you sell a dated item, beware of the buyer who must have it immediately. Suppose your high bidder is purchasing a ticket, and he's leaving town in just four days. There may not be time for you to receive his payment and then send him the tickets. "Can't you please just send it today? I promise that your payment is in the mail! I'll even throw in a few extra bucks." Don't be caught up in someone else's time troubles. Stick with your standard business model and don't be drawn into the hurry-up trap.

3. **Extortion** It sounds bizarre but some buyers will threaten you to try to make you sell your item at a certain price or under certain conditions. If you don't do as they say, they'll make sure you get ten negative feedbacks (or something just as obnoxious). If you ever get this kind of message, keep a copy of the e-mail you received and send it to your Internet auction's security personnel. Users caught making threats of this nature will often be immediately suspended from further participation in the auction site.

2. **Bid siphoning** This is the process that unscrupulous sellers use to make money from your customers. They contact people

bidding on your item and offer to sell a similar item to them at a price lower than the current bid. You may never know about this unless an honest buyer makes you aware of it. If this happens, get as much evidence as you can (e-mails) and send it to your Internet auction security personnel.

1. **Vanishing buyers** Because there are so many new people entering the Internet auction market, you're going to run into a few that don't really have a clue that bidding is a commitment. They bid without thinking and then when they win, they panic. Instead of trying to work it out with you, they will simply become invisible. They won't answer e-mail. In fact, with e-mail accounts being free and easy to get, they'll probably change their e-mail account and you'll never hear from them again.

For cases when a buyer fails to follow up on his purchase, your only recourse may be to relist your item and apply for a refund of your eBay Final Value Fee. When you request a credit for a sale that was not completed due to nonpayment by the bidder, the bidder faces automatic consequences for not completing the transaction. Bidders reported for nonpayment via eBay's automated online credit request system face the following warnings and suspensions:

1. First offense: warning
2. Second offense: warning
3. Third offense: warning and 30 day suspension
4. Fourth offense: indefinite suspension

As an honest seller, it helps you and your fellow sellers if you properly report buyers who are misusing the system.

CONTROLLING BUSINESS RISKS

Two people are given the same opportunities for starting a business. One makes a million dollars and the other loses his shirt. What caused the difference? It could have been the choice of what merchandise to sell, how to sell it, what kind of service to offer customers, or a host of other subtle factors. Business is inherently risky. It constantly requires attention. Those who pay attention to the details of business can lower their risks and keep their profits growing.

Although success strategies have been studied by many researchers, so far no one has discovered a fail-safe formula. However, there are a few characteristics of successful men and women in business that can help any enterprise reduce risk and achieve success. These characteristics, as applied to the Internet auction business, are:

- ✔ **Know the marketplace.** Internet auctions are a new and evolving phenomenon. This book gives you a basic understanding of how they work, but you must continue to watch the marketplace to determine how ongoing changes will affect your chances for success.

- ✔ **Understand the buyer's desires and motives.** Know your customers. The most successful sellers are usually those who concentrate on a single niche. They know their merchandise well and know who wants to buy it. This gives them the ability to write meaningful and enticing ads, keep customers happy and coming back for more, and reduce returns and complaints.

- ✔ **Keep fresh and enthusiastic.** Internet auction purchases are usually for fun items, not the necessities of life. Therefore, keep your auctions upbeat and entertaining. Keep your e-mails lighthearted and make your customer feel comfortable working with you.

- ✔ **Pay attention to details.** Run your business. Never let your business run you. Have procedures and strategies defined, in place and ready to use for every type of situation you can think of. That way the day-to-day operation of your business can be made routine, allowing you to use your creativity and energies for growth.

- ✔ **Persevere.** Business is a competition and those who put up more auctions, sell better quality merchandise, create more enticing ads, and treat customers better than anyone else will be the winners. Many now-successful businesses began as small enterprises that were constantly pushed forward by the energy and vision of one person.

What will you do with the current opportunities available in Internet auctions? The field is young enough and ripe enough for innovation so that anyone can step in and become a major player. It doesn't require a college degree or a background in business. If you can discipline yourself to learn all you can about Internet auctions and enthusiastically follow reasonable business practices, then you'll be able to control your risks and enjoy a successful business.

SUMMARY

Your best defense against fraud and your best strategy for success is knowledge. Keep a watchful eye on the Internet auction marketplace. Beware of criminals who are out to make a quick buck. Hang out in chat rooms and learn about how to avoid new scams. Continue to research other auctions to see what's selling and what's not. Control your own risks by operating your business with honesty and good judgment, and you'll be able to make your enterprise into whatever you want it to become.

Chapter

14

Making a Living on Internet Auctions

P eople sell products on Internet auctions for a variety of reasons. Some sellers use Internet auctions as an electronic garage sale, some use it to buy and sell items for their personal collections, and some use it to generate ongoing income. Those who decide to make a business of Internet auctions take their selling to a different and higher level than those who do it as a hobby. In previous chapters you've seen how to identify and acquire goods to sell, how to operate an auction, and how to deal with customers. This chapter is about using those skills every day to develop income that can supplement your current job or business or even provide you with a full-time income.

LEARNING FROM THE EXPERTS

One of the best ways to build a new Internet auction business is to learn how other successful people have done it. The following stories illustrate how a few sellers were able to make it to the big time. (A few names and circumstances have been changed slightly in these stories.) For some of these sellers, their business provides a good supplemental income and for others it is their primary source of income. These stories illustrate just a sample of the variety of people that have started businesses as a result of Internet auctions. There are still plenty of products to sell and plenty of ideas to try out.

The Movie Guy

John liked movies. His story begins a few years ago when he was looking for a particular movie titled *Electric Dreams* (a 1984 comedy about a love triangle between a man, a woman, and a computer). As he was browsing around his local video store, he found a prerented copy of the movie for $5. Curious about what it would sell for on e-Bay, he was surprised to find copies of the same movie selling for $15 to $20. This gave him an idea. He bought several more of the prerented movies, put them on eBay, and made a tidy profit. That was just the beginning. John located other sources of videos and purchased them from video stores, individuals, and at auctions. In fact, he eventually bought out most of the stock of his local video store when they went out of business. He's now sold more than a thousand videos on eBay and his business continues to grow.

What does John recommend for new eBay sellers? Specialize in selling products you know something about. One of the factors he thinks makes his video business successful is that he specializes in tapes that are out of print. He recommends that you offer a product you know people will want, give them plenty of good information about the item, include a picture in the ad, and be completely honest about its condition. In dealing with customers you should always be courteous, answer all questions promptly, have a quick turnaround, invite your customers to come back to your auctions again, leave positive feedback for good buyers, and ask your customers to leave positive feedback for you. His favorite sale was to a young couple who had watched a particular Disney movie every year at Christmastime. When they began to have kids they went looking for the out-of-print movie and finally found it in one of John's auctions. It made someone's Christmas very special and gave him a warm feeling as well.

The College Student

Valerie was attending college in the United States, but since she was a foreign student, she couldn't get a job. However, after studying the situation, she began looking around for some way to make a few bucks. That's when she discovered eBay. Now all she needed was something to sell. Fortunately, there was an off-price bookstore that sold new books for $5 or less. Economics taught her that if she could sell these books for more than she paid for them, she could make a profit. Therefore, she purchased a few books and began an auction business. Within six months, she'd sold several hundred books and had made $6,000 profit. Not bad for a part-time job!

Valerie recommends that you keep track of your sales by printing out the auction page for each auction and putting it in a binder. Also print out your list of auctions (which you can display from My eBay) and mark this list when you receive payments. This will help you see who has paid and who hasn't. Valerie also recommends that you leave positive feedback for every customer and encourage them to leave you positive feedback as well. However, if you run across a deadbeat customer, just lick your wounds and go on. Be wary of leaving negative feedback for these customers because they will often retaliate and leave you negative feedback. It's not worth it to damage your reputation as a seller. To help build up repeat business, Valerie keeps a growing list of customers and e-mails them about new auctions she thinks they might be interested in. They don't teach this kind of stuff in college!

The Elvis Impersonator

Elvis is alive and well on eBay. Rumor has it that he operates his Internet auction business out of the basement at Graceland and goes by the name of Tim. His story begins in 1996. The King was operating a video store when he first found out about eBay. At this time, there were only a few thousand eBay auctions being held each day. Elvis, being the innovator that he is, experimented by selling a few videos, antiques, and other items. His ads were more than just vanilla descriptions. They were lighthearted and humorous. For example, to spice up the description for a cooking pot he'd picked up at a thrift store in Frank Sinatra's old neighborhood, he wondered if maybe Frank had eaten out of it years ago. Who knows? It made interesting reading at least. After he'd sold everything he could find in his basement, Elvis began looking for more merchandise. In the evenings, he drove his 1959 Cadillac El Dorado to local antique auctions. He'd purchase a trunk full of items and sell them the next week for a considerable profit. However, as eBay grew (and more antique dealers began selling on eBay) it became harder to find wholesale antiques. As a result, Elvis had to diversify into other categories. He purchased a few men's ties at a flea market, and when they sold well, he began finding other wholesale sources for ties. Now he sells dozens a week. In total, Elvis has sold over 10,000 items and ranks as an eBay superstar in anyone's books.

In a recent rare interview, Elvis gave some advice to new eBay sellers. Sellers who make a full-time living on eBay usually work twelve hours a day, seven days a week. (Which is one reason he hasn't had time to do any concerts lately.) In order to work efficiently, make your job as easy as possible. Sell items that are easy to mail and hard to break. Because most of the purchases on eBay are for fun items, keep your auctions and corre-spondence lighthearted and humorous. Relax. Don't get hung up on the occasional buyer who is slow to pay or who never pays. If you have a problem with a buyer, do one follow-up e-mail and then move on. When shipping items, use the United States Post Office and insure everything that's expensive. If you have an unhappy customer, just refund their money quickly and move on. What kind of product sells best? Elvis rec-ommends that you stay away from everyday merchandise. Find something with character—something stupid, nostalgic, or cute. Create an obviously fictionalized story about its history—like the antique Christmas ornament that *might* have hung on Santa's tree at the North Pole. However, always under-describe your products so the buyer will be pleasantly surprised at how good the item really is. This creates goodwill and repeat customers. Make the experience fun for the buyer and always treat him with the kind of respect you'd want to receive.

The Father and Son

John was playing poker one night in January 1998 when a friend told him about Internet auctions. At that time he'd worked in the hardware busi-ness for 20 years and also had experience selling a variety of products at gun shows. The concept of selling products through an Internet auction intrigued him. After studying the situation, he decided to jump into this new e-business with both feet. He purchased a computer and signed up with eBay in March 1998. He took "Omaha" as his eBay ID, which is the name of the particular poker game he'd been playing when he first heard about eBay. It took John about a month to figure out how to put pictures in his ads, but once he got the process down, he started selling like wild-fire. Using his knowledge of hardware suppliers, John was able to pur-chase an ongoing supply of items to sell. After a little more than a year on eBay, John was holding 500 to 600 auctions and making about $35,000 in sales every month. To supplement his sales on eBay, John maintains a web site called closeoutsupply.com where he sells his merchandise directly to users. All of this has made John so busy that he recently had to build a new workshed in his backyard and hire a few people to help him handle the workload.

John has helped several other people get started in their own Inter-net auction businesses and he has a few tips for new sellers. His first rec-ommendation is to get a good digital camera because a good picture is a necessity for selling your items. John's second suggestion is that you need to create effective titles for your auction ads. Without a good ad title, you'll never bring buyers to your auction. He also recommends that you concentrate on selling items you're interested in and know something about. When you look for items to sell, buy them as close to the source as you can. If you're buying domestic products, buy from the factory. If you're buying imports, buy them from the primary importer. Never use the Reserve Auction feature, only charge your customer the postage required to send the product, leave your customers positive feedback, and ask them for the same. It's worked for John—he was recently listed as having the third highest feedback rating of any eBay seller. John uses the Quicken software program to keep up with his sales, but he doesn't spend time trying to trace down deadbeat customers—he's too busy processing orders for those who come through with payments. John sees a bright future for Internet auctions with eBay continuing to be the leader. His bets for the second best auction sites are Yahoo! and AuctionUniverse.

Shortly after John began selling on eBay, his son John H. (eBay ID "Widget") followed suit. However, Widget conducts his business a little differently. Since Widget is more comfortable using computers than his dad, he's taken a more automated approach to this business. Instead of entering ads by hand, Widget uses eBay's Mister Lister feature to upload ads in bulk. Because Widget operates his eBay business as a supplement to his full-time job, he's tried to simplify each transaction. For example, he charges a flat postage and handling fee ($3.50) on every sale. He also offers customers the opportunity to pay for the transaction through a secure web site (where the customer can also select other items to purchase at the same time). After sending the merchandise and before filing away the paperwork, Widget automatically leaves positive feedback for his customer. The results are impressive. Working only part-time, Widget has been able to amass a feedback record that puts him in the top twenty-five eBay sellers.

The Nurse Turned Entrepreneur

Susie is a nurse who found herself on the other side of a needle. While recuperating from an illness in the spring of 1997 she started surfing the Internet. A new and smallish site that intrigued her was eBay. She studied information about how to buy and sell merchandise through auctions and decided it would be a fun activity she could do while she recovered. But what could she sell? After considering a number of the categories she decided that pottery appealed to her. Since she knew little about it, she took a self-guided crash course to find out what types were popular and how they should be graded. Purchasing pottery from local auctions and estates, Susie's business quickly prospered. In fact, it wasn't long until she was making more on eBay than she was as a nurse. Over the past two years she's had to become more creative about finding items to sell since so many people are discovering eBay.

Today, Susie manages to hold about 50 auctions a week under the eBay ID "susie-n-texas." Her advice to new sellers is to operate your business with the philosophy that the customer comes first. You never know who might be a repeat customer. Keep in mind that customers "recommend" you with their positive feedback. Susie is very customer-oriented, and it shows. In her two years she's never received a bad check. Although she does have a few buyers each month that don't come through with payments, most of her clientele are prompt and friendly. Since she deals with valuable and breakable items, she takes extra care in packaging her merchandise. She double-boxes her items and prefers to send them through the United States Post Office. Using this technique, she's experienced very few instances of breakage. She charges her customers postage plus some packaging costs. To insure safe passage for some of her fragile items, she sometimes has to charge for special packaging materials. However, if she finds that she's charged too much for handling she sends a refund check to her customer for the overcharge amount. Operating her eBay business keeps Susie very busy and she sometimes needs help to get all the work done. But in the long run, it's been more fun than giving shots and emptying bedpans.

CREATING AN ONGOING INTERNET AUCTION BUSINESS

You've surely heard the old adage *"buy low and sell high."* That's exactly what these entrepreneurs have done. They find items they can purchase at wholesale prices and sell at close to retail. However, the key to their achievement is not just in finding a few items they can sell at a profit, but in finding an ongoing supply. Another old maxim in the retail business is *"replicate success."* It is critical to your success that you find some money-making system that you can replicate.

Buy Low, Sell High Principle   Find items you can purchase at wholesale prices and sell at close to retail. The key to success is not just in finding a few items you can sell for a profit, but in finding an ongoing supply of these items.

Replicating success means that once you find a business process that works, you do it over and over again for as long as the process is viable and makes a profit. For example, you shouldn't have to figure out on each new auction if a $1 opening bid will bring in bidders or not. Experience will teach you one way or the other. You shouldn't have to figure out the best way to mail each product. You'll already have a standard, quick, and inexpensive way to do it. You shouldn't have to come up with clever new ways to create a winning auction ad. You should know the information that it takes to sell what you offer. The bottom line is this—if you can standardize your business operation, you'll save yourself time, money, and headaches.

Replicate Success   Once you find a business process that works, you do it over and over again for as long as the process is viable and makes a profit.

For example, when the folks at McDonald's cook french fries they don't just toss a handful of frozen fries into the grease and watch them until they look done. They have a *prescribed* amount of fries that they cook at a *prescribed* temperature for a *prescribed* amount of time. Because they do the same process over and over again, they get consistent results. Your strategy for creating an ongoing business should be to come up with similar procedures that will consistently bring you profitable sales. Once you discover your own formula for selling items, replicate it as many times as you can. Use 80 percent of your energy to milk your successful procedures as long as possible. Use the other 20 percent to experiment with a few other items to see if you can come up with another star seller you can replicate. In this way, you'll stay on track with your best sellers while hedging your bet for the future.

SUMMARY

There are two major components to making a business out of Internet auctions. First, you must find a category of items that you can purchase cheaply and sell for a profit. Secondly, you must be able to successfully repeat similar auctions over and over again. Once you've come up with these two elements, your success will only be dependent upon your willingness to spend the time and energy to make it happen.

Other Auction Resources

Although eBay is the clear leader in general Internet auctions there are hundreds of other auctions available online. A few of the other auctions offer substantial opportunities for buyers and sellers, but many others are small and struggle to attract new participants. As you look for auction venues that fit your buying or selling needs, you may consider looking beyond eBay to see what these other sites offer. For sellers, you may also want to look at auction resource sites for help on building your own auction business. This chapter describes some of the major auction sites and resources available to you on the Internet.

POPULAR OPEN AUCTIONS

Open auctions offer the mostvariety of merchandise. Because they allow individual sellers to place auctions there is no limit to the imagination of what can be sold. However, because these auctions are so diverse, they often don't have the ability to really specialize in a particular item. eBay, Yahoo!, and Amazon are the three most popular auctions in this category. There are a number of other emerging auctions that also fit this bill. Buyers and sellers alike should visit each of these sites to determine which of these auctions best serve their particular scope of interests. Some of the notable open auction sites (in alphabetical order) are:

✔ **Amazon (auctions.amazon.com)** If you've purchased anything from the Amazon bookstore in the past, you're already registered for Amazon's auction. (You will be given the opportunity to select a User ID and password to use for bidding.) Not surprisingly, Amazon is strong in books, although it still does not have as many at auction as eBay. Another way Amazon is attracting business is with alliances to established sellers. For example, the famous Sotheby's auction house has teamed up with Amazon to offer authenticated fine art in Amazon auctions.

✔ **Auctionaddict (auctionaddict.com)** This site is similar to the eBay auction model. Sellers and buyers must register before participating. However, Auctionaddict does not charge sellers a listing fee, only a fee when the item sells. It also goes beyond the realm of auctions and allows you to create an electronic storefront where you can sell items directly to consumers without the auction format.

✔ **AuctionUniverse (auctionuniverse.com)** Although this site is much smaller than eBay, it is growing and holds promise because it is liked by both sellers and buyers. Several of the site's strongest categories are collectibles, automobiles, and jewelry. AuctionUniverse offers collectible editorial content from trusted sources such as White's Guide to Collectibles and ToyFair in its Collector Hubs. The site has extensive and easy-to-access help pages and impressive search capabilities. AuctionUniverse is owned by the Classified Ventures and was recently affiliated with *USA Today*.

✔ **CityAuction (cityauction.com)** The purpose of CityAuction is to enable buyers and sellers to find each other in their own geographical region. It has several thousand auctions daily, a small inventory, and no presence in some categories. CityAuction is owned by Ticketmaster.

✔ **eBay (ebay.com)** This site has millions of items at auction all the time. It allows you to sell your own merchandise. Registration on eBay is free. Merchandise is placed at auction by individuals or businesses. Auctions last seven days, although some last three, five, or ten days. Most items sold are single quantity, although some auctions are for multiple items—these are called Dutch Auctions. Once an auction is won, it is up to the buyer and seller to arrange payment and shipping. eBay never has possession of the merchandise—it only acts as the auction host. Users can leave feedback about one another, and in this way, you can determine if a buyer or seller has consistently been prompt and business-like in his transactions. eBay began as a site for Pez collectors and has retained a collector's bent since its beginning, even though its offerings now include such diverse items as mobile homes, jewelry, and computers. If you're looking for a unique item or a collectible, eBay should be the first place you look. eBay has the widest variety of any auction on the Web.

✔ Excite (auctions.excite.com) This site is also patterned after eBay in many ways. You must register to buy or sell. Excite supports an "AutoBidder" similar to eBay's proxy bids. One difference in the Excite auction is the use of the extended end-of-auction feature. This means that if there is a bid within the last ten minutes of the auction's end, then the auction is automatically extended by another ten minutes. This prevents "sniping" and allows live bidders to continue to bid against one another until all but one gives up. Excite began as a search engine site but it has grown to include a number of shopping links, chat rooms, and financial resources.

✔ FairMarket Network (www.fairmarket.com) This is collection of private-label merchants, portals, and online community auction sites connected through a shared database of goods and services. The FairMarket Network is a marketplace for both vendors selling new and refurbished high-quality merchandise as well as a collection of person-to-person auctions. Major auction sites that have teamed up with FairMarket include AltaVista, MSN (Microsoft), Excit, and Lycos. Some of the private merchants who sell goods at auction through the FairMarket network include Bid1Travel, CompUSA, Damark, Dell, Outposts, VH-1, and others. This network gives users access to several auctions at once, including both open and store auctions. If successful, it could eventually become the primary competitor to eBay.

✔ Gold's Auction (goldsauction.com) This is a friendly auction site featuring general merchandise, good auction support, and a chat room. Its auctions and rules are similar to eBay's.

✔ Yahoo! (auctions.yahoo.com) This site is second only to eBay in terms of the number of users and variety of items offered. Yahoo! used its popular search engine site to tap into a large market of users, resulting in a large and well-run auction site. One way that Yahoo! differs from eBay is that it requires that sellers enter a credit card number in order to be able to sell. This additional identification for sellers is meant to be a deterrent for unscrupulous dealers. Yahoo! has great search capabilities and a list of categories only rivaled by eBay.

Although eBay is by far the most dominant of all Internet auction sites, several other sites continue to vie for the auction dollar. The strong sites such as Amazon and Yahoo! will directly compete with eBay, but many of the other sites may have to find some unique way to challenge the leader. For example, some of the smaller auctions may choose to combine forces in the future. For additional information on other auction sites, refer to "Additional Auction Resources" later in this chapter.

POPULAR STORE AUCTIONS

As described in Chapter 1, Store Auctions are operated by a business with the primary purpose of selling its own merchandise. More and more businesses are learning that they can reach a large audience and sell items at close to retail prices by putting their merchandise on Web auctions. The advantage to the buyer is that all of the transaction takes place directly with the online store. You don't have to worry about contacting the seller and negotiating terms. Online Store Auctions almost always accept credit cards and offer some kind of warranty. The top online Store Auctions (in alphabetical order) are:

- ✔ **Bid.com (bid.com)** Canada's largest store auction site specializes in computers, digital cameras, jewelry, sports equipment, and home electronics. Ships products both in Canada and the United States. Products are mostly new or refurbished.

- ✔ **DealDeal (dealdeal.com)** This is a consignment auction that features consumer electronics. Virtually all of the items are new, and there are usually multiple items for sale in each auction. You must join in order to bid and you must give them credit card information. When you win an auction, your payment goes directly to DealDeal. You are essentially buying from a retailer and one advantage is that you're offered some technical support for your purchase.

- ✔ **Egghead (surplusauction.com)** This site features new and refurbished computer equipment as well as consumer electronics, jewelry, and home and garden products. To register to bid, you must include a credit card number. Most Egghead auctions have multiple quantities for each item auctioned, so you can indicate with your bid how many of an item you want. A number of Egghead's auctions are daily, so there are typically a number of new items for sale every day. It is difficult to evaluate the sales on Egghead since it does not routinely post the winning prices on completed auctions. You also cannot tell who is bidding or how many of the quantity have been specified in previous bids. However, many products purchased from Egghead retain some warranty, from a 30 day mail-in warranty (typically on refurbished devices) to full factory warranties on some new merchandise. Egghead began as a computer retailer in 1984 and made the transition over to an Internet-only business in 1998. Go to Egghead when you want a bargain on new or refurbished computers or consumer electronics, and when you want to pay by credit card.

✔ **Onsale (onsale.com)** This site offers mostly consumer electronics, sports and fitness products, and travel packages. If you are a manufacturer or dealer, you can also arrange to sell items through the Onsale auction site.

✔ **uBid (ubid.com)** This auction house features excess, refurbished, and new merchandise (mostly consumer electronics) through live-auction bidding. uBid's Internet storefront displays a continuously-evolving inventory of products. It is owned by Creative Computers.

WHAT AUCTION SITE HAS WHAT YOU'RE LOOKING FOR?

With so many auction sites available, how do you know which site contains the types of items you're looking for? There is no single answer. However, the following information will help you understand what kind of products may be found on several of the most popular auction sites.

In a recent comparison of open auction sites, fifteen items were selected (with unique keyword names) and searches were performed. Table 15.1 shows the results of those searches. Notice that this is simply a snapshot of one day's activity, and that the numbers will change from day to day. However, this table will give you an idea of the level of activity on each auction site.

Keywords were chosen to represent a variety of merchandise types. Mavica (Sony), Playstation, Compaq, Iomega, and Minolta represent consumer electronics and computers. Lionel, Fostoria (glassware),

TABLE 15.1 Comparison of Open Auction Sites						
Keyword	eBay	Amazon	Auction Addict	Auction Universe	Excite	Gold's Auction	Yahoo!
Mavica	223	6	0	1	2	0	65
Playstation	2378	61	3	16	42	5	2905
Compaq	1327	68	7	12	53	0	439
Iomega	416	35	1	19	25	1	282
Minolta	1066	19	1	1	7	4	66
Lionel	3902	45	1	1	10	20	321
Fostoria	1519	14	1	0	0	20	58
Disney	15554	873	25	188	142	57	7454
Smoochy	355	32	2	42	49	1	152
Yankees	2968	130	1	44	13	5	1920
Mariners	647	34	0	6	8	0	1707
Tolkien	223	29	1	1	2	0	28
Steinbeck	130	45	0	0	1	1	23
Gretzky	1879	74	5	33	47	2	486
Elvis	4293	269	17	49	31	24	464
Total	36880	1734	65	413	432	140	16370

Disney, and Smoochy (Ty Beanie Baby) are representative collectibles. Yankees and Mariners are sports teams, Tolkien and Steinbeck are authors, and Gretzky and Elvis are famous personalities. For the total number of auctions in this survey, it's easy to see why eBay is considered the auction site leader. To find out which sites are potentially good sites for items you intend to buy or sell, do a quick keyword search on these popular auction web sites to perform a similar evaluation on your own.

SPECIALTY AUCTIONS

Some auction sites are intentionally limited. These specialty auction sites focus on one particular class of merchandise. Here's a list of a few interesting specialty auction sites:

✔ **Arrowhead Auctions (arrowheads.com/auction)** An auction site specializing in artifacts, particularly from North America.

✔ **Guitar Auction (guitarauction.com)** Auctions for used, new, and vintage guitars by Martin, Gibson, Fender, Takoma, and others. Also includes auctions for other musical instruments, music books, and supplies.

✔ **Just Glass (justglass.com)** Specializes in glassware. The site lists more than thirty categories from art glass to Vaseline glass.

✔ **Mister Vintage (mistervintage.com)** Specializes in the vintage collectibles market only.

✔ **Pottery Auction (potteryauction.com)** Specializes in American art pottery, including dinnerware.

✔ **Replay Toys (replaytoys.com)** Specializes in vintage toys, including action figures, dolls, comics, and video games.

✔ **Teletrade (teletrade.com)** Features fine art and collectibles and both online and phone-in bidding. Categories include coins, stamps, fine art, diamonds, sports cards, and memorabilia.

✔ **The Chicago Wine Company (tcwc.com)** Specializes in fine wines. Purchases are directly from the Chicago Wine Company, rather than from individual sellers.

✔ **Auto Auction (uautobid.com)** A site dedicated to selling new and used autos that also includes an auction feature.

This is merely a sampling of some of the interesting specialty auctions on the Web. For a more complete list, consult the auction resource sites listed below.

ADDITIONAL AUCTION RESOURCES

With so much auction activity on the Web, it's hard to keep up with what's available. Not surprisingly, several auction help sites have cropped up on the Web. These sites provide up-to-the-minute news about auctions, how-to tutorials on using the Web, and links to hundreds of auction sites. Some of the sites you might find useful are:

✔ **Alan's Auction Resource Site (www.alanelliott.com/auction)** An auction resource site that provides information and links to the most popular auction sites plus links to auction information that is particularly useful to sellers.

✔ **AuctionAssistant (www.blackthornesw.com/Bthome)** This is the home of the AuctionAssistant software program that can help you build professional-looking auction ads.

✔ **Auction Explorer (expressdev.com)** If you're a buyer and you want to search more than one auction at a time, you can use the Auction Explorer. Download the trial copy from this site.

✔ **Auction Tribune (auctiontribune.com)** This site is like an auction newspaper. It covers auction news and contains links to auction sites and resources.

✔ **Auction Watch (auctionwatch.com)** This site keeps you up to date on the latest auction news and provides articles on current auction topics.

✔ **Auctionpix (auctionpix.com/ebay)** An auction image hosting site that also contains a general list of auction help sites and links to major auctions.

✔ **Honesty (www.honesty.com)** A resource for auction counters that you can place in your auction ads.

✔ **Online Business Resources (auction.pagetogo.com)** Contains links to a number of online auctions and resources for both auctions and e-commerce businesses.

✔ **Pongo (pongo.com)** If you need help using Web features in your auction ads (such as graphics, HTML, links, etc.) this is the place to go for tutorials.

✔ **Shareware (shareware.com)** Go to this site and perform a search on "auction" to find the latest auction-oriented shareware software.

There are many other sites containing help for Internet auctions and the list is growing daily. Using these sites as a beginning, you'll be able to find a tremendous amount of information to help you establish your own auction business.

SUMMARY

Auctions and auction resources on the Internet continue to grow and expand. Those sites that have established an early presence on the Web will probably remain the major players in Internet auctions, but new ideas and sites continually test the old ones. Use the resources listed in this chapter to keep up with the constantly changing Internet auction industry.

Is it time you jumped on the bandwagon? Although there are millions of auctions being held this minute, there is still room for more. The entire industry is still in diapers. As online auctions mature, there will be new opportunities, new rules, and new risks. With the information you've learned in this book you already have the resources in hand to put you at the front of the race. What are you waiting for? Go ahead! Now is the time for you to get started in Internet auctions.

Index